Health Policy and the Public Interest

This book was motivated by a lack of a suitable textbook for a course Health Policy, which the author has taught for many years. He wanted a book that is less technical and more informative and insightful than the books available about the direction of health policy reform, which needs to ensure: (1) universal protection in basic healthcare; (2) provision of greater choice; (3) efficient production and consumption of healthcare services; (4) financial sustainability of the healthcare system. Defining the public interest as the welfare of the "representative individual" with no vested interest who imagines himself to have equal chance of being anyone in society, this book explores alternative ways of finance and delivery, the optimal interface between the public healthcare sector and the private healthcare sector, and that between public insurance and private insurance.

The book includes a theoretical but non-technical section that distinguishes between the stock of health and functional health, proposes a utility maximizing/behavioral framework to explain behavior and the role of health policy and investigates the nature of risk and alternative insurance mechanisms. The book illustrates the application of this framework with a number of country studies, covering a large range of healthcare systems from the American and the European systems to various Asian systems as well as those of Australia and New Zealand. The survey of country experiences reinforces the theoretical conclusions about the role of the public healthcare sector and social insurance and that of the private market.

The book highlights the importance of, and the workability of, "pricing right" and "capping right": pricing standard or basic healthcare services at the right price can contain both demand-side and supply-side moral hazard and lead to more efficient production and consumption of healthcare services; capping annual eligible healthcare expenses will provide effective protection against financial risks. The proposal of a lifetime healthcare supplement offers greater choice. Private caregivers and insurers supplement the public healthcare system by offering more choices and premium services, as well as additional protection.

Lok Sang Ho, Professor of Economics and Director of the Centre for Public Policy Studies, Lingnan University, is the author of *Public Policy and the Public Interest* and *Health Care Financing and Delivery: A Model for Reform* and has published about 90 academic papers in journals and book chapters, as well as various other books (as joint editor or author) covering a broad spectrum of areas in public policy. Professor Ho has always been active in community and professional service. He served as President of the Hong Kong Economic Association for eight years through 2007 and was one of the key figures who founded the *Pacific Economic Review*. Prior to his academic career he had worked in the Ontario Ministry of Treasury and Economics and the Ontario Economic Council. Holding a PhD from the University of Toronto, he had taught at York University and the Chinese University of Hong Kong before joining Lingnan. He writes a weekly column in *China Daily*, Hong Kong edition and occasionally contributes articles to Seeking Alpha, a well-known financial website, on policies related to financial markets and macroeconomic management.

Health Policy and the Public Interest

Lok Sang Ho

Routledge
Taylor & Francis Group
LONDON AND NEW YORK

First published 2013
by Routledge
2 Park Square, Milton Park, Abingdon, Oxon OX14 4RN

Simultaneously published in the USA and Canada
by Routledge
711 Third Avenue, New York, NY 10017

Routledge is an imprint of the Taylor & Francis Group, an informa business

British Library Cataloguing in Publication Data
A catalogue record for this book is available from the British Library

Library of Congress Cataloging in Publication Data
Ho, Lok-sang.
Health policy and the public interest / Lok-sang Ho.
p. cm.
Includes bibliographical references and index.
1. Medical policy. 2. Public interest. I. Title.
RA395.A3H6 2012
362.1–dc23 2012010927

ISBN: 978-0-415-66480-6 (hbk)
ISBN: 978-0-203-09562-1 (ebk)

Typeset in Times New Roman
by Wearset Ltd, Boldon, Tyne and Wear

MIX
Paper from responsible sources
FSC www.fsc.org FSC® C004839

Printed and bound in Great Britain by
TJ International Ltd, Padstow, Cornwall

Contents

Illustrations

Figures

Tables

Foreword

David R. Phillips

Professor Lok Sang Ho is well known in Hong Kong as an authority on health care and welfare financing, on health policy and on public policy more generally. He has taught and researched these topics for almost two decades at Lingnan University in Hong Kong, and in other universities and countries prior to that. He has investigated the nature, strengths, weaknesses and evolution of policy in many systems internationally. His teaching and public presentations on policy topics are invariably stimulating to students and wider audiences. He is a very popular teacher in the social sciences at Lingnan University in Hong Kong. He is also in constant demand as a commentator in the local newspapers and radio, and a guest of honor and speaker on health policy in such organizations as the Hong Kong Management Association and Lions Clubs. His approach is marked by originality and clarity, and the novelty and insightfulness of his recommendations for policy changes and improvements. His areas of work over the years have been complementary to my own interests in global health, social epidemiology and social gerontology. As his colleague for a decade and a half, I have frequently enjoyed and appreciated hearing his suggestions concerning many areas of public policy. I am especially pleased to have been given the opportunity to introduce this well-written, innovative and informative book.

Health policy, to the WHO, refers to decisions, plans and actions that are undertaken to achieve specific health care goals within a society. This leaves considerable room for differentiation within and between the health policies of different nations, and in individual places over time – for policies are rarely fixed and most are in a state of continuous evolution. Policies can define what the future of health services should look like. They can set out priorities and resources to be allocated to different sub-sectors and health conditions and sometimes to different types of population groups and localities (for example, groups or places defined as being in greater or lesser relative need). Policies may relate to the delivery and funding of health care as a whole, and subsidiary policies will often focus on specific themes or issues within the sector, such as training, public health, health promotion and health education, pharmaceuticals, complementary therapies, and the like. Lok Sang Ho has also added another important feature, in the concept of policy efficiency, discussed in chapter 10. This concept implies a policy should be evaluated in terms of its efficiency of achieving intended goals in relation to the resources committed (he notes, for example, the United States' health system may be regarded as relatively inefficient in this respect: huge resources are committed to health but achieving relatively poor and uneven outcomes).

Health systems are of many sizes and forms and have evolved to meet the needs of existing populations. Moreover, whatever their scale and nature, systems universally need to adapt to often rapidly changing demographic, health and financial circumstances. Health policies all experience a similar evolution and it is clear that some are more likely to be successful in planning the capacity and capability to meet future changes and in serving the public interest within affordable parameters. Given this enormous variety and shifting landscape, how can we analyse the key features of policies, assess how they are performing and identify "winners"? In this book, Lok Sang takes on the daunting task of assisting us to do this, by summarising, analysing and comparing the features of a range of international health care systems operating under differing funding and political systems. He does this with his customary originality and clarity of discussion and presentation, always referring back to the conceptual and analytical framework introduced in the first four chapters of the book.

The health policy in any nation naturally evolves in the context of the nation's functional health and health stock, and also under the broader socio-economic and political circumstances of the place and time. Yet all the systems examined in this book (which, apart from China, are principally from the richer nations) are facing essentially very similar challenges for their health policy contexts but they present considerable variety in their approaches. All are facing similar trends in health care, public health and epidemiology. These include emphasis on health promotion, prevention and education; increasing reliance on health care technology; the blurring of the boundaries between health care and social care; and an inexorable trend towards current and future "epidemics" of non-communicable diseases and conditions such as dementias. The global increases in non-communicable diseases have, unfortunately, in effect not always been counterbalanced by an elimination of infectious diseases. The potential for pandemics, likely of mainly viral aetiology, is widely recognised and there is currently a lack of effective medicines to deal with these classes of disease. There is also growing antibiotic resistance, so that WHO and others presage a time when humanity will effectively be left without a drug arsenal to combat many common bacterial diseases. These trends have serious, often dire, implications for health policy, costs and effectiveness, underscoring a need for greater incentives in prevention, as emphasized in this book.

Almost all contemporary policies are developed in settings that are subject to increasing financial pressures and considerable escalation in health care costs. Trends – some might say fads – such as health sector reform and a focus on sustainability are often interjected as crucial to the policy context. Policies are also almost universally set in countries experiencing considerable socio-economic and demographic change, principally the ageing of their populations, which affect both their health profiles and their long-term revenue and tax bases. Many affect both their health profiles and their long-term revenue and tax bases. Many developed country health systems are in economies already facing, or soon to face, diminishing tax bases and increasing "dependent" populations, which in the future will mainly comprise older rather than younger cohorts.

The health and epidemiological trends mentioned above also emphasise the increasing interrelations of health policy with other areas of public policy, a borderland with which Lok Sang is very familiar and on which he has produced much innovative research. Health policy is inevitably influenced by political dogma and increasingly related to areas such as fiscal policy, social welfare, education, housing, nutrition, pensions, and infrastructure. How effectively these different sectors mesh and cooperate varies considerably amongst the systems he examines. He reminds us that rarely are sub-areas "seamless", even within health policy itself, so there will almost certainly be many and greater barriers and discontinuities between health sector policy and that for other areas, many of which have traditionally considered themselves as independent sectors. Lok Sang has many years' rich experience of analysing how public policies can be reshaped, reformulated and improved to meet the public interest – including the years when he worked for the Ontario Government and the now defunct Ontario Economic Council, and this knowledge is brought to bear in the scene-setting and case-study chapters in this book.

Health Policy and the Public Interest provides a refreshing, clear approach to the complex evolution and interactions of policy and its ultimate affordability, sustainability, and efficacy. In this book, Lok Sang Ho helps us to assess how well policies in different places meet the requirements of the "public interest". To do this, he draws on his decades of experience and dedication as a teacher, researcher and practising economist. The book also shows clearly Lok Sang's original and essentially humanistic thinking about what makes policy "good" for the public, and how it can be improved within levels of affordability and practicality. Very importantly, he ponders how policy is likely to be fit for purpose in the future. Students, researchers and practitioners at many levels of knowledge will benefit enormously from reading this work.

David R. Phillips
Lingnan University
June 2012

Preface

All over the world, governments of all stripes are searching for a healthier healthcare system: one that is financially sustainable over the long term, that promotes prevention, that optimizes the resources in diagnostics, treatment, and research, and that provides healthcare of an acceptable quality that is financially accessible to all who need it when they need it. Most of the healthcare systems in existence – from that on the Chinese mainland and that in the Hong Kong Special Administrative Region in the East to the United Kingdom and the United States in the West – are in a state of crisis or near-crisis. Sustainability is a major concern. "Reform" is the buzz word. The Singapore system, with a mandatory private medical savings plan subsumed under the Central Provident Fund dubbed "Medisave," a risk-pooling mechanism to provide catastrophic care called "Medishield," and an endowment fund dubbed "Medifund" to provide care to the poor who have not the means to save a sufficient amount for health protection, is sometimes touted as a model for the world. Even though it does offer many attractive features, it also has a number of pitfalls. Foremost is that in a substantive sense the state takes over the individual's right as to how he would spend his money. Moreover, with so many different components, each requiring separate administration, it is not a "seamless system." There will be a separate chapter on the Singapore system in this book which the interested reader can turn to later.

If Singapore's system is not the best, what is? There is obviously no perfect system. But a system that promises acceptable and dependable quality, accessibility to all, financial sustainability and efficiency should not be too much to ask. These qualities appear to be the qualities that any decent healthcare system MUST have. These qualities are the least to be expected of a healthcare system, if we are genuinely concerned about the public interest.

The public interest, for the purpose of this discussion, and as defined in *Public Policy and the Public Interest*, a sister companion to this volume, refers to the "*ex ante* welfare of the representative individual" – a hypothetical person who has no prior identity, who could be anyone in the community and thus could potentially be helped or hurt by a policy, who ponders a collective decision, and must decide if one policy arrangement is preferred to another. Thus the public interest must be judged by an "impartial judge" who has no vested interests to defend. Since we would not want to be the unfortunate one who is denied needed care for any reason, and would not like to be given care that is not effective in dealing with a health problem, both *accessibility* and *quality* are basic. Since this protection is highly valued by anyone in society facing the possibility of a health problem, it is clearly imperative that the protection is *fiscally sustainable*. Since wastefulness is a "deadweight loss" – a net social loss – *efficiency* is also a basic requirement expected of any decent healthcare system.

In an earlier volume published in 1997,[1] I proposed that there is a perennial trilemma between three competing goals: *quantity* (accessibility, or the availability of the care to as many people as possible), *quality* (the quality of the care that an individual gets, the higher the better), and *least burden* (minimizing the burden or in other words the opportunity cost of the resources committed to healthcare). Fiscal sustainability and efficiency are obviously related to least burden, and are central to many of the healthcare reform initiatives around the world in recent years.

It will be maintained in this book that the world's experience with alternative healthcare systems has suggested that the *excessive burden insurance* (EBI) system, or alternatively *excessive burden protection* (EBP), combined with an "incentive-conscious" pricing strategy for healthcare services, is emerging as an economically viable option that is grounded on human nature as we know it. The EBI is already in practice in Australia, in Sweden and in Taiwan, with variations, and generally with considerable success. The system can be adapted to any country, subject to political feasibility. The system has commanded widespread public satisfaction and support. EBI features public provision of key medical infrastructure and prevention; self-paid medical treatment of covered services up to a yearly spending limit; public insurance against "excessive medical expenditures"; and is compatible with joint provision of medical care services by both the public and the private sectors. The pricing of healthcare services in the marketplace may or may not be regulated. Supplementary medical insurance plans are often available in the private market to soften the possible medical spending burden within the spending threshold and to procure superior or state-of-the-art care that is not covered. It will be argued, in the chapters to follow, that while private healthcare providers should be encouraged, a publicly provided, non-profit, healthcare system should always serve as the backbone for healthcare. The basic argument is that private providers must be good enough to attract patients to use their services even in the presence of a well-run public healthcare system. In the absence of a reliable public healthcare system, citizens will feel insecure, since they would have no alternative other than what is available in the private market. They would be at the behest of the profit-making healthcare providers.

EBI can be supplemented with what may be called the *lifetime healthcare supplement* (LHS). The LHS, also called Lifetime Choice-core supplement (LCS), features an individualized contingent account that allows the individual to withdraw publicly provided funds for medical care purposes up a lifetime limit, subject to matching input from the patient. Details are presented in Chapter 11: The way forward.

While the policy recommendation is clear, this book will also cover and evaluate alternative financing schemes, mainly through scrutinizing country experiences. The survey of country experiences will, it is hoped, convince readers that EBI makes eminent sense and is simple to administer.

It is rare for a textbook like this to make specific policy recommendations. But if theory and evidence suggest that these policy recommendations make sense, why shy away from it? Readers are, of course, welcomed to challenge any of the ideas presented in this book, and the author is prepared to respond to such challenges through a platform that will also serve as a teaching and learning tool for students.

It is useful to first spell out some basic assumptions and postulates.

It is postulated that both the users and the providers of health services are rational entities. This does not mean that they all have perfect foresight and can make the best decisions all the time. This simply means that they will respond to incentives in a way that would maximize their own *ex ante perceived* welfare – necessarily as understood by themselves. Yet what is rational to them personally at the moment of the decision making need not be the best decision in the end even for themselves, and more importantly, need not be rational for society as a whole. It is a challenge to policymakers in health policy to align the personal interests of service suppliers and users with the public interest.

It is postulated that with the right incentives and given the necessary autonomy, medical professionals will exercise a high degree of professionalism so that they will combine high quality care. Medical professionals are in a better position than bureaucrats or anyone else to determine what medical decisions are worthwhile and what are not, although they may not be as aware of the other needs of society as bureaucrats who oversee a spectrum of policy areas and therefore may not be as sensitive to costs as policymakers with a wider policy portfolio. Still, unless well justified through a careful cost–benefit comparison of restraining the autonomy, medical professionals should be given as much professional autonomy as possible. In a system that respects and rewards professionalism medical professionals will translate the resources allocated for medical services into higher quality services and achieve the professional satisfaction that will further given them the motivation to perform even better.

While no one is in the position to speak for the entire society on the question of what level of medical care is the right one, we need to look for a mechanism that is acceptable to society for determining the level and the extent of medical care that should be publicly provided. Individuals may then determine privately for themselves what additional medical services that they want to procure over and above the publicly provided level.

In Chapter 1 we will describe the distinction between functional health and stock of health. We will also examine the changes of the health stock over the life cycle. Chapter 2 will provide a general framework of health policy analysis. It consists of a theory about household choice and thus household behavior; and then proceeds with a theoretical overview of alternative insurance mechanisms. Chapter 3 will look at other special topics associated with insurance, such as moral hazard, adverse selection and risk sharing. We will also throw light on the debate over private versus public insurance. A taxonomy of alternative healthcare financing mechanisms will be given to highlight the place of insurance in the healthcare financing equation. In Chapter 4, we shall look at the criteria for the evaluation of health policy and the methods of such evaluations. Chapter 5 will look at the policy experience and the debate in Hong Kong, Taiwan and mainland China. Chapter 6 will focus on the National Health Service of the United Kingdom, and that of Canada, as examples of a "bureaucracy-led model" and will explore what constitutes the interface between the market and the government that is in the best "public interest." Chapter 7 will be devoted to a study of the Singapore system, while Chapter 8 will examine the healthcare system in New Zealand and in Australia. Chapter 9 will look at the experience in several European countries, particularly France, Germany and Sweden. Chapter 10 will be devoted to an analysis of the American system and the ongoing policy debate. Finally, Chapter 11 will draw conclusions and summarize the findings of this book.

Abbreviations

ACC	Accident Compensation Corporation
AME	*L'Aide Médicale d'Etat*
AV	Annual value
CDC	Center for Disease Control and Prevention
CHIP	Children's Health Insurance Program
CHT	Canada Health Transfer
CMU	*Couverture Maladie Universelle*
CPF	Central Provident Fund
CSSA	Comprehensive Social Security Allowance
CUPE	Canadian Union of Public Employees
DFA	Drug and Food Administration
DHB	District health board
DRG	Diagnosis Related Group
EBI	Excessive burden insurance
EBP	Excessive burden protection
EHD	Equivalent healthy day
EMSN	Extended Medicare Safety Net
FRI	Fee-reducing health insurance
GBPS	Global Budget Payment Scheme
GST	Goods and services tax
HMO	Health Maintenance Organization
HPP	Health production possibility frontier
HRA	Health reimbursement arrangement
HSA	Health savings account
HYE	Healthy year equivalent
IDAPE	Interim Disability Assistance Program for the Elderly
LCS	Lifetime Choice-care Supplement
LHS	Lifetime healthcare supplement
MBS	Medicare Benefit Schedule
MCC	Medisave contribution ceiling
MMS	Minimum Medisave sum
PbR	Payment by results
PBS	Pharmaceutical Benefits Scheme

PCPS	Primary Care Partnership Scheme
PHIAC	Health Insurance Administration Council
PHO	Primary health organization
PPO	Preferred provider organization
QALY	Quality adjusted life-year
SPR	Singapore Permanent Resident

1 Functional health and the health stock

1.1 Introduction

Since Grossman published his groundbreaking piece on the concept of health capital in 1972 economists have applied the concept both theoretically and empirically with much success (Bercowitz *et al.*, 1983; Karatzas, 1992, Picone *et al.* 1998). However, most authors have not made a clear distinction between "functional health" and health stock. The original paper by Grossman (1972) had assumed – largely for expediency – that "health services," i.e., the benefits that arise from the health stock in each period and another term for "functional health," is directly proportional to the stock of health. Henceforth, however, authors typically assume that a larger stock of health must imply a larger flow of health services. For example, Picone *et al.* (1998), uses health stock rather than functional health as an argument in the utility function *in each period*, which would not make sense unless in each period the service flow is directly proportional to the stock. Folland *et al.* (2010) are more explicit about the distinction between health stock and functional health, but are certainly mistaken in the statement that: "The greater one's stock of health [is], the greater the number of healthy days, up to a natural maximum of 365 days [will be]" (p. 141). The assumption that flows are directly related to stocks is often correct, but as demonstrated below is not always true. The concept of functional health is not unfamiliar among researchers in the health sciences (Hornbrook and Goodman, 1996; Kington and Smith, 1997), but is seldom explicitly discussed in the economics literature. This chapter will fill this gap.

The health of a person can be looked as a condition that can improve or deteriorate as the individual recovers from or falls into sickness. This "condition," however, is actually a stream of functioning capability that we can refer to as *functional health.* In contrast to functional health, the *health stock* of a person can change without the individual's noticing it. The health stock can be looked at as a store of such capability that can serve the person into the future. This store may change without our noticing. Perhaps a tumor is developing in its early stage. Perhaps some blood vessels are blocking. Perhaps the individual is infected with HIV or a parasite. In other words, the individual can function at a normal level, i.e., "functional health" may still be at a high level, and yet his stock of health may be quietly falling.

Some drugs are known to increase functional health momentarily, but at the expense of the stock of health. Under influence from the drug, an individual may perform better, concentrate better and enjoy a feeling of better well-being. Yet he may be drawing down his stock of health. Functional health has many aspects: the general feeling of well-being, the faculties of sight, hearing, smell, taste, touch, speech and mobility. Since severe pain distracts and disables, a pain killer will improve functional health, but a strong pain killer, such as morphine, can damage the stock of health. Similarly steroids can quickly improve functional health, but can also produce side effects that may undermine health over the long term.

The distinction between health stock and functional health is useful in discussions relating to health policy because there is an obvious need to balance measures devoted to improving or maintaining the health stock and measures devoted to improving functional health. The choice over these two aspects of health is related to the discount rate (time to translate future benefits to the present). If the rate of discount is higher, implying stronger time preference for the present, functional health will be given greater weight relative to the health stock. If the rate of discount is lower, on the other hand, replenishing or protecting the health stock will be given greater weight. A high rate of discount is one of the reasons why some individuals choose to take drugs that may enhance their functional health in the short term but may hurt the stock of health over the longer term.

Proposition 1.1: Distinction between functional health and health stock. Functional health is a flow, and flows have a time dimension. Functional health is a service provided by the health stock. In general, a larger health stock can be expected to provide more years of functional health. The reverse, however, is not true. Very high functional health in a particular year does not necessarily mean that the stock of health is high. One could feel fine and could function extremely well without realizing that one's health is being eroded by some unknown illness.

In general, given the state of technology, the health stock will inevitably depreciate over time. Appropriate healthcare, however, can slow down the speed of this depreciation. But this must involve various kinds of sacrifice. There is in principle a different "*optimal rate of depreciation* of the health stock" for different members of society. The optimal rate of depreciation is defined as occurring when the marginal cost involved in slowing depreciation is equal to the marginal benefit. This marginal cost may be an out-of-pocket expenditure, the cost of a drug, for example. It may also be the opportunity cost of a change in lifestyle, which may be quite personal and subjective. Health policy should allow each person to achieve his optimal level of depreciation of the health stock by making an intelligent, informed choice and by affording him the means of making such choices. These aspects of optimization are extremely complex and they involve many decision makers in both the private and the public sectors weighing the benefits against the costs of healthcare, and weighing the benefits and costs of alternative lifestyles.

> **Proposition 1.2 Optimal health stock depreciation**
> The optimal rate of health stock depreciation is achieved by adjusting behavior, typically aspects of lifestyle, so that the marginal benefit of slowing depreciation in terms of the value of a longer life over the longer term, is equal to the marginal cost of that preventive behavior, either in terms of the sacrifice in enjoyment of an activity or in terms of a direct outlay.

1.2 Functional health as a "good"

We can measure functional health in a year as the number of "equivalent healthy days" (EHDs) in that year.[1] An EHD is a day of "normal functional health." A day with a loss of functional health may be discounted and treated as a fraction of a day of normal health. Because functional health contributes to the quality of life, which may involve many different dimensions, the concept of functional health is not exactly the same as the related concept of "*quality adjusted life-year* (QALY)" (Broome, 1993). In the rest of this book we will focus on EHD instead of QALY. EHD is considered an input along with market goods and services in consumption activities (also called "household production"[2]) that yield the "consumption attributes" X which affect utility. We can draw the "*(functional) health production possibility frontier*" (HPP) applicable to one individual as shown in Figure 1.1.

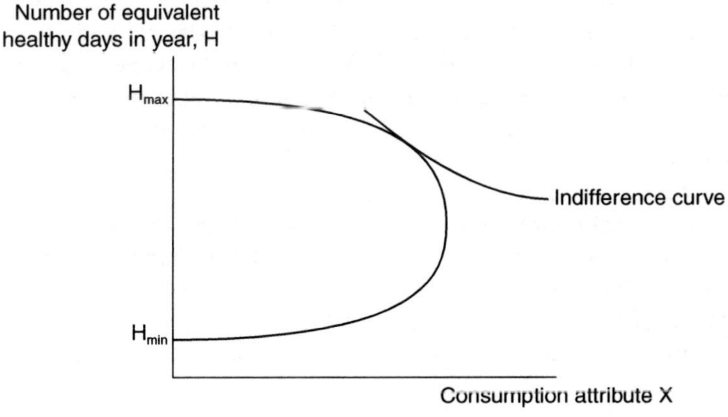

Figure 1.1 Functional health production possibility frontier.

Here H_{min} is the number of EHDs that would occur even when there is no healthcare input allocated for the purpose of increasing health. Starting from this level, suppose some medical input is now used to increase functional health. Because functional health is needed to enjoy life it is possible to increase the enjoyment of consumption attribute X while at the same time enhancing H. Beyond a point, however, it is possible to increase functional health only at the expense of X. Finally, there is a limit to which medical input can be used to enhance the number of EHDs and this is represented as H_{max}. H_{min}, H_{max}, and the curvature of the production possibility frontier depend on the stock of health of the individual at the time as well as the state of medical knowledge.

We can now superimpose the indifference map onto the diagram. We can then easily see that optimality in the sense of utility maximization subject to the (functional) health possibility frontier generally implies that functional health will not normally be maximized. The simple reason is that beyond a certain point improving functional health carries a price in terms of the enjoyment of other goods and services. While it is generally not in the interest of utility maximization to maximize functional health in a year, it will be in the interest of long term utility maximization to conserve health, i.e., to slow down depreciation of the health stock. Again, however, there is an optimal rate of health stock depreciation. Reducing the rate of depreciation brings a return in terms of greater functional health in the future, but it also carries a cost in terms of loss of some consumption opportunities.

In general, as the individual's stock of health depreciates over the course of his life we expect that the HPP will drift downwards. In the short term, it is also possible for the HPP to shift down with the working of some random factors such as the outbreak of some epidemics.

1.3 Prevention versus treatment

The stock of health generally depreciates over the life cycle of a person. Depreciation may be slowed down both by prevention and by treatment. Prevention reduces the chances of health threatening events, so that episodes of rapid depreciation in the health stock will be minimized. Treatment reduces the impact of health threatening events that have already taken place. Treatment may help restore functional health, and may also restore the health stock or save it from dangerous depletion.

It is common to say that prevention is better than cure. This is often true in the sense that once a health threatening event has taken place, often irreparable damage to the health stock may be unavoidable, but the health threatening event may actually be avoidable. However, from the policy point of view, optimal resource allocation between prevention and treatment will occur when *at the margin* the benefits of prevention and treatment are the same. This is illustrated in Figure 1.2.

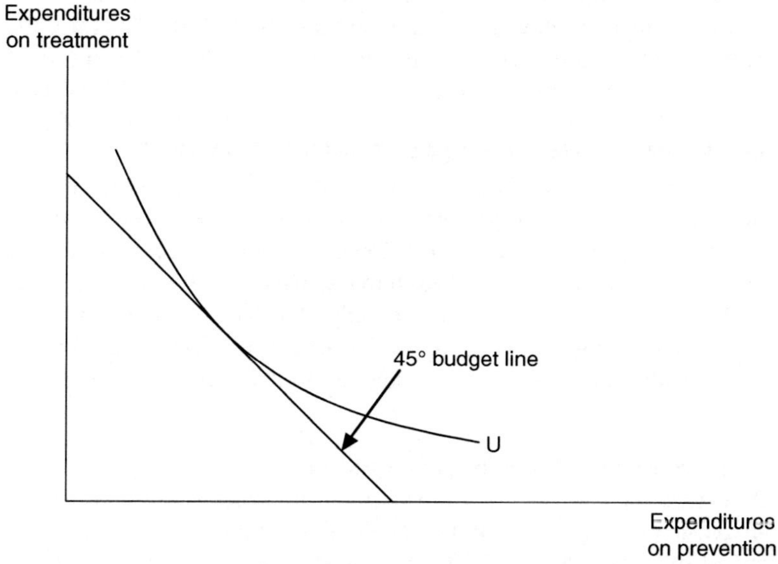

Figure 1.2 Optimal balance between cure and prevention.

Proposition 1.3 Optimal prevention and treatment
When allocation is optimal, the marginal benefit of a dollar spent on prevention should be equal to the marginal benefit of a dollar spent on treatment.

1.4 The relationship between medical knowledge/technology and the health stock

The stock of health of a person is defined as the potential of functional health stream that would accrue to that person. This potential, obviously, is related to the *state of medical knowledge and medical technology*. There was a time when tuberculosis could not be cured. Someone diagnosed as having the disease was expected not to live very long. His stock of health would then be quite low. A person with exactly the same conditions today, however, may be cured and may expect to live many more years. Both the functional health and the physiological conditions of the person then and that of the person now may be quite the same. Yet their potentials for life are vastly different. Hence the stock of health of a person with the *same* biophysical conditions today would be *much higher* than that of someone, say, two generations ago.

Defined as such, the stock of health is, given the state of medical knowledge and medical technology available to the person, generally largest at birth and will generally decline over time. A medical breakthrough, or improved access to medical care on account of better financial conditions, will, however, raise the stock of health. Further, appropriate healthcare can slow down the speed of depreciation of the health stock. Someone who contracts a serious illness from which he will recover of his own accord would experience a significant dip in functional health but his decline in the stock of health proceeds smoothly without a commensurate drastic decline. Someone who falls ill or is injured badly in a traffic accident and needs medical intervention to survive experiences an immediate decline in both functional health and stock of health. Access to medical attention, however, allows his stock of health to rise back. Finally, someone who contracts the HIV virus and someone in the early stages of a malignant tumor experience no decline in functional health in the beginning, but already suffer a great loss in the health stock assuming that they fall ill in a few years or months.

Proposition 1.4 Medical knowledge and health
Because a person with access to improved medical technology is expected to live longer, improving access to and the quality of medical care through technological breakthroughs will increase the health stock of the people living in the community.

Proposition 1.5 Depreciation of the health stock
Given the state of medical knowledge and the access to healthcare, health stock generally keeps depreciating by the day, as reflected by the decline in life expectancy as one ages. The rate of depreciation, however, may be slowed down by a healthier lifestyle and better medical care.

"*Investing in health,*" then, may carry two meanings. First, it may refer to society investing in medical discovery and in greater access to healthcare. Second, assuming one kind of lifestyle as norm, it may refer to an individual's adopting a healthier lifestyle compared to this norm as investing in health, as this will enhance the life expectation and the quality of life in his remaining years. Given the state of medical knowledge, the state of access to healthcare, and the lifestyle adopted, an individual can only accept the fact that the health stock declines inexorably by the day.

We propose to measure functional health in a year as the number of EHDs in that year. In order to derive this measure, days of attenuated health have to be discounted and then added to the days of normal health. This is obviously related to the "*healthy year equivalent*" (HYE) concept (Gafni and Birch, 1997, Birch *et al.*, 1998).

Investing on medical discovery, access to healthcare and adopting a healthy lifestyle to slow down the depreciation of the health stock will all involve a sacrifice. In principle, for society there is an optimal rate of investment in medical discovery and an optimal rate of investment in access to healthcare, and for the individual, there is an optimal rate of depreciation of the health stock.

1.5 Stock of health over the life cycle

The stock of health typically declines from birth in the sense that life expectancy declines as one ages. Note that death probability initially declines and then quickly rises from the age of ten for males and from the age of 11 for females. The probability of death is always higher for males than for females at all ages, leading to a higher life expectancy for females than for males. Table 1.1 presents a *Life Table* that shows how *life expectancy* and *death probabilities* (*survival probability* = 1 minus *death probability*) change over the life cycle.

Life expectancy is always defined with respect to the age of a person. Life expectancy is typically highest at birth[3]. It tells us the number of years on average the person at that age can live through. The table shows how many of 100,000 live births survive after the expiry of each complete year for each of the genders.

It may be noted that the death probability falls for children as they grow up to the age of 10–11, and then begins to rise! The speed of rise is very slow at first, and it accelerates noticeably after one reaches one's mid-fifties. The decline in the health stock is not only reflected in the decline in life expectancy but also in the increase of *morbidity*, which is a loss of functionality.

However, the advent of morbidity varies tremendously from person to person. There is much evidence that lifestyle, quite apart from genes and circumstances, affects both the mortality rate and the morbidity rate.

One of the goals of health policy is "*compression of morbidity*," so that the person stays healthy and functional until very close to the very end, with a very short period of morbidity. Given the huge costs of caring for the very old, compression of morbidity has the potential of reducing healthcare costs tremendously, quite apart from the direct benefits of more healthy life-years. The hypothesis that a healthier lifestyle can contribute toward compressed morbidity was supported by a recent study.[4]

1.6 Conclusions

Human longevity has been rising over the years, testifying to the improvement in the human condition brought about by modern science and technology. Table 1.2 shows that the American population has been enjoying an increase in life expectancy and is now living longer than any time in history. American females born in 2007 expect to live up to 80.4 years while American males up to 75.4 years.

But improvement in public hygiene, particularly the improved availability of clean water, is at least as important as the improvement in medical science and technology. The health stock as well as functional health has therefore been rising for much of humanity in the past century. However, for an individual,

Table 1.1 A life table for the American population from age 0 to age 65

Age	*Probability of dying between ages x to x + 1* q_x	*Number surviving to age x* l_x	*Number dying between ages x to x + 1* d_x	*Person-years lived between ages x to x + 1* L_x	*Total number of person-years lived above age x* T_x	*Expectation of life at age x* e_x
0–1	0.006761	100,000	676	99,406	7,793,398	77.9
1–2	0.000460	99,324	46	99,301	7,693,992	77.5
2–3	0.000286	99,278	28	99,264	7,594,691	76.5
3–4	0.000218	99,250	22	99,239	7,495.427	75.5
4–5	0.000176	99,228	17	99,219	7,396,188	74.5
5–6	0.000164	99,211	16	99,203	7,296.969	73.6
6–7	0.000151	99,194	15	99,187	7,197,766	72.6
7–8	0.000140	99,179	14	99,173	7,098,579	71.6
8–9	0.000124	99,166	12	99,159	6,999,407	70.6
9–10	0.000105	99,153	10	99,148	6,900,247	69.6
10–11	0.000091	99,143	9	99,138	6,801,099	68.6
11–12	0.000094	99,134	9	99,129	6,701,961	67.6
12–13	0.000132	99,125	13	99,118	6,602,831	66.6
13–14	0.000209	99,112	21	99,101	6,503,713	65.6
14–15	0.000314	99,091	31	99,075	6,404,612	64.6
15–16	0.000426	99,060	42	99,039	6,305,537	63.7
16–17	0.000529	99,018	52	98,991	6,206,498	62.7
17–18	0.006270	98,965	62	98,934	6,107,506	61.7
18–19	0.000715	98,903	71	98,868	6,008,572	60.8
19–20	0.000796	98,832	79	98,793	5,909,705	59.8
20–21	0.000882	98,754	87	98,710	5,810,911	58.8
21–22	0.000963	98,667	95	98,619	5,712,201	57.9
22–23	0.001017	98,572	100	98,522	5,613,582	56.9
23–24	0.001034	98,472	102	98,421	5,515,060	56.0
24–25	0.001023	98,370	101	98,320	5,416,639	55.1
25–26	0.001003	98,269	99	98,220	5,318,320	54.1
26–27	0.000990	98,171	97	98,122	5,220,100	53.2
27–28	0.000983	98,074	96	98,025	5,121,978	52,2
28–29	0.000988	97,977	97	97,929	5,023,952	51.3
29–30	0.001005	97,880	98	97,831	4,926,023	50.3
30–31	0.001030	97,782	101	97,732	4,828,192	49.4
31–32	0.001060	97,681	104	97,630	4,730,460	48.4
32–33	0.001099	97,578	107	97,524	4,632,831	47.5
33–34	0.001146	97,471	112	97,415	4,535,307	46.5
34–35	0.001201	97,359	117	97,300	4,437,892	45.6
35–36	0.001264	97,242	123	97,180	4,340,592	44.6
36–37	0.001340	97,119	130	97,054	4,243,412	43.7
37–38	0.001434	96,989	139	96,919	4,146,358	42.9
38–39	0.001548	96,850	150	96,775	4,049,438	41.8
39–40	0.001685	96,700	163	96,618	3,952,664	40.9
40–41	0.001836	96,537	177	96,448	3,856,045	39.9
41–42	0.002000	96,360	193	96,263	3,759,597	39.0
42–43	0.002188	96,167	210	96,062	3,663,334	38.1
43–44	0.002400	95,956	230	95,841	3,567,272	37.2
44–45	0.002629	95,726	252	95,600	3,471,431	36.3
45–46	0.002864	95,475	273	95,338	3,375,831	35.4
46–47	0.003107	95,201	296	95,053	3,280,493	34.5
47–48	0.003369	94,905	320	94,745	3,185,440	33.6
48–49	0.003661	94,586	346	94,412	3,090,694	32.7
49–50	0.003984	94,239	375	94,052	2,996,282	31.8
50–51	0.004337	93,864	407	93,660	2,902,230	30.9
51–52	0.004709	93,457	440	93,237	2,808,570	30.1
52–53	0.005091	93,017	474	92,780	2,715,333	29.2
53–54	0.005474	92,543	507	92,290	2,622,553	28.3
54–55	0.005863	92,037	540	91,767	2,530,263	27.5
55–56	0.006275	91,497	574	91,210	2,438,496	26.7
56–57	0.006726	90,923	612	90,617	2,347,286	25.8
57–58	0.007220	90,311	652	89,985	2,256,669	25.0
58–59	0.007773	89,659	697	89,311	2,166,684	24.2
59–60	0.008389	88,962	746	88,589	2,077,353	23.4
60–61	0.009081	88,216	801	87,816	1,988,784	22.5
61–62	0.009839	87,415	860	86,985	1,900,968	21.7
62–63	0.010657	86,555	922	86,094	1,813,983	21.0
63–64	0.011534	85,632	988	85,139	1,727,890	20.2
64–65	0.012491	84,645	1,057	84,116	1,642,751	19.4

Source: *National Vital Statistics Reports*, 59(9), September 28, 2011, online, available at http://www.cdc.gov/nchs/data/nvsr/nvsr59/nvsr59_09.pdf

Table 1.2 Cohort life expectancies at birth by sex, race and year of birth, 1929–2007, United States[a]

Year of birth	*All races*			*White*[c]			*Black*[d]		
	Both sexes	*Male*	*Female*	*Both sexes*	*Male*	*Female*	*Both sexes*	*Male*	*Female*
2007[b]	77.9	75.4	80.4	78.4	75.9	80.8	73.6	70.0	76.8
2006[b]	77.7	75.1	80.2	78.2	75.7	80.6	73.2	69.7	76.5
2005[b]	77.4	74.9	79.9	77.9	75.4	80.4	72.8	69.3	76.1
2004[b]	77.5	74.9	79.9	77.9	75.4	80.4	72.8	69.3	76.0
2003[b]	77.1	74.5	79.6	77.6	75.0	80.0	72.3	68.8	75.6
2002[b]	76.9	74.3	79.5	77.4	74.9	79.9	72.1	68.6	75.4
2001[b]	76.9	74.2	79.4	77.4	74.8	79.9	72.0	68.4	75.2
2000[b]	76.8	74.1	79.3	77.3	74.7	79.9	71.8	68.2	75.1
1999	76.7	73.9	79.4	77.3	74.6	79.9	71.4	67.8	74.7
1989	75.1	71.7	78.5	75.9	72.5	79.2	68.8	64.3	73.3
1979	73.9	70.0	77.8	74.6	70.8	78.4	68.5	64.0	72.9
1969	70.5	66.8	74.4	71.4	67.7	75.3	64.5	60.6	68.6
1959	69.9	66.8	73.2	70.7	67.5	74.2	63.9	61.3	66.5
1949	68.0	65.2	70.7	68.8	66.2	71.9	60.6	58.9	62.7
1939	63.7	62.1	65.4	64.9	63.3	66.6	54.5	53.2	56.0
1929	57.1	55.3	58.7	58.6	57.2	60.3	46.7	45.7	47.8

Sources: United States Life Tables, 2007 by Elizabeth Arias, National Vital Statistics Reports, 59(9), September 28, 2011, online, available at: www.cdc.gov/nchs/data/nvsr/nvsr59/nvsr59_09.pdf.

Notes

a Alaska included as from 1959 and Hawaii as from 1960.

b Life expectancies for 2000–2007 were calculated using a revised methodology.

c Figures by race exclude data for residents of New Jersey.

d Prior to 1970, data for the black population are not available. Data shown for 1900–1969 are for the non-white population.

health stock is almost monotonically declining with time, even though functional health tends to be maintained at a fairly high level. With the advent of the study of epidemiology it is now increasingly realized that lifestyle has much to do with the speed at which the health stock depreciates. Preventive care has to be undertaken at an early age if it is to be most effective, but the incentive for preventive care at an early age has been compromised by a high discount rate among the young people, who have grown dissatisfied with many of the things that they are confronted with and who are also under peer pressure to behave in certain ways.

Health policy has to confront the constraint of human nature, and health policy cannot be cost-effective if it does not go hand in hand with the education and cultural policy that help restore a respect for life. A respect for life will bring down the discount rate for the individual, and will automatically lead to more preventive care at an early age, since people with a longer perspective would eat healthier, avoid dangerous activities and generally adopt a healthier lifestyle. Of course more information about the relationship between lifestyle and health, and about food and health, and public education about prevention also constitute part of health policy.

We have noted that aging normally leads to higher healthcare expenditures, but the rate at which this happens varies considerably from place to place. In the United States, where out-of-pocket healthcare expenditures for the elderly is significantly reduced by Medicare but taken over by taxpayers, where private health insurance plans are expensive and where workers are increasingly denied of employer-provided health insurance, the relative as well as absolute healthcare cost per capita for the aged is higher by far than that in other nations. Differences in policy and in institutions have a huge effect on the "cost premium" of the elderly over that of the younger population, underscoring the significant effects of policy and institutions on human behavior.

Review questions

1 Is there anything conceptually wrong with the common question asked in field surveys: "what is your health status?"
2 "The health stock depends solely on both the physical and mental conditions of a person." Do you agree?
3 "The health stock depreciates as one ages. It never rises." Do you agree?
4 Why is knowledge of the life-table important for health policymakers?
5 Is population aging a major reason for the escalation of healthcare costs? What do Figure 1.3 and Table 1.3, below, tell us?

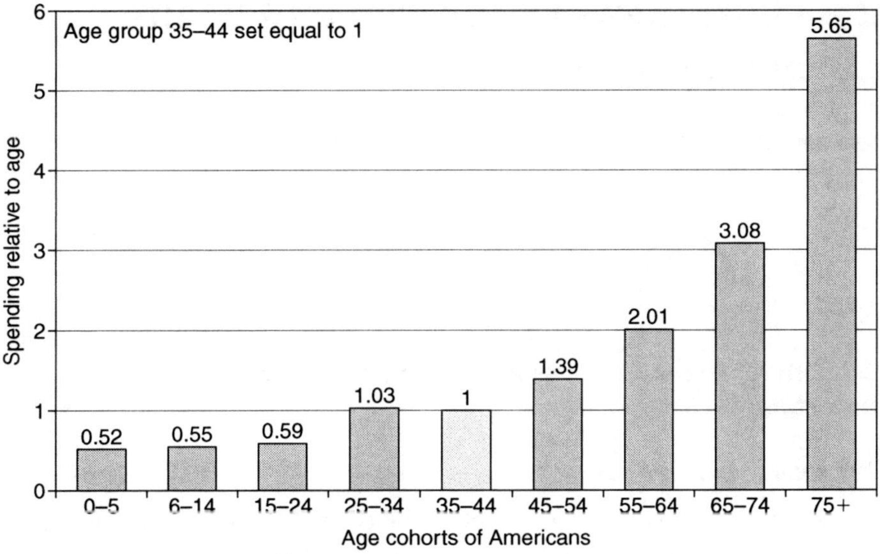

Figure 1.3 Relative per capita health spending by age, 1999.

Table 1.3 Healthcare benefit age profiles

	0–14	*15–19*	*20–49*	*50–64*	*65–69*	*70–74*	*75–79*	*80+*
Australia	0.60	0.57	0.64	1.00	1.81	2.16	3.90	4.23
Austria	0.28	0.28	0.46	1.00	1.42	1.75	1.98	2.17
Canada	0.43	0.61	0.65	1.00	2.45	2.44	4.97	7.54
Germany	0.48	0.43	0.58	1.00	1.52	1.80	2.11	2.48
Japan	0.44	0.22	0.43	1.00	1.70	2.20	2.76	3.53
Norway	0.57	0.34	0.52	1.00	1.70	2.21	2.69	3.41
Spain	0.57	0.39	0.48	1.00	1.46	1.73	1.97	2.11
Sweden	0.43	0.43	0.63	1.00	1.50	1.50	1.96	1.99
United Kingdom	1.08	0.65	0.76	1.00	2.07	2.07	3.67	4.65
United States	0.88	0.82	0.77	1.00	5.01	5.02	8.52	11.53

Source: Kotlikoff, L. and C. Hagist (2005) "Who's Going Broke? Comparing Growth in Healthcare Costs in Ten OECD Countries," NBER Working Paper no. 11833.

2 A framework for risk and health policy analysis

2.1 Utility maximization as *ex ante* utility maximization in an uncertain world

Perceptions and behavior

Economists often assume that people are rational. To the extent that people have feelings, and that they all want to live happily, the assumption makes sense, because no one will knowingly reduce their own welfare, other things being equal. But to assume that people could actually maximize welfare as if they were all well informed about the consequences of their actions would be out of place with reality. Still, we can safely assume that people would maximize "*ex ante* perceived" welfare. That is to say: they would do whatever they can to get the best results as they anticipate at the moment. But in practice they often fail to maximize actual welfare because their perceptions may be flawed, or because they simply do not have the information to make the right choice.

It is important to realize that we live in an uncertain world. Accidents are sometimes unavoidable and one's health stock as well as one's functional health may therefore suddenly decline. Some unknown virus may be lurking somewhere and could strike any time. Crimes can also cause injuries, as will natural disasters. The fact is that we face so much uncertainty that it is difficult to tell how much healthcare services one may need.

The previous paragraph describes things that are out of our control, but there are things that are within our control, and we do also observe people engaging in behaviors that are harmful or even would put them in serious danger. Alcoholism, smoking, substance abuse, unsafe driving habits, car racing are cases in point. There are also problems like pathetic gambling and family violence. We can see that good self-control is not inherent in human nature. These phenomena may suggest that people may not be rational after all. Some of these behaviors directly increase healthcare expenditures. Controlling healthcare expenditures would require us to deal with all these behaviors, and that implies that education, training and rehabilitation to promote or to help people regain self-control must be part of health policy or health promotion strategy.

Proposition 2.1 The extent of health policy
Health policy is not limited to healthcare, public hygiene, and public health, but has to encompass many other areas include education, road design, building safety, environmental planning, crime prevention, food safety, etc.

Proposition 2.2 "Bounded rationality"
Given the flawed perceptions and weaknesses inherent in human nature, attempts to maximize utility may not be successful. Still, people respond to incentives, and behavior is often predictable. Rationality is subject to limitations and is therefore "bounded."

The representative individual approach to evaluating health policy

Individuals may find themselves "hijacked" by their "inferior selves" and suffer a loss of utility as a result, but policymakers must act rationally, and that means acting with full awareness of social costs and social benefits. The idea is that whatever policy is adopted must be expected to bring more benefits than costs. Because there will always be uncertainty, and because the distribution of benefits and costs are uneven, therefore, policymakers must maximize the *ex ante* utility for the "*representative individual*." By representative individual is meant a hypothetical individual who has no fixed identity: we simply imagine ourselves to be blind to our identities but that we could be anyone in the community, including the unfortunate ones. If there was an equal chance for us to be anyone, including such unfortunate ones, what policy options and what kind of institutional arrangements would we like to have in our society? It is proposed that the task of the policymaker is to maximize the *public interest* defined as the *ex ante* welfare of this representative individual and this can only be done *ex ante*, meaning that we feel most comfortable with the policy that we choose *ex ante*. This approach allows us to have much clearer choices in making key policy decisions. An example will clarify the concept. Consider a city with a population of seven million, such as Hong Kong in 2011. Should we spend $7 million on one patient to cure a rare and crippling disease (assuming that the cure is totally effective) that is expected to hit one person out of the seven million population each year? If we imagine that the disease randomly strikes on anyone in the city, then since spending only $1 per capita a year can eliminate a real and serious threat, the city should certainly spend the money. The cost of $1 per person per year should be far smaller than the *ex ante* loss of welfare due to the *threat* of an untreated crippling illness.[1]

Proposition 2.3 *Ex ante* utility maximization
Policymakers should take an impartial position, imagining that they could be anyone in the community, and among policy or institutional design options that are available, preference should be given to the one offering the highest *ex ante* utility.

Proposition 2.4 Public interest
The public interest is defined as the *ex ante* welfare of the representative individual, i.e., the hypothetical person who had no vested interest at all and who had an equal chance to be anyone in society, pondering over the prospects and possibilities that he faced. The hallmark of the public interest is therefore that it be considered impartially, i.e., without being biased by one's own position, endowment and interest.

2.2 Why health is of value

Health is important both because it is valued by households (in this book "household" and "individual consumer" are used interchangeably) and because it is valued by employers. Health is also of value because when the population enjoys good health generally, the nation is seen as stronger and enjoys a sense of national pride.

Households undertake "*household production*," which is the process of transforming consumption of goods and services purchased in the marketplace and other inputs into enjoyable final objects of consumption (such as a feeling of togetherness, the wonderful taste of good food, relaxation, excitement, fun, etc.) We can envisage "*healthy days*" or "*healthy time*" as such an input. In the absence of healthy days or healthy time no one can enjoy a picnic, a concert, a theatrical performance, a packaged tour, or a dinner party with friends and relatives. To take full advantage of the good things offered by nature or modern science and technology one has to be healthy.

Proposition 2.5 Household production
Households use inputs purchased from the market as well as their own time to produce the final qualities or attributes that matter to their utility. This activity generally benefits from and sometimes requires good health.

Households also value health for its own sake. A state of excellent health clearly makes one feel good. Indeed it also makes other members of one's family feel good. Conversely, poor health makes a person and his immediate family members feel bad.

Healthy days or healthy time is also an input in commercial production or social production. The lack of health lowers productivity and increases absenteeism.

Because of the advent of modern science and technology, *the value of health is increasing by the day*. Modern science and technology has raised the potential productivity of workers and has made available new goods and services that were formerly unthinkable. This has raised the opportunity cost of healthy days lost because of sickness. In general, if the opportunity cost of healthy days has gone up, we should devote more resources to health, other things being equal. For this reason, an increase in the proportion of the public budget devoted to healthcare in itself may be appropriate and is not necessarily a cause for alarm.

Proposition 2.6 Increasing value of health over time
The advent of science and technology has allowed people to do much more with their time, provided that they are healthy. The value of healthy time has grown tremendously through history, and is expected to continue to grow well into the future.

2.3 Household behavior

Households are assumed to behave as if they are maximizing a quantity that can be expressed as a mathematical function. This function is called an "objective function," and is defined over some decision variables. So they choose those variables in order to maximize the value of the objective function. This objective function need not correspond with the real utility function of the household, and can be called a "decision utility function."[2] Only with perfect information will this correspond with the real utility function. Households' maximizing behavior is subject to a number of constraints, which include such things as the availability of goods and services in the marketplace, wages and prices, their health stock and functional health at the time, and the opportunities of healthcare and work at the time.

One key area in health policy lies in educating the public about the relationship between health and various lifestyle decisions. Such public education will help reduce the gap between the decision utility function and the actual utility function.

Proposition 2.7 Health education and health policy
Educating people about the relationship between lifestyle and healthcare decisions on the one hand, and their health outcomes on the other hand, will help them make wiser decisions so they will be in a better position to maximize their welfare.

Another key area in health policy lies in making arrangements to deal with the uncertainty that people face. To simplify the discussion, let us consider the simple case of the probability of being "fortunate" (i.e. healthy) at P_i and that of being "not fortunate" at $(1-P_i)$ where $i=0$ when the individual is working and $i=1$ when the individual has retired. Further, we assume that worry over risk or anxiety is a "*mental bad*" and that it enters the utility function of the household. Readers will find a discussion of "mental goods" and "mental bads" in Ho (2001, 2012), as well as Becker and Rubinstein (2004). Becker and Rubinstein did not use the term "mental bad" but explained that "Introducing fear as an argument into the utility function we allow uncertainty to affect persons' utility and well-being" (p. 3). Introducing mental goods and mental bads into the utility function represents a big departure from traditional economic analysis of utility and particularly of behavior under risk. Under the traditional analysis, with utility defined over only physical goods, people are assumed to maximize expected utility. Risk aversion is seen as a reflection simply of the shape of the utility function. A *prospect* offering a higher expected value of utility based on physical goods ("*expected utility*") would then always be preferred to one offering a lower expected utility. Once anxiety (a mental bad) directly enters the utility function, a prospect offering higher expected utility is not necessarily preferred.

In Figure 2.1, we assume that an individual faces two alternative prospects, one with (U_L, U_H) as outcomes in the unfortunate and fortunate scenarios, respectively; the other with (U_L', U_H') as outcomes. The segment of the 45° line between the possible outcomes shows the expected utility corresponding to the different combinations of probabilities for the alternative outcomes. Thus E(U) is the expected utility for $(U_L, U_H; 1/2, 1/2)$, where 1/2 is the probability of both the unfortunate and the fortunate outcomes. We now assume that the prospect

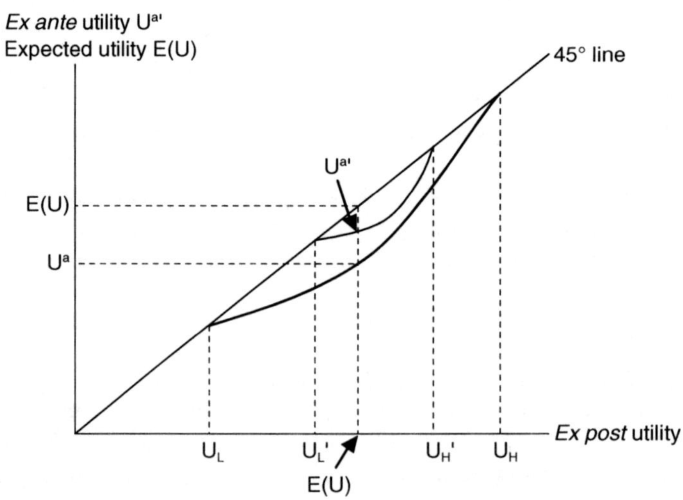

Figure 2.1 Prospective or *ex ante* utility = expected utility − disutility of mental bad.

with (U_L', U_H') as outcomes offers exactly the same expected utility. The way the diagram is drawn, the probability of U_H' is lower than that of U_L'.

We postulate that provided that anxiety enters the utility function, and that anxiety increases with the dispersion of the outcomes, the individual will choose the prospect offering a smaller dispersion of the outcomes. This can be demonstrated by making reference to the curved lines, which trace out the *ex ante* utility of the two prospects at different combinations of probabilities. At the extreme points, i.e., U_H' and U_H, since the probability of being fortunate = 1, *ex ante* and expected utilities are identical and are simply equal to U_H' and U_H respectively for the two prospects. When being fortunate is no longer a certainty *ex ante* utility falls below expected utility and assumes the curved lines as illustrated, because the mental bad "anxiety" takes its toll.

Thus we can define prospective or *ex ante* utility as expected utility minus the disutility of the mental bad associated with the prospect. When the probability of being fortunate approaches unity, anxiety approaches zero, and so *ex ante* utility approaches the almost certain U_H. Similarly, when the probability of being unfortunate approaches unity, the misfortunate is almost a certainty. Again, *ex ante* utility approaches the almost certain U_L. In between these cases, the mental bad is at work. Subtracting the disutility of mental bad yields the *ex ante* utility, which is depicted by the curved line. This disutility of mental bad is obviously smaller when the dispersion of the outcomes is smaller.

Proposition 2.8 Mental bad and *ex ante* utility
Anxiety over the possibility of the "worst case" scenario may undermine *ex ante* utility because it is a mental bad. *Ex ante* utility is equal to expected utility minus the disutility of the anxiety and may be enhanced by policies that narrow the dispersion of the outcomes.

Proposition 2.9 Risk and health policy
An important area of health policy lies in reducing the anxiety of people who will worry over the possibility of being hit by health problems and by the huge expenses of healthcare.

As Figure 2.1 and Figure 2.2 suggest, maximizing *ex ante* utility is not the same as maximizing expected utility. Two situations with the same expected utility should not be considered equivalent. Policymakers need to build in mechanisms so that utility will not decline too much during misfortunes. This suggests a need for some kind of insurance, so that when misfortune strikes the individual gets help, so that utility decreases by less. In a sense, we may say that insurance provides peace of mind and provides a "mental good" that enhances utility *ex ante*.

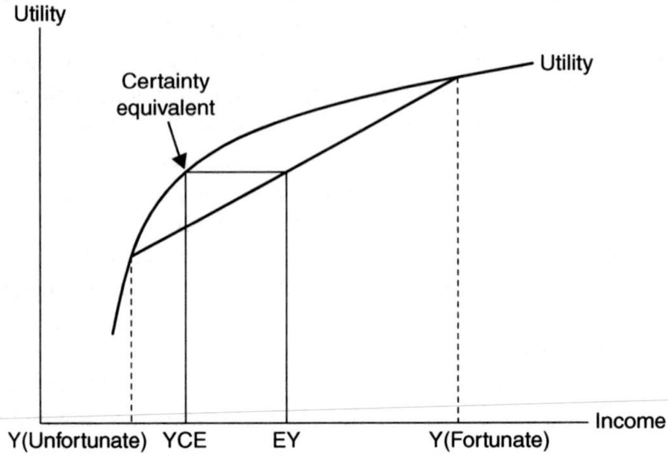

Figure 2.2 Decision making under expected utility framework.

We can therefore define *ex ante* utility for a prospect with a favorable outcome and an unfavorable outcome as expected utility minus the disutility over perception of risk. In a two period model, with working years (period $i=0$) followed by retired years (period $i=1$), *ex ante* utility function is equal to:

$$U_0(F)\times P_0+U_0(N)\times(1-P_0)+U'_0(R_0)+U_1(F)\times P_1+U_1(N)\times(1-P_1)+U'_1(R_1) \quad [2.1]$$

where perceived risk in the two periods R_0 and R_1 are related to the probability distributions of U_0 and U_1, each of which are *ex post* utilities conditional upon fortune (F) or misfortune (N), while U' is the *ex ante* utility of the mental bad associated with perceived risks (with a negative value). Because a distribution with a bigger dispersion is more risky, it is associated with less (*ex ante*) utility, than one with a smaller dispersion.

Further, in the event of "not fortunate," it is assumed that optimal healthcare expenditures is m' in the event of "fortunate," optimal healthcare expenditures is m. Meanwhile all equilibrium variables including functional health and health stocks will be different. The budget constraint for the "most fortunate" case is:

$$\mathbf{c_0P_{0c}}+m_0+\gamma(\mathbf{c_1.P_{1c}}+m_1)\leq W.h_{L0}\,(1-\text{tax rate}) \quad [2.2]$$

which simply says that the sum of consumption expenditures($\mathbf{c_0P_{0c}}$) and healthcare expenses (m_0) during the working years and the present value of consumption expenditures and healthcare expenses during retirement ($i=1$) must be no greater than labor income after taxes.[3] Labor income is assumed to be the only income available and the household is assumed not to own any asset that can be

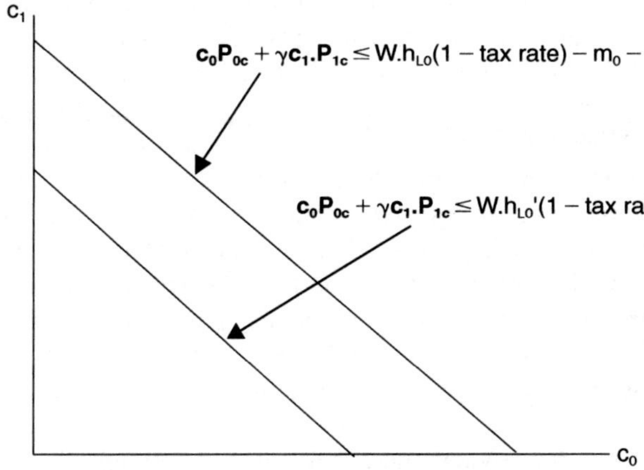

Figure 2.3 Budget constraints under different scenarios.

turned into purchasing power: h_{L0} is the time spent working and W and the wage rate per unit time. γ translates future retirement income into the present.

The budget constraint for the "most unfortunate" case (i.e. poor health in both periods) is:

$$c_0P_{0c} + m_0' + \gamma c_1P_{1c} + \gamma m_1' \leq W.h_{L0}'\,(1 - \text{tax rate}) \qquad [2.3]$$

In the most unfortunate case, not only will the budget constraints more binding, but because of poorer health, the individual suffers a further loss of utility because of fewer working hours (h_{L0}'), while consumption attributes X and functional health h are both lower.

According to a study by a research team from Harvard University, medical problems caused 62 percent of all personal bankruptcies filed in the United States in 2007.[4] Underscoring the inadequacy of market-based health insurance products, they also found that 78 percent of those filers had medical insurance at the start of their illness, including 60.3 percent who had private coverage, not Medicare or Medicaid.

Proposition 2.10 Healthcare expenses and welfare
Healthcare expenses represent a major cause of personal bankruptcies and pose a significant risk to individuals and worry over huge healthcare expenses undermines *ex ante* utility.

2.4 Efficient production of health

The rate of depreciation of health is the joint outcome of private activity and public policy. At the same time, the stock of health is increased whenever there is a medical advance that permits effective treatment of an ailment. Note that this increase in the stock of health is not associated with any physical change on the part of the people. Further, to the extent that private and public healthcare expenditures are substitutes, the more healthcare input is provided by the public sector the less privately procured input will be necessary. Within the private sector, households and healthcare providers interact with consequences on health, and they interact in an environment that is determined by public policy. For example, if the government requires everyone to subscribe to a health insurance plan, or if the health insurance plan is subsidized, healthcare behavior will certainly change. Health policy generally will modify the budget constraint faced by households. By changing prices and costs and the perception of risk, the incentives of both households and caregivers will be changed. By direct reallocation of resources, the amount of total spending on healthcare will also be changed.

From the public policy point of view, there is the central problem of structuring incentives so that (1) medical inputs are used efficiently in enhancing or preserving the health stock; (2) households adopt a lifestyle taking full account of the true social costs.[5] In this regard the following peculiarities about healthcare must be noted.

First, while the consumers of healthcare services are households, households have very *limited information* on their own health status and the quality of healthcare provided by different physicians. Above all, they do not know what kind of healthcare service is most appropriate to their situations. Consumers of healthcare services generally depend on medical professionals to advise them about what treatment or diagnostic procedures are needed. Thus we have a case of "*information asymmetry*." They need well trained doctors to look after their health. A key question is whether doctors do indeed look after their health disinterestedly. Physicians in private practice make their living by having patients visiting them. The interest of physicians in earning an income and the interest of patients in having a healthy life thus generally stand in conflict. Moreover, the interest of physicians in making a living and the interest of insurance companies also stand in conflict. These considerations represent what is called a *principal–agent problem*. Can we rely on physicians to be an agent to champion for the patient's best interest? Can we rely on physicians to be an agent for insurance companies to spend on a patient only when necessary and appropriate?

Proposition 2.11 Information asymmetry in the healthcare market
Consumers of healthcare services generally rely on doctors to advise them what healthcare services are needed. Without knowing the basis as to how doctors reach their judgments, they have difficulty knowing if doctors' advice, diagnoses and prescriptions are accurate.

Proposition 2.12 Principal–agent problem
The interests of caregivers in the marketplace and those of patients do not align, giving rise to a possible conflict of interest on the part of caregivers which gives rise to the principal–agent problem, i.e., the possibility of caregivers as the "agents" of patients not really serving the interests of the "principals" who appoint them to look after their health.

Second, medical expertise, drugs and medical technology are all very expensive. With an aging population the cost of medical care is projected to continue to increase rapidly well into the future. Who is to tell if expenditures are well spent? What are the criteria to tell if expenditures are well spent?

Third, medical care needs are of two kinds: chronic or episodic. Needs arising from existing chronic health problems are *uninsurable* in the private market because no insurer would offer a policy that is known to be money-losing. But are the chronically sick to be left to fend for themselves? Should the government provide them with healthcare, and if so, on what terms?

Fourth, episodic health problems are insurable, but they are subject to the problem of "*moral hazard*" in the sense that insured people may take fewer preventive steps to avoid health problems, may seek treatment without comparing expected benefits and costs, and may more readily respond positively to medical doctors' advice for diagnostic procedures or treatment without considering the appropriateness of such procedures or treatment. This latter is related to the phenomenon of *supply-side moral hazard.* That is: caregivers may supply more services than is appropriate for patients, with a view to pocketing financial gains. Regarding supply-side moral hazard in China, Prof. Gu Xin of Beijing University's School of Government had this to say:

> Why do I say over-care is pervasive in China?... China's utilization rate of antibiotics is the world's first; China's propensity to use Caesarean section in delivery is the world's first; China's use of intravenous injections is the world's first; and China's use of stents in heart surgery is the world's first.[6]

Definition: moral hazard

Demand-side moral hazard occurs when people change their behavior once they feel protected by insurance, whether such insurance is formal or informal. It is predicated on an excessively low price paid by the consumer. Supply-side moral hazard occurs when suppliers of a service over-supply the service in pursuit of profit. It is predicated on an excessively high price received by the producer.

Fifth, healthcare, whether of the preventive or the curative type, has *external effects*. Thus, improved immunity against a disease achieved by injection of a vaccine among part of the population will benefit the rest of the population, because their chances of contracting the disease will also come down. Effectively curing a patient of tuberculosis will also reduce the chances of the disease spreading to other victims. In terms of our model, we can say that even though the random factors may be taken as given and external to individual households, they may actually be affected by their joint behavior. Thus more drunk drivers in the street would increase the unfavorable random factor increasing the chance for traffic accidents to adversely affect one's health.

Efficient production of health and efficient supply of insurance must include credible ways of dealing with moral hazard, incentives and externalities.

Marginal cost pricing

Economists believe that marginal cost pricing is the most efficient because under free and informed choice consumers will buy a product or a service whenever its value is higher than the price paid. Marginal cost pricing implies that consumers will buy a product or a service whenever the value derived from consumption is higher than the marginal cost. Marginal cost pricing may imply that the provider cannot recover the overhead or fixed costs. Marginal cost pricing also implies that suppliers of a service will only be compensated for the direct costs expended when they supply the service.

Under market based fee-for-service, typically charges are well over marginal cost, offering the provider a huge mark-up that helps cover fixed costs, including malpractice insurance premiums, and yields a profit.

2.5 Fee-reducing insurance versus excessive burden protection

Before we analyze the relative superiority of these two approaches, we stipulate that efficiency requires healthcare services to be set at levels reflecting the direct marginal costs of services. Such pricing would minimize moral hazard[7] from both the demand side and the supply side. As is well known, asymmetric information and agency problems characterize the healthcare market and may lead to overcharges and supply of unnecessary services if patients have no choice other than attending private clinics and private hospitals. Vaithianathan (2006) shows that under imperfect competition insurance markets could lead to health cost inflation. On the other hand, Lu and Hsiao (2003) observe that, by "reducing overcharges, duplication and overuse of health services and tests, transaction costs, and other costs" Taiwan was able to contain the possible cost explosion that might be expected when a single payer national insurance plan was introduced. For the purposes of formal analysis, we shall assume that health services are charged at standard rates equal to direct marginal costs. This allows us to focus on the implications of the two forms of insurance, absolving from information asymmetry problems.[8]

Fee-reducing health insurance (FRI) offers patients the opportunity to get healthcare at a fraction of the standard charge or actual direct cost. There may be different kinds of fee-reducing insurance plans: a plan to cover consultation, a drug plan, a dental plan, etc. FRI plans are typically funded by insurance premiums, and they may involve deductibles or co-payments. Deductibles are the amounts that the patient pays each time he makes a claim before the insurance benefits kick in. Co-payments are the shares of the cost that the patient must pay along with the insurance agency. Even with co-payments, under FRI patients pay a fraction of the true direct costs when they use a service. They are therefore more likely to comply with doctors' advice for a second visit or for tests than otherwise.

In contrast to FRI, EBP requires the patient to be responsible for the direct cost of healthcare up to an annual cap or ceiling. Because it also covers patients with pre-existing or chronic conditions it is not just an insurance plan. Before total eligible spending hits the cap, patients pay the normal charges, so the incentive to utilize services prudently is preserved. After having paid the threshold amount patients pay nothing for the rest of the year when they use EBP-covered services. But at that point they normally have genuine needs, and moral hazard is usually not a serious issue.

Administratively, EBI works very simply with the modern smart card. The annual cap is a deductible that applies to total cumulative healthcare expenditures within the year. The smart card tracks and remembers all eligible expenditures[9] in the year, as well as providing a "key" for access to the full medical history of the patient. EBI therefore provides the backbone to a "seamless" insurance and healthcare plan, allowing ALL eligible expenses, including drugs, consultation, diagnostics, dental care, etc., to be included, and facilitating care and coordination. Conceptually, the annual deductible represents "affordable burden"; expenditures beyond the annual cap represent "excessive burden" and are totally absorbed by the government.

Both FRI and EBP can, if mandated, be universally accessible to citizens. However, reduced fees may still be burdensome. Under FRI patients who are chronically ill or who suffer from catastrophic events may still have to face a burdensome and unpredictable healthcare bill, while the reduced charges may cause the healthy to use more resources than is optimal. Because a large number of generally healthy patients pay less and use more services, the resources available for the sicker people will be less, rendering the quality of care lower than that under EBI for the group that need the most care. This implies that in terms of effective protection from true risks, EBP is superior to FRI both because patients are protected from excessive burden, and because the quality of care will be better under EBI. A more formal demonstration is provided in Appendix 2.1.

In principle, both FRI and EBI can be sustainable if the withdrawals from the system (i.e., the benefits) are commensurate with the payments into the system (premiums, fees and any subsidy from the general tax revenue). But because FRI triggers more moral hazard than EBI, it will require greater inputs in terms of premiums and fees to generate the same outputs (protection). In other words, while FRI and EBI can both be sustainable, the cost of FRI will be higher or the degree of protection will be lower than can be obtained under EBI.

Under FRI as under EBI, it will be necessary to spell out what services are covered and what are not. One attraction of the EBI is that it crystallizes the fact that the higher the annual cap is, the more resources will be paid into the system and so the greater can be the potential coverage. The community can make a collective decision over the trade-off between the annual cap and the coverage. Moreover, the community can make a collective decision over how much concession it would like to give to the poor, who can be given the benefit of both a lower cap and lower fees. Under the EBI, members of the community are also free to buy fee-reducing insurance for "within-cap" spending and for "beyond EBI coverage" benefits. So the EBI is very versatile, allowing choice and participation on several fronts.

Finally, a big benefit of the EBI is its simplicity. There is no need to differentiate different kinds of healthcare expenses as long as they are considered part of a standard healthcare package. Each person can have one central file, covering both medical history and spending record. The central file can be accessed by any authorized medical personnel with approval by the patient on the production of a smart card. It provides the basis for "seamless care." Moreover, provided that the annual spending cap is reasonably high and the fees can reflect to an extent the direct costs of care it is even possible to dispense with the collection of the insurance premiums and thus to fund it with the general tax revenue.

Proposition 2.13 EBI

EBI or EBP protects the individual or the household from having to spend beyond what is considered too much to bear on healthcare. It goes hand in hand with a user-fee that is sufficient to reduce moral hazard and requires simply capping all eligible healthcare expenses within the year. It may be funded by an insurance premium from the insured or from the general tax revenue. It is related to the high deductible insurance plans available in the marketplace.

Among publicly maintained healthcare systems, those in Sweden, Australia, Taiwan, mainland China and Switzerland are among those that provide some form of EBI, either on a national or a sub-national scale. In Sweden, the high cost ceilings that cap medical expenses for individuals over any 12-month period are actually ridiculously low and stand at 900 kroner for services (not much more than \$100) and 1,800 kroner for drugs (about \$250) as of 2011.[10] Beyond such thresholds, the state comes in and completely shelters the individual. In the case of China, a WHO working paper (2002) portrayed the new health financing system introduced in some urban areas[11] as consisting of three tiers: *medical savings accounts*; out-of-pocket deductibles; and social insurance accounts (the "three tier system").

> The beneficiaries pay for healthcare from their MSAs until all money in the accounts has been spent. Then a further deductible at a specified percentage of their annual wage has to be paid out-of-pocket before the social risk-pool fund (SIA) comes in. Beyond the deductible amount, the patients are still responsible for a co-payment that declines as a share of the medical costs as they increase. There is finally an upper limit on the total annual out-of-pocket payment depending on the individual's annual income, above which social insurance covers all expenses.
>
> (Hanvoravongchai, 2002: 24–25)

This is obviously a more complicated system of EBI than that explained in our examples, but when there is a big dispersion of incomes across a big nation such as China, setting the annual cap as a percentage of the average annual wage income for the local community may be a sensible approach., and appears to be the more prevalent approach more recently.[12] For the application of the EBP principle in the other countries, please refer to the relevant chapters that follow.

The Chinese adaptation of the Medical Savings Accounts appears to be quite attractive. It provides some assurance that patients under EBI will have funds to pay for at least a portion of the amounts up to the annual deductible. The co-payments further help conserve the healthcare funds. In a country where public funding for healthcare is tight the *MSA-cum-co-payment* arrangement complements the EBP.

Optimal cost sharing and the Lifetime Choice-care Supplement

Newhouse (2006) raised an important issue, asking what constitutes optimal cost/risk sharing between the patient and the insurer. Under EBI patients have to pay full marginal costs of care. Will this discourage them from seeking medical help leading to delays in detection and treatment? One way of ameliorating this effect[13] is, instead of charging at full marginal cost below the threshold and charging nothing above the threshold, to charge at, say, 75 percent of full marginal cost up to some point, and then 25 percent beyond that point, and then finally nothing beyond the ultimate threshold. The prospect of reduced and ultimately zero charges will encourage people to seek timely care that may save costs over the long run. In any case, educating people about the right attitude to take in regard to medical care is important and should have a place in health policy.

The subject of cost-sharing or risk-sharing appears to be even more important as we consider the more costly kinds of care that cannot be covered in the standard EBI plan. The emergence of costly diagnosis and treatment[14] for various health problems over the years and the rising expectations of the community for quality healthcare have rendered it necessary to limit coverage in the basic healthcare plan. Yet few patients can take full responsibility for costly medical intervention or diagnosis, while few governments are in the position to offer such protection to everybody. This gives rise to a cost-sharing proposal, namely the "*Lifetime Choice-care Supplement*" (LCS).

The proposal of the LCS is to partially subsidize patients in need of expensive diagnostics or treatment. Put simply, it makes available an amount of $X for each citizen over his lifetime for spending on costly healthcare and diagnostics that are not covered in the standard healthcare plan. This $X, like the MSA, is nominally set aside in a personalized account and is specific to each eligible member of the community. It is nominally set aside in the sense that it may or may not be taken up. If it is not taken up, it will revert to the general revenue. It is different from the MSA in that the funds come from the government rather than from the individual's own savings. To minimize moral hazard, the individual must match withdrawals from the LCS with his own spending.[15] This provision mirrors the requirement in China that patients covered by the "three-tier system" pay a fixed 20 percent co-payment on expensive diagnostic services.

The LCS scores high on all the five criteria mentioned. First, it follows the universality principle and is simple to administer. Subject to the fiscal conditions of the economy, the LCS will be set at a sustainable level. The supplement clearly provides greater choice and enhances protection over what is available under EBI. The LCS has two built-in features that will help contain moral hazard: individuals are subject to a lifetime budget constraint, they know that money withdrawn from the LCS now means less protection in the future; co-payments will discourage abusive use of the funds. While some may say that this arrangement may not help the very poor, co-payments can be reduced for them and the scheme also does not rule out other explicit redistribution measures to help the poor. Some may also argue that the rich should not be eligible for the benefits. But as long as the tax system is progressive, the rich are supporting the system and there will be no free lunch for the rich as a group.

2.6 Conclusions

Pauly and Goodman (1995) proposed combining the medical savings account with a form of catastrophic insurance. By softening the burden of the fees at the time a patient uses the healthcare services with an MSA and covering only catastrophic needs, insurance premiums can be significantly reduced. They propose to offer people incentives to put the savings from lower premiums into an MSA. Their proposal has some parallels to the EBI plan but also some distinct differences.

First, on parallels, they are obviously also concerned about excessive burden, since paying for catastrophic care is the most onerous among healthcare services. Most catastrophic health insurance plans specify the kinds of services covered, such as hospitalization upon specified diseases or needs. But costs on otherwise non-catastrophic services can build up and become onerous.

They also proposed "tax credits for catastrophic coverage and MSAs as the only (minimal) government interventions" (p. 131). Since pre-existing conditions such as AIDS, diabetes, emphysema, heart disease, multiple sclerosis and schizophrenia would not normally get covered from a catastrophic health plan, they leave open the question of how to deal with those who already suffer such problems. While the present volume agrees with Pauly and Goodman over the benefits of an MSA in assisting patients to cover their deductible payments, public interest considerations would lead us to recommend a universal EBP plan that will cover people with pre-existing and chronic conditions as well.

Rather than opting for a "minimal" intervention, because of the unique nature of the healthcare market we recommend that the government should completely fund the fixed costs of public hospitals and should charge patients direct costs up to their yearly spending thresholds, while underwriting all standard care costs beyond such thresholds. These charges and payments should be collected by the public hospitals, and add to the direct yearly allocations as financing. The government will collect standard premiums to finance the EBI. This is not to say that patients must use the services of public hospitals. Following the principle of maximum patient choice, they may, if desired, opt for private hospitals, but when they do so and pay higher than standard charges, they are allowed to count only the standard charges toward their annual spending threshold. When their spending exceeds the annual threshold, the government will also pay only the standard fees and charges if they continue to opt for private hospital services.

Beyond standard basic care this chapter puts forward a proposal along the line of "Money Follows the Patient." The LCS for eligible citizens, it relies on two mechanisms to contain possible demand-side moral hazard, namely the lifetime budget constraint and the co-payment. The design provides a cap on the potential burden of the government. It gives citizens the option to buy costly care that would otherwise be beyond their affordability. The co-payment also encourages patients to scrutinize the nature and quality of the services, thus offering a check on possible supply-side moral hazard.

These cost-sharing arrangements and EBP appear promising as key ingredients in an ideal healthcare policy, as they offer choice and protection while preserving the incentives to use healthcare resources efficiently.

Appendix 2.1 Superiority of EBP over FRI

An example will illustrate the superiority of EBP over FRI. Suppose in a community of P people, every year uP are hit by misfortune ("unfortunate") and $(1-u)P$ people are not hit by misfortune ("fortunate"). It takes \$F annually to care for the fortunate ones (F will be called the *medical fee* or *cost for the fortunate*), and \$nF to care for the unfortunate ones each year, where n is a multiple of F (n will be called the "*misfortune multiple*"). By assumption, the probability of being fortunate and that of being unfortunate are $(1-u)$ and u respectively. Under EBI with an *annual deductible cap* D, the patient pays the lesser of D and F annually if he is "fortunate" (i.e., F) and the lesser of D and nF annually if he is "unfortunate" (i.e., D). Thus the total amount that will be raised through charges from the entire population works out to:

$$F(1-u)P + D.uP \text{ since } nF > D > F \qquad [A2.1]$$

Since F and nF are the true annual direct costs of caring for each fortunate and unfortunate patient respectively, the premium required to finance the EBP scheme, assuming zero *loading cost*,[16] works out to (total healthcare spending minus fees collected from the fortunate and the unfortunate people, then divided by population):

$$[F(1-u)P+nFuP-F(1-u)P-DuP]/P. \quad \text{[“the actuarially fair EBI premium”]} \qquad [A2.2]$$

The individual's annual healthcare cost is equal to the EBP premium plus the out-of-pocket cost, and is equal to:

$$[F(1-u)P+nFuP-F(1-u)P-DuP]/P+F \quad \text{if he is fortunate,} \qquad [A2.3]$$

$$[F(1-u)P+nFuP-F(1-u)P-DuP]/P+D \quad \text{if he is unfortunate.} \qquad [A2.4]$$

Under pure FRI, there is no deductible amount. Assuming that the discount factor is d, the actual annual charges payable after the discount is $(1-d)F$ for the fortunate ones, and $(1-d)nF$ for the unfortunate ones.

The required premium under FRI ("the actuarially fair FRI premium") then becomes:

$$[F(1-u)P+nFuP-(1-d)F(1-u)P-(1-d)nFuP]/P=F(1-u)+nFu-(1-d)F(1-u)-(1-d)nFu \qquad [A2.5]$$

Since the fortunate and the unfortunate pay the same premium, the individual's annual healthcare cost inclusive of the health insurance premium under fee-reducing insurance becomes:

$$[F(1-u)+nFu-(1-d)F(1-u)-(1-d)nFu]+(1-d)F \quad \text{if he is fortunate,} \qquad [A2.3'] \text{ and}$$

$$[F(1-u)+nFu-(1-d)F(1-u)-(1-d)nFu+(1-d)nF \quad \text{if he is unfortunate.} \qquad [A2.4']$$

For simplicity let us first assume that the behavior of the insured and the incidence of health hazards do not change with the kind of insurance. We will relax this assumption later.

By differentiating the risk premiums under EBI and FRI with respect to u and n, we can see how the risk premium changes when the misfortune multiple increases and when the probability of misfortune increases.

$$\frac{\partial Eqn(A2.2)}{\partial u} = nF - D \qquad [A2.6]$$

This shows that under EBP when the chances of misfortune u increase, the premium goes up by the excess of nF over the annual deductible D. An increase in the annual deductible can neutralize any increase in pressures to raise premiums.

$$\frac{\partial Eqn(A2.2)}{\partial n} = Fu \qquad [A2.7]$$

Thus under EBP an increase in the misfortune multiple n will raise the premium. This effect will increase with the probability of the misfortune u and the medical cost for the fortunate F. Similarly we can work out how the premium under FRI varies when u and n change:

$$\frac{\partial Eqn(A2.5)}{\partial u} = -F + nF + (1-d)F - (1-d)nF = \qquad [A2.8]$$
$$nF - dF - (1-d)nF = (n-1)dF$$

How much the FRI premium rises when the probability of misfortune u rises depends on the discount offered d and the medical cost for the fortunate F, as well as the misfortune multiple n.

$$\frac{\partial Eqn(A2.5)}{\partial n} = Fu - (1-d)Fu = dFu \qquad [A2.9]$$

Equation A2.9 shows that apart from the medical cost base F and the chances of misfortune u, the magnitude of the discount offered will directly impact on the insurance premium as the misfortune multiple increases.

We can work out the ratio of the unfortunate scenario cost to the patient to the fortunate scenario cost to the patient. This will be called the "*risk ratio.*"

Risk ratio under EBI

$$= \frac{F(1-u) + nFu - F(1-u) - Du + D}{F(1-u) + nFu - F(1-u) - Du + F} \qquad [A2.10]$$

Risk ratio under FRI

$$= \frac{F(1-u) + nFu - (1-d)F(1-u) - (1-d)nFu + (1-d)nF}{F(1-u) + nFu - (1-d)F(1-u) - (1-d)nFu + (1-d)F} \qquad [A2.11]$$

In general, if D is smaller than (1 − d)nF the risk ratio will be bigger under FRI than under EBI.

Let us now turn to a numerical example.

$$\text{Min}(D, F) \times (P-U) + \text{Min}(D, nF)U = F(P-U) + DU \text{ since } nF > D > F$$

Since F and nF are the true annual direct costs of caring for the fortunate and the unfortunate respectively, the premium required to finance the EBI scheme, assuming zero loading cost, works out to:

$$[F(P-U) + nFU - F(P-U) - DU]/P \qquad \text{["the actuarially fair EBI premium"]}$$

The individual's annual healthcare cost is equal to the EBI premium plus the out-of-pocket charges. Thus:

$$[F(P-U)+nFU-F(P-U)-DU]/P+F \quad \text{if he is fortunate, and}$$

$$F(P-U)+nFU-F(P-U)-DU]/P+D \quad \text{if he is unfortunate.}$$

Now consider the pure Fee Reducing Insurance. Assuming that the fee reduction discount factor is d, the actual annual charges payable is $(1-d)F$ for the fortunate ones, and $(1-d)nF$ for the unfortunate ones.

The required premium under FRI then becomes:

$$[F(P-U)+nFU-(1-d)\,F(P-U)-(1-d)nFU]/P$$ ["the actuarially fair FRI premium"]

The individual's annual healthcare cost inclusive of the health insurance premium under fee-reducing insurance becomes:

$$[F(P-U)+nFU-(1-d)F(P-U)-(1-d)nFU]/P+(1-d)F \quad \text{if he is fortunate, and}$$

$$[F(P-U)+nFU-(1-d)F(P-U)-(1-d)nFU]/P+(1-d)nF \quad \text{if he is unfortunate.}$$

Let us first assume that the behavior of the insured and the incidence of health hazards do not change with the kind of insurance. We will now turn to a numerical example.

In a community of 100,000 people, all are insured. 99,000 people (99 percent) in each period are fortunate, and 1,000 people (1 percent) are unfortunate. The misfortune multiple is 10. Thus it costs ten times as much to care for the unfortunate as to care for the fortunate. Suppose the cost of caring for a fortunate person is $10,000. Table A2.1 and Table A2.2 present the charges and costs borne by the fortunate and the unfortunate under EBI and FRI respectively at different annual caps and discount factors. They indicate that the two kinds of insurance would generate identical stakes when the EBI annual deductible (the cap) stands at $10,000 and when the FRI discount factor rises to 100 percent. The discount factor d at 100 percent means that FRI reduces charges to zero. Clearly, under these assumptions there will be a serious problem of moral hazard. On the other hand, even at 50 percent discount ($d=50$ percent), the "risk ratio" would still be over 5, meaning that when one is hit with misfortune, total healthcare cost would be over five times as high as when one is not.

Assuming that people are risk averse, EBI when $D=\$10,000$ clearly dominates over FRI when $d=10$–90 percent because greater welfare is associated with smaller risks, other things being equal.[17] When d rises to 100 percent, the FRI risk ratio does fall to 1 and becomes identical with that of EBI when $D=\$10,000$. However, the assumption of behavior neutrality when healthcare charges are so heavily discounted will certainly be untenable.

Table A2.1 Excessive burden insurance when misfortune multiple = 10 and probability of misfortune = 1 percent

Amount of annual deductible D (the "Cap") (a)	*Charges paid by fortunate (b)*	*Charges paid by unfortunate (c)*	*Premium or per capita financing required (d)*	*Minimum individual pays (e)*	*Maximum individual pays (f)*	*Individual's expected cost (g)*	*Risk ratio (h) = (f)/(e)*
10,000	10,000	10,000	900	10,900	10,900	10,900	1.00
20,000	10,000	20,000	800	10,800	20,800	10,900	1.93
30,000	10,000	30,000	700	10,700	30,700	10,900	2.87
40,000	10,000	40,000	600	10,600	40,600	10,900	3.83
50,000	10,000	50,000	500	10,500	50,500	10,900	4.81
70,000	10,000	70,000	400	10,400	60,400	10,900	5.81
60,000	10,000	60,000	300	10,300	70,300	10,900	6.83
80,000	10,000	80,000	200	10,200	80,200	10,900	7.86
90,000	10,000	90,000	100	10,100	90,100	10,900	8.92
100,000	10,000	100,000	0	10,000	100,000	10,900	10.00

Notes

Population of 100,000 is assumed as in the text. Behavior neutrality assumed. Social cost of healthcare for each unfortunate person = \$100,000 = 10 × social cost of healthcare for a fortunate person. Individuals pay full direct costs of care up to the cap. Risk ratio = Total Cost to Individual if Unfortunate divided by Total Cost to Individual if Fortunate. Expected cost = Sum of these Costs weighted by the probabilities of misfortune and fortune.

Table A2.2 Fee reducing insurance when misfortune multiple = 10 and probability of misfortune = 1 percent

Discount factor d (a) (%) (h) = (f)/(e)	*Charges paid by fortunate (b)*	*Charges paid by unfortunate (c)*	*Premium or per capita financing required (d)*	*Minimum individual pays (e)*	*Maximum individual pays (f)*	*Individual's expected cost (g)*	*Risk ratio*
10	9,000	90,000	1,090	10,090	91,090	10,900	9.03
20	8,000	80,000	2,180	10,180	82,180	10,900	8.07
30	7,000	70,000	3,270	10,270	73,270	10,900	7.13
40	6,000	60,000	4,360	10,360	64,360	10,900	6.21
50	5,000	50,000	5,450	10,450	55,450	10,900	5.31
60	4,000	40,000	6,540	10,540	46,540	10,900	4.42
70	3,000	30,000	7,630	10,630	37,630	10,900	3.54
80	2,000	20,000	8,720	10,720	28,720	10,900	2.68
90	1,000	10,000	9,810	10,810	19,810	10,900	1.83
100	0	0	10,900	10,900	10,900	10,900	1.00

Note

At 100 percent discount, stakes under FRI would be identical with stakes under EBI with an annual cap at $10,000, *assuming no moral hazard.*

First, as d rises the incentives for self-protection or preventive care will fall, because the marginal benefits from such self-protection, in the form of savings in healthcare costs at the margin, are reduced. Second, as indicated in Table A2.2, the required insurance premiums increase as the rate of discount rises. When people have paid a large insurance premium in the first place, there is an incentive to try to "get even" with the insurers and demand more services than necessary. In contrast, pure EBI does not protect an individual from healthcare costs unless they become excessive. Such high levels of spending only come after the patient has paid the cap amount and are typically associated with hospitalization and even surgical operations. Any moral hazard problems associated with EBI tend to be smaller.

One can use the framework of Von Neumann and Morgenstern to demonstrate that expected utility under EBI is indeed higher than expected utility under FRI. For example, for EBI (D=\$10,000) and FRI (d=10 percent), assuming that the initial income without illness is \$200,000 and that the insurance premiums are actuarially fair, the expected income is \$200,000−\$10,900=\$189,100 under both EBI and FRI. Under FRI, the stakes can be summarized as (\$200,000−\$91,090=\$108,910, \$200,000−\$10,090=\$189,910). Under EBI the stakes become (\$200,000−\$10,900=\$189,910 always) which is identical with the expected disposable income after healthcare expense. With a concave utility function expected utility will be higher under EBI than under FRI, as shown in Figure A2.1. Even ignoring the disutility of the mental bad from perceived risks, EBI generates higher utility. Because of the greater likelihood of moral hazard

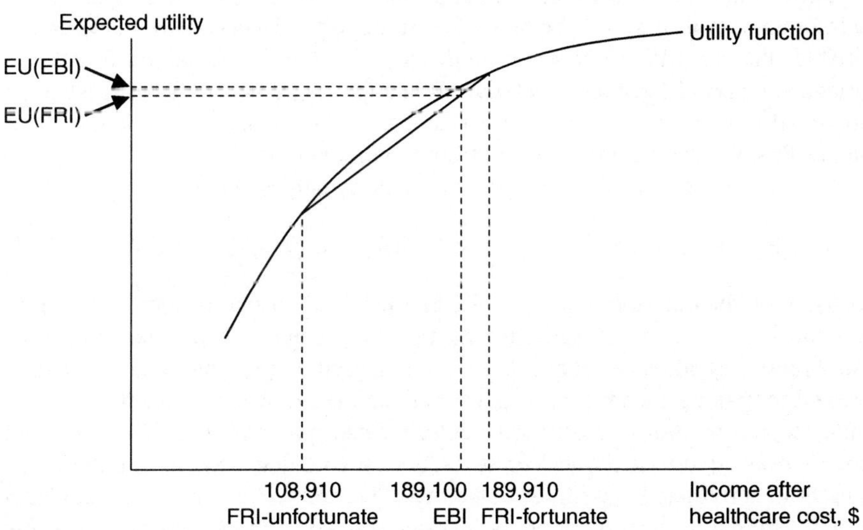

Figure A2.1 Under EBI insurance income is always \$189,100 and yields higher utility than FRI under the Von Neumann–Morgenstern framework (assuming gross annual income = \$200,000) even ignoring disutility of risk.

under fee reducing insurance, actual claims are likely to be much higher under fee reducing insurance, leading to inefficiency.

Appendix 2.2

One common theory provides that utility depends on consumption attributes **X** (the qualities that matter in the utility function) produced through various household activities **A**, "health status" H, and time devoted to work L. Bold letter indicates "vector", or an array of quantities. In a one-period model the utility function can be depicted as follows:

$$U(\mathbf{X}(A_1, A_2, \ldots); H; L) \qquad [A2.12]$$

A problem with this approach is that "health status" is really not a clear concept. Is it a flow? Is it a stock? Given that it is a one-period model, and assuming away uncertainty, there may not be much difference between functional health (a flow) or stock of health, so this may not be a problem.

In a more realistic setting, say if we consider a two-period world with a Working Period and a Retired Period, and allowing uncertainty, we may choose to write:

$$U_0(\mathbf{X}_0(\mathbf{A}_0(\mathbf{c}_{0a}, \mathbf{h}_{0a})), h_0, h_{L0}, e_0) + \lambda U_1(\mathbf{X}_1(\mathbf{A}_1(\mathbf{c}_{1a}, \mathbf{h}_{1a})), h_1, 0, e_1) \qquad [A2.13]$$

Note that utility in the second period is subject to an uncertainty discount factor λ and that no work is rendered in the second period (post-retirement). If there is a chance of non-survival in the second period, λ can be interpreted as the probability of survival. It should be noted that in period 0 decisions are made on the variables that are within one's control during that period. The values of decision variables in period 1 are only tentative. When the future becomes the present the individual may revise his decision variable since he has new information about the health stock that he has inherited from the first period.

We may consider the following health stock dynamics equation:

$$H_1 = H_0 - \delta(\mathbf{A_0}, m_0, g_0, h_{L0}, t_{hc0,} H_{0,} e_0) = \delta(\mathbf{A_1}, m_1, g_1, 0, t_{hc1,} H_{1,} e_1) \qquad [A2.14]$$

Focusing on the decision making in the first period, households maximize utility by choosing the kinds of activities $\mathbf{A_0}$ that they engage in and deciding how much time they allocate among the various activities ($\mathbf{h_a}$), the amount of time devoted to earning income (h_{L0}), as well as the time devoted to healthcare (t_{hc0}). Total income is allocated between *health-related goods and services* (m_0) and *other market goods and services* (**c**) – the latter being used as inputs in the household activities. Households make these decisions in an environment that is largely external to them but more or less determined by the government. g_i is the government-provided healthcare in period i.

Equation A2.14 simply says that the health stock at the beginning of period 1 is equal to the health stock at the beginning of period 0 minus the depreciation of the capital stock, while depreciation depends on the lifestyle (activities A_0), privately provided medical input m, publicly provided medical input g, hours worked h_L, healthcare time t_{hc}, health stock H_0 at the beginning of period 0 as given by the biophysical conditions and the state of technology, and random, environmental factors e.

The entire health stock is assumed to depreciate away in the second period.

Additional constraints include the following:

budget constraint $\mathbf{c_0 . P_{0c}} + m_0 + \beta(\mathbf{c_1 . P_{1c}} + m_1) \leq W.h_{L0}(1 - \text{tax rate})$ [A2.15]

That is, the present value of consumption expenditures and medical expenditures must not exceed after-tax labor income, β being the discount factor for expenditures in the second period.

household production functions $\mathbf{X_0(A_0(c_{0a}, h_{0a}))}, \mathbf{X_1(A_1(c_{1a}, h_{1a}))}$ [A2.16]

This says household activities **a** require market goods **c** and activity time **h** and that these activities give rise to the qualities that enter the utility function.

The functional health production function in the two periods:

$$h_0 = f(\mathbf{A}_0, m_0, g_0, h_{L0}, t_{hc0}, H_0, e_0) \quad [A2.17]$$

$$h_1 = f(\mathbf{A}_1, m_1, g_1, 0, t_{hc1}, H_1, e_1) \quad [A2.18]$$

Functional health, measured in EHDs, is the result of lifestyle **A**, h_{Li}, the healthcare plan (M, t_{hci}), publicly provided healthcare input (g), random factors and the initial health stock.

time allocation constraint $\Sigma_a h_{ai} = h_i - h_{Li} - t_{hci}$ for $i = 0, 1$ [A2.19]

Household production activity time is what "healthy time" remains after deducting working time and healthcare time. Healthcare time include time spent in activities like washing hands, tooth brushing and flossing, visiting doctors, exercises, etc.

Tax rate, government healthcare spending g, all market prices and the state of medical technology as available in both the private and public sectors.

From this model we can solve for the maximized equilibrium utility:

$$U^* = U_0(\mathbf{X}_0(\mathbf{A}_0(\mathbf{c_{0a}}^*, \mathbf{h_{0a}}^*)), h_0^*, h_{L0}^*) + \beta U_1(\mathbf{X}_1(\mathbf{A}_1(\mathbf{c_{1a}}^*, \mathbf{h_{1a}}^*)), h_1^*, 0) \quad [A2.20]$$

Optimal healthcare plan $= (m_0^*, t_{hc0}^*)$ and (m_1^*, t_{hci}^*) [A2.21]

Optimal functional health: $h_0^* = f(\mathbf{A}_0^*, m_0^*, g_0, h_{L0}^*, t_{hc0}^*, H_0, e_0)$ [A2.22]

$$h_1^* = f(\mathbf{A}_1^*, m_1^*, g_1, 0, t_{hc1}^*, H_0 - \delta_0^*, e_1) \quad [A2.23]$$

Optimal health stock depreciation: $\delta(A_0*, m_{0*}, g_0, h_{L0}*, t_{hc0}*, H_0, e_0)$ [A2.24]

$\delta(A_1*, m_1*, g_1, 0, t_{hc1}*, H_1, e_1)$ [A2.25]

where the asterisks indicate equilibrium optimal values given the exogenous variables.

Even under this simple framework, because of random factors e_0 and e_1, all decision variables including $\mathbf{c}_a$, $\mathbf{h}_a$, m, h_L, t_{hcs}, t_{hch} are also subject to stochastic influences. So all decision variables are conditional or contingent on the random events.

Review questions

1 What is the nature of health risks for individuals?
2 What is the nature of risks for the government in providing healthcare for its citizens?
3 What is the rationale for capping healthcare costs, and that for charging fees for the use of healthcare services?
4 Compare the advantages and disadvantages of the Fee Reducing Insurance and the EBI. Look at a high deductible healthcare plan as advertised by an insurer. Is it the same as the EBI discussed in the text?
5 Distinguish moral hazard from adverse selection. Is there anything in common between them?

3 Insurance, moral hazard and adverse selection

3.1 Introduction

Insurance is like a good because it brings utility. In particular, insurance brings peace of mind. By buying an insurance policy, the insured person pays a premium in exchange for the protection in the covered period. Something is sacrificed; something is gained. There are two things that are gained. One is peace of mind. This is an immediate benefit. The other is the savings in cost or the compensation against losses that are contingent on the insured state of the world materializing. This is a contingent benefit.

The demand for insurance responds to the premium charged just as the demand for a good responds to its price. But the demand for insurance also depends on the odds involved. In general, human nature being what it is, people want insurance whenever there is a large risk – by large risk is not meant here a large probability for a small loss but a positive probability for a big loss. People want protection from the threat of a big loss. Insurance is usually a profitable business because people are willing to pay a premium – even if they know the insurer is making a profit and that a policy is actuarially unfair. This suggests that "*mental bads*" like anxiety and worry over possible misfortunes carry a real cost to society and that insurance brings net social benefits.

3.2 Moral hazard

The *RAND Health Insurance Study* was conducted by the RAND Corporation in the period 1971–1982[1]. It was a huge social experiment, involving 2,750 families and more than 7,700 individuals, all under 65, and all ineligible for Medicare. They were chosen from six US sites across the United States with a 4:2 urban–rural ratio. They were randomly enrolled in different health insurance plans, encompassing four different levels of co-payment: 0 percent, 25 percent, 50 percent and 95 percent. The fifth plan was a non-profit, *Health Maintenance Organization*[2] (HMO)-style group cooperative. Enrollees in this plan were offered free care. In each case out-of-pocket spending was capped at $1,000 per year or X percent of income, whichever was lower, where X could be 5 percent, 10 percent, or 15 percent for the poor.

The results showed that co-payments reduced the use of nearly all health services. In general, participants who are required to pay made one to two fewer physician visits annually and had 20 percent fewer hospitalizations than those with free care. They also demand less of other types of services, including dental visits, prescriptions and mental health treatment. Consumers in the HMO-style cooperative had 39 percent fewer hospital admissions than consumers with free care in the fee-for-service system, but they had similar use of outpatient services. Individuals who need to pay spend less on healthcare compared to those who do not, and the savings came from abstaining from the use of services rather than from lower prices. Those with 25 percent coinsurance spent 20 percent less than participants with free care, and those with 95 percent coinsurance spent about 30 percent less. Reduced use of services resulted primarily from participants deciding not to initiate care. Once patients entered the healthcare system, cost sharing only modestly affected the intensity or cost of an episode of care, suggesting that doctors take charge once patients are under their care.

The analysis found that although cost sharing reduced the use of care across the board it did not appear to have reduced the quality of care, except for the poorest and the sickest. For this group, it was found that free care improved the control of hypertension, leading to a 10 percent reduction in mortality for those with hypertension. Free care marginally improved vision and increased the likelihood of the poorest seeking dental care. Free care also appeared to reduce the prevalence of serious symptoms among the poorest.

It should be noted that the RAND study involved too short a time span (3–5 years) to track down the possible effects of co-payments on prevention. It is possible that apart from reducing demand cost-sharing may additionally reduce healthcare costs by promoting a healthier lifestyle, though this did not emerge from the study.

The RAND insurance study shows that the demand for medical care is responsive to the price of medical care even though the elasticity of demand is not very high. However, there is more to moral hazard than just utilization of medical services alone. There is moral hazard on the supplier's side, and there is moral hazard on preventive lifestyle.

Figure 3.1 shows that health insurance, by reducing the loss due to the insured event, will shift the marginal benefit of prevention curve down, leading to a decline in the prevention effort. This means a less healthy lifestyle. This has been particularly relevant in recent years, as we observe a rise in lifestyle-related illnesses, such as hypertension and diabetes.

Economists see *demand-side moral hazard* comprising two categories:

a endogenous probability of claims. Less preventive care may lead to a higher probability of claims. This is less of a problem if the insured event is painful, such as injury from a traffic accident, although there is still the problem of fraud. On the other hand, if the insured "event" is a desirable surgery, such as plastic surgery for greater "beauty," then insurance will not work because it will certainly induce more "needed services."

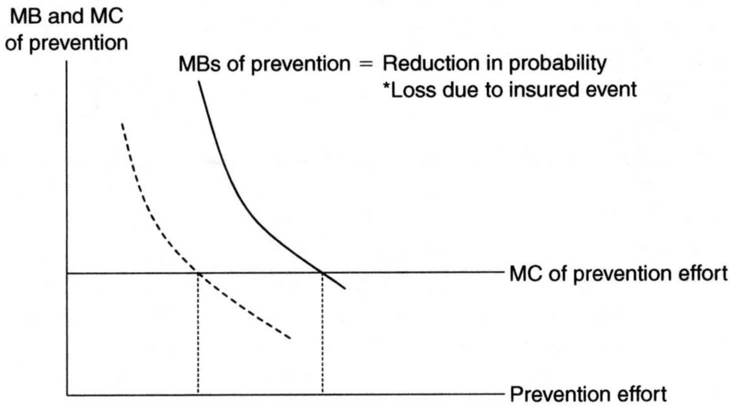

Figure 3.1 Effect of moral hazard on prevention.

b endogenous claims. To the extent that services are covered, larger claims may be made, and this in part may be related to moral hazard on the supplier's side, as when a patient files a claim, it is at least as likely that the service rendered is initiated by the service provider as that it is initiated by the patient.

Supplier Induced Demand or *supply-side moral hazard* is clearly related to the fact of asymmetric information and is an example of a "principal–agent problem" or "agency problem." The patient has to depend on doctors for whatever medical services they need. When providing services is financially attractive some doctors may provide them irrespective of whether the patient needs them or whether they are in the best interest of the patient. There is also the possibility that doctors charge higher fees on patients covered by insurance. From this perspective, it is clearly in the interest of insurance companies to spell out a payment schedule for various services rendered.

Proposition 3.1 Asymmetric information and principal–agent problem
The principal–agent problem is caused by asymmetric information between the principal who has a task to perform and the agent who is asked to perform the task for the principal. Because the interest of the principal and that of the agent may not align, the agent is likely to behave in a way that deviates from the interest of his principal.

3.3 Insurance, risk sharing and risk pooling

The concept of insurance is based on the principle of risk pooling: each member in a group faces risks, but the risks are not correlated, so that each individual is independently exposed to the potential loss. If risks are not correlated, then it is possible to translate the probability of loss P for each individual into a proportion P of a group suffering the loss.

The presence of uncorrelated risks is the key to insurance. If risks are correlated, so that one person suffering a loss implies a higher likelihood for another to suffer a loss, then we can no longer assume that the probability of a person's suffering the loss can translate into a percentage. It will be very difficult to work out a premium that will be profitable for the insurance company.

In general, people are more worried about a prospect involving bigger loss and smaller probability than one involving smaller loss and higher probability. Insurance mainly deals with the former. Typically, when losses are sufficiently big, everyone will become risk averse. The fact that there is a market for insurance and that insurance can be profitable suggests that two prospects with equal expected value may well be regarded differently by an individual by virtue of the different risks involved.

Proposition 3.2 Risk pooling as the basis of insurance
When risks are uncorrelated the probability of an insured event readily translates into the proportion of people affected by the insured event. This allows the calculation of an insurance premium that will cover the cost of claims and generate a profit.

In general, we may write:

Loss* Probability of Loss + Administration Cost + Normal Profit = Insurance Premium.

If administration cost and normal profit are non-existent, then the insurance policy can be said to be actuarially fair. The sum of Administration Cost and Normal Profit is called the *loading fee* of the insurer.

Sometimes risks may be unduly high, and several insurance companies may jointly underwrite a risk. This is in order to protect each of the insurance companies from the unlikely, yet possible, eventuality of having to pay a huge compensation when the insured event occurs. This is called risk sharing.

Insurers may require the insured person to share a part of the cost of the insured event by co-payments and deductibles. Co-payment is the payment that has to be made by the insured each time he makes a claim. Deductible is the amount that the insured person must pay on his own first, before the benefit kicks in. Deductible can be in the form of a deductible per claim or a deductible per year.

Insurance covers a risk, which means a potential loss that may occur with some probability. A pre-existing condition is not a risk, and is not insurable.

3.4 Adverse selection

Insurance companies face a number of problems, apart from unexpectedly large claims. They try to limit excessively large claims by putting a ceiling to the amount of claims. They also try to contain the moral hazard problem by co-payment requirements and deductibles. Insurance companies depend on doctors to take care of their clients who have purchased health insurance from them. But doctors' interests and insurers' interests do not align, giving rise to a principal–agent problem or simply an agency problem.

One way to get around this is to provide healthcare services along with providing insurance coverage. An entity that offers both is an HMO. Because the insurer supplies the healthcare services too, there is no worry that excessive claims or unwarranted claims will be made. Indeed, HMOs try to offer preventive care, so that the insured people will not get sick and will not need the medical services to treat their ailments. HMOs have the incentive to offer prevention, and may in principle help contain medical care costs.

Another problem that insurance companies may face is the problem of adverse selection.[3] Consider the following:

Here the individual is assumed to be initially in position A, with probability P of getting sick and then effectively suffering a big loss in income in the relevant period. The flatter and the steeper lines are actuarially fair transformation lines for a low risk group (P is small) and for a high risk group (P is big) respectively. The fair risk transformation line is defined by the condition: Compensation * Probability of Compensation + Loading Cost = Premium.

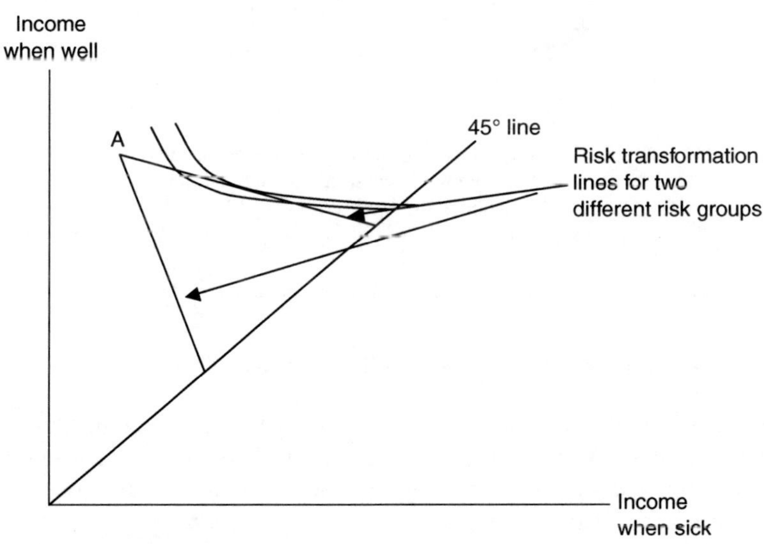

Figure 3.2 Risk transformation lines offered by insurance.

The individual's indifference curve coincides with the risk transformation line if he is "globally risk neutral." But normally, we may expect the usual shape, in which case the individual is risk averse at first, then becomes risk neutral, then becomes risk loving. To the left of the equilibrium point the person is risk averse, since he prefers to take less risk. When the indifference curve is tangent to the transformation line he is risk neutral. Further to the right he becomes risk loving, and prefers less protection.

Based on this framework, it is easy to prove Proposition 3.3:

Proposition 3.3 Instability of a pooling equilibrium
A "pooling equilibrium" that involves the same premium charged to two risk groups that are unknown to the insurers is not stable, and a stable equilibrium is likely to be suboptimal.

A *pooling equilibrium* refers to an equilibrium with both high risk and low risk individuals covered under the same terms. It is something like point P below:

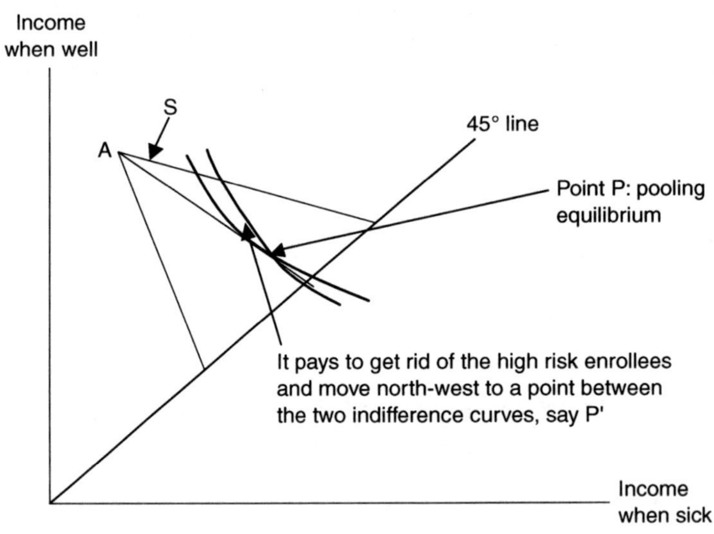

Figure 3.3 What happens after some insurers have moved to P′?

Any insurer at P will find it attractive to move northwest to a point like P′, where high-risk enrollees would leave, creating a profit. But other insurers would have to follow suit, and soon the story repeats itself. A migration northwest is followed by still other insurers. Eventually a stable "*separating equilibrium*" is reached in the suboptimal zone S for the low risk ones while the high risk ones have to put up with S_H.

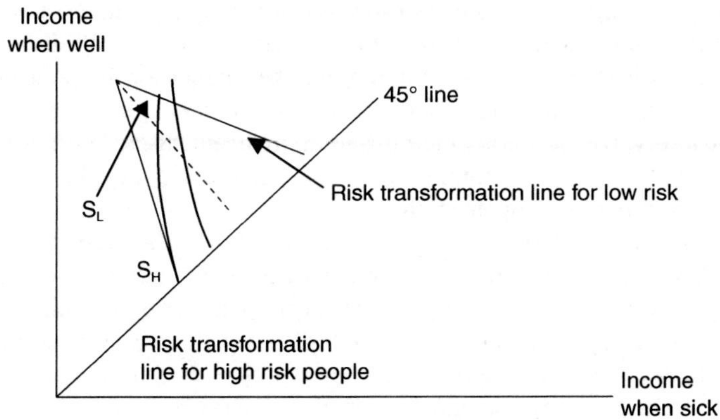

Figure 3.4 The separating equilibrium with different plans for high and low risk patients.

The phenomenon of *self-selection* assures that the good risks choose cheaper plans and bad risks choose high coverage plans and is known as *adverse selection*, because it goes against the interests of the insurer. But the above story does not describe the distinction between expensive plans that offer potentially big compensation versus cheap plans that offer small compensation. The earlier discussion focuses on high probability of compensation but not big compensation. Ignoring the "loading cost" of the insurance company that covers administration

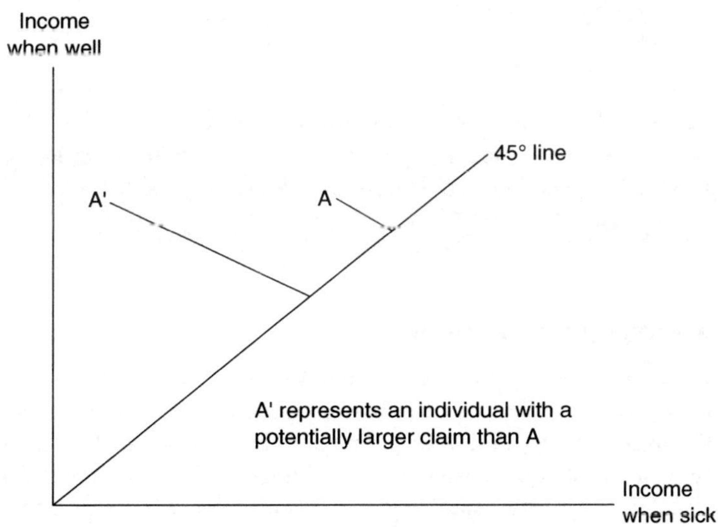

Figure 3.5 Equal probability but different claims.

cost and normal profit, a fair premium must provide Premium = Probability * Compensation, implying that the slope of the risk transformation line equals the probability of the compensation and should be the same when probability is the same. If probability is small, then the premium will be smaller for the same compensation. If A' is a high risk person and A is a low risk person in terms of loss and NOT probability, we can depict their different predicaments as in Figure 3.5, where the slopes of the risk transformation line are the same and depict an identical premium per dollar of compensation.

This suggests that the slope of the risk transformation line should be the same if the probability of loss and therefore compensation is the same. The person with "high risk" in this sense pays a premium at the same rate *per dollar protected*, but wants to buy more protection. A higher coverage plan will attract bigger risks. However, in this case when compensation is directly related to the amount of premium paid adverse selection is not a concern because given the same probability, the profitability of the insurance policy for big or small risk would be the same. Thus the adverse selection problem refers generally to insurance plans attracting enrollees with higher probability of making claims when the insurer *cannot* distinguish between them, or when the insurer cannot charge bigger claimants bigger premiums. Insurance companies typically deal with the problem of adverse selection by opting for *group insurance*, which will include everybody in the plan regardless of risks.

Proposition 3.4 Adverse selection and higher probability of claims
Adverse selection is associated with asymmetric information under which people with higher probability of claims who are unknown to the insurer are more likely to enroll than people with lower probability of claims.

Proposition 3.5 High risks in the sense of big claims
High risks in the sense of bigger payout in the event of a claim will NOT cause the adverse selection problem if the probability of the claim is known.

3.5 Private versus public insurance

Insurance plans are generally financed by premiums. This is certainly true of private plans but may also be true of public plans. However, public plans may fund a public insurance program wholly or partially with taxes. As was mentioned before, Compensation * Probability of Compensation + Loading Cost = Premium. Since public plans usually do not have to include profit and save advertising or marketing costs, potentially public plans can be cheaper than private plans. Some economists, however, may argue that private companies may be more cost-conscious and may therefore be more efficient. There is no evidence that private plans are necessarily more efficient than public plans. On the other hand, the costs of a market-driven health insurance market are well known. One commentator thus described the market-driven health insurance market in the United States:

> In 1999 *The New England Journal of Medicine* published a study that found it cost $300 billion annually to administer various health insurance plans. It takes some three million clerks and managers to run our healthcare system; that's nearly four times the number of doctors practicing medicine in the United States. It costs between $8 and $18 to file each insurance claim, and a third of them have to be refiled.[4]

In the United States, there have been complaints that insurance companies may find all kinds of reasons not to honor a claim and that they may even drop patients from the plans at a time when they need the protection. To guard against abuses, regulatory agencies have to closely monitor and to investigate such complaints. In some countries, such as Switzerland, purchasing a private health insurance plan was mandatory, and it is possible to ban an insurer from dropping anyone. But this will add to the cost of private insurance plans.

However, private insurance plans do serve useful purposes. Typically, public health insurance plans have to be limited in their coverage, and so private insurance companies can fill the gap. Public health insurance plans should not interfere with the principle of choice: i.e., people should have the choice to buy the kind of insurance plans that they want. For this reason, it is proposed that public health insurance plans offer "basic care," to which individuals can top up as they prefer with whatever additional coverage that they want.

It is proposed that the basic plan should be a public one, which has the advantage of being a genuine "group plan" for the entire population. No one will be excluded from coverage because of an existing condition and as long as an ailment falls within the scope of coverage no one needs to worry that protection will be capped. The public insurer will cover the costs of "standard care" for as long as the patient needs it as long as the condition falls within the domain of coverage. This brings up the question of what constitutes "standard care," which is a subject that the society should come to an agreement on, fully aware of the costs of extending coverage and the costs in terms of higher taxes. We will explore this issue in the next chapter.

In Canada, health insurance systems are run by provinces, which run a single payer system, but doctors charge fees strictly according to the schedules determined officially. It is apparent that price fixing is an important element in controlling healthcare costs under single payer plans. This is not surprising, because claims are likely to be bigger if doctors are allowed to charge fees that are paid by the insurer. But price fixing must not be too extensive. In order to promote innovation, it is desirable to have some flexibility. Thus, it makes sense to allow caregivers to set their own fees on services beyond standard care and to let the private market develop policies to cover for non-standard care for those willing to pay for them.

3.6 Conclusions

Problems of moral hazard and *adverse selection* are real and can never be eliminated, and therefore pose serious problems for *both* insurers and patients. For a private insurance plan to survive, it would have to dump all the big risks and the big claimants. But insurance will not be very useful if it cannot insure against big risks, and if private insurance avoids all the potential big risks, then it cannot serve society very well. The "representative individual," pondering the possibilities behind a veil of ignorance, would feel uneasy – leading to a welfare loss.

If problems of moral hazard and adverse selection are serious, the insurance companies will need to charge higher premiums, and that will be bad for those who take preventive care, who do not cheat and who are low-risk.

Commercial insurers typically want to put a ceiling on how much they will pay out in the event of a claim. This means that even individuals with commercial insurance will continue to have risk exposure that is not covered.

Commercial insurers cannot insure against patients with known chronic illnesses that are costly to care for. So the chronically ill and those with "pre-existing conditions," will never be covered by a commercial insurance plan, unless the government somehow mandates it. Patients born with defects and their families, will have a hard time trying to procure the appropriate care.

Commercial insurers have a "built-in" aversion to paying out claims, particularly when the claims are large. In practice, they have been found to try to avoid honoring their obligations by digging out "pre-existing conditions" or other reasons to discredit a claim.

There is often a belief that commercial insurers are somehow more efficient than the government, but given that commercial insurers often reject patients in need of insurance and given the fact that they spend large amounts on marketing and in discrediting claims, there is a case for the government to be the "insurer of the last resort" for "basic healthcare needs" – which will need to be defined, and which we will deal with in the next chapter. If private health insurance provides only supplementary insurance for specified needs, they help by making more choice available for patients. If they offer plans that cover user charges within the yearly spending cap, their liability per patient will be limited; or if they offer plans that cover specified needs beyond what is covered by the government healthcare policy they also promote choice to those willing to pay for the extra choices. This is certainly welfare-enhancing.

Review questions

1 Why are premiums for group insurance generally lower than those for individuals?

2 Is group insurance unfair? Mandatory insurance is an extreme form of group insurance. In what sense is mandatory insurance fair or unfair? How can group insurance be justified from the point of view of public interest?
3 What is the rationale for a "waiting period" before an enrollee in an insurance plan may enjoy the benefits of some specified coverage?
4 Can we describe all people as basically risk-averse?
5 Compare the advantages and disadvantages of fee reducing insurance plans versus those EBI plans.
6 Compare the advantages and disadvantages of a single public healthcare plan versus a myriad of private healthcare plans competing in the marketplace.

4 Health policy evaluation

4.1 Introduction

The single most important criterion to judge if a policy is successful is whether or not it brings net benefits to the community. But this begs the question of what constitutes a benefit and what constitutes a cost. There are generally conflicting goals, and in order to assess if a policy ultimately benefits society *all* of the effects have to be considered, and more specifically, all of the effects on all people have to be considered. Following our earlier discussion on the representative individual, we propose that we have to consider the impact of the proposed policy on everyone in the society, while forgetting our own personal identity and our own personal interests. This approach is very useful, even though it may still be criticized as imprecise. While we would accept that the proposed approach is imprecise, we would argue that it nevertheless goes a long way toward fairly considering many of our key issues, and that it is consistent with an important concept of justice.

4.2 The objectives of healthcare policy: confronting the perennial trade-off among quality, financial accessibility and least burden in healthcare

In principle, we want to seek the *optimal allocation of resources to healthcare*. That is to say, we want to allocate resources to healthcare as long as the resources thus allocated produce more benefit than that arising from alternative uses, such as housing and education. The value of the alternative uses forgone, or the "opportunity cost" of resources allocated to healthcare represents the *total burden* placed on the entire society.

In general if we are willing to accept the increase in burden involved, we can, by increasing the resources allocated to healthcare, improve both the *quality* of healthcare and the *quantity* of healthcare services. In the absence of such increase in resources allocated to healthcare, we can improve quality only at the expense of quantity, or quantity only at the expense of quality. For now let us interpret quality narrowly as the amount of healthcare services received by one person and quantity as the extension of the services to more people. The latter

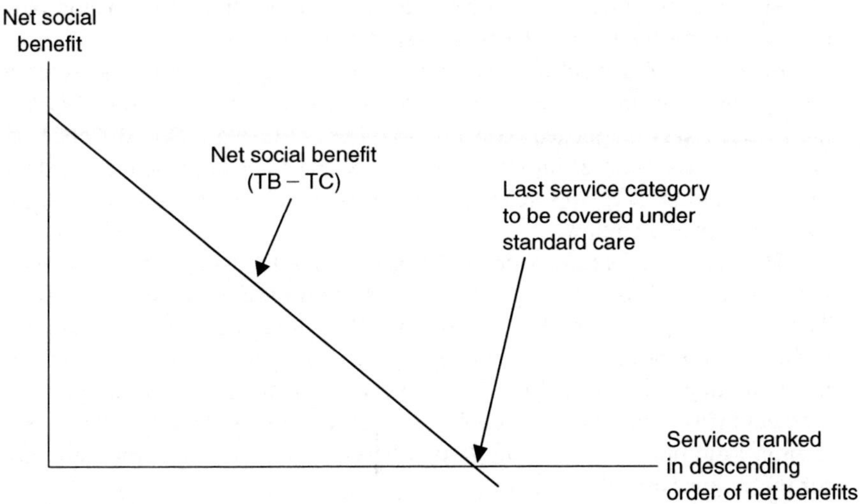

Figure 4.1 The limits of publicly provided care are defined where net social benefit vanishes for the representative individual (TB = total *ex ante* benefit of the service; TC = total expected cost).

would correspond to *financial accessibility*. Given the resources allocated to healthcare, one can provide better care per patient or better access to care. This inevitably begs the question of what services are covered, and what is the level or standard of the services provided if covered. Suppose the latter question has been answered by specifying the "standard care." The first question can then be answered with Figure 4.1.

Figure 4.1 shows that cost–benefit comparisons should determine the boundary between what is publicly provided care and what is not. Publicly provided care would be universally accessible care. Universally accessible care however is not necessarily free care, but it should be affordable care in a substantive sense.

Accessibility is a universal concern of healthcare reform initiatives everywhere. The reason why people value accessibility is that when one gets sick and is desperately in need of medical care, excessive financial burden can ruin the lives of the entire family. Because the fate of people suffering from excessive financial burden is so horrible, using the representative individual approach, we would all support accessibility as a basic policy goal in health policy. Still, even though a service is publicly provided and should be universally accessible, in practice universal access is still limited by resources, leading to the need for waiting in queues, or for long distance travel for getting a service.

Here is the testimony of Sojourners, an active and socially conscious religious group in the United States promoting the cause of justice:

> Robin Beaton is a 59-year-old retired registered nurse who bought an individual insurance policy when she started her own business. Earlier this year she offered this testimony at a congressional hearing:
>
> "In May 2008, I went to the dermatologist for acne. A word was written on my chart and interpreted incorrectly as meaning pre-cancerous. Shortly thereafter, I was diagnosed with Invasive HER-2 Genetic Breast Cancer, a very aggressive form of breast cancer. I was told I needed a double mastectomy. When the surgeons scheduled my surgery I was pre-certified for my two days hospitalization.
>
> "The Friday before the Monday I was scheduled to have my double mastectomy, Blue Cross red flagged my chart due to the dermatologist report. The dermatologist called Blue Cross directly to report that I only had acne and please not hold up my coming surgery. Blue Cross called me to inform me that they were launching a five-year medical investigation into my medical history and that this would take approximately three months. I was frantic. I did not know what to do or where to turn. I knew I could not pay for the surgery myself...
>
> "Next, I found out that my insurance was completely canceled; this was devastating."

Sojourners further voiced support for the Obama healthcare reform initiatives:

> The major proposals for healthcare reform would prohibit insurance companies from arbitrarily canceling insurance and from denying needed care due to pre-existing conditions. This would ensure that all people have access to the care they need, when they need it. If this provision existed, Robin could have had her surgery at an earlier time, before possibly critical months had passed by.

The total amount of resources allocated to healthcare in many countries is a result of both public and private decision making. The former is achieved through a budgetary process which may be highly political, involving a change in taxes collected or a cutback in some other government-provided services. The latter is achieved in the marketplace through the interaction of producers and consumers of healthcare services in the context of the government regulatory regime.

Proposition 4.1 Determination of standard or basic care coverage
Healthcare resources, which may be allocated between quality of healthcare and financial accessibility to healthcare, should be increased as long as the benefits to be enjoyed by the representative individual are larger than the cost of the resources involved in terms of the sacrifice of other socially desirable goods and services. Cost–benefit considerations will determine the limits of "standard care" to be provided publicly.

Now let us relax the earlier assumption that we have solved the question about what should constitute "standard care." Interestingly, we can use the same diagram, Figure 4.1, to answer this question just as well. But we will have to relabel the horizontal axis as service standard for service i. Again when the net marginal benefit for improving service standard as perceived by the representative individual vanishes to zero, no further increase in service level is called for.

We may note that some countries have chosen to cap the total amount of public funds in providing for healthcare. To an extent such caps give the government some protection from ongoing political pressure to increase public spending on healthcare. But this may not be socially optimal if this implies people may be denied needed care in the event of emergency. People may worry about this a lot and welfare may be lost.[1]

Governments generally have a large impact on how much is allocated privately on healthcare as well. The regulatory environment, in particular laws relating to advertising and insurance, will influence how much is spent on healthcare within the private sector.

Given the total resources allocated to healthcare, two questions immediately follow. The first pertains to the sharing of the burden among members of society. We will seek the *optimal sharing of burden*, the meaning of which will be explored shortly. Another question is the *optimal allocation of healthcare resources on different aspects of healthcare*. Of particular interest is the allocation between preventive medicine and treatment. In addition, another question, referred to earlier, is if we should provide basic care to more people (*accessibility to basic care*), or *quality* care to some people selected on the basis of some criteria (for example first come first served).

Proposition 4.2 Efficient allocation between treatment and prevention
Resources should be allocated to preventive medicine as long as the benefit is larger than that arising from devoting the same resources to treatment.

Proposition 4.3 Efficient allocation between financial accessibility and quality
Resources should be allocated to improve financial accessibility as long as the social benefit is larger than that arising from devoting the same resources to enhancing quality.

We may consider that healthcare service users, taxpayers and users of non-healthcare government services jointly finance the provision of healthcare. Users can pay directly when they use the healthcare services or can pay for the use of such services by subscribing to a health insurance scheme. Taxpayers contribute to the financing of healthcare when general tax revenue is used to finance publicly provided healthcare services. Finally healthcare services may be financed by cutting back other public services.

The *principle of least burden* says that the burden of providing for healthcare services should be allocated among taxpayers (who pay taxes), users of public services (who may suffer a decline in the quality of some public services), and healthcare service users (who may have to pay fees, insurance premiums, or suffer a decline in the quality of medical services) in such a way that the cost to society is minimized. This means that, if the social cost of assigning \$1 of burden to patients is lower than the social cost of assigning \$1 of burden to taxpayers, we should assign the cost to patients. It also means that if the social cost of assigning \$1 of burden to patient A is higher than that of assigning to patient B, the burden should be assigned to B rather than to A. Finally, it further requires that if the social cost of cutting \$1 of healthcare spending is lower than the social cost of cutting \$1 of education spending, healthcare spending should be cut. Conversely if the social cost of cutting \$1 of healthcare spending is higher than that of cutting \$1 of education spending, that \$1 should be allocated on healthcare services rather than education services.

In recent years there is much discussion about the *user pays principle*. It is widely believed, and economists are reputed to uphold it, that making users pay for what they consume is both equitable and efficient. Actually such a belief is misplaced. The user pays principle is valid only *at the margin*. That is to say, if users consume *more* of a service, they should pay for the cost of the services thus used up. If they are not willing to pay for the service, then presumably the cost is higher than the value of the service. The resources involved should be saved for alternative uses. Because most public services involve high fixed costs, there is a difference between users paying for marginal costs and users paying for the total costs. In general marginal costs are much lower than average costs. If users have to pay for the average cost of everything they will reduce their demand drastically – they will refrain from using a service even if the marginal benefit is higher than the marginal cost. Many facilities will be underutilized. The society will end up not having those facilities and services at all.

Suppose university students have to pay for the full average cost of university education; patients have to pay for the full average cost of hospital services; passengers have to pay for the full average cost of the mass transit system; motorists have to pay for the full average cost of roads and highways. We will end up underutilizing all of these services, leading to gross inefficiency and waste.

In general, then, in the interest of efficiency, subject to the governments being able to finance the overhead costs infrastructure users should only pay for the marginal cost. A complication and caveat is that taxes are costly to raise, involving collection costs, compliance costs, and above all distortion costs – the costs of distorting the behavior of consumers, wage-earners and investors. Hence economists talk about "optimal deviations from marginal cost pricing" (Baumol and Bradford, 1970). In any case it is hoped that we have established the case for the sharing of costs between users and taxpayers.

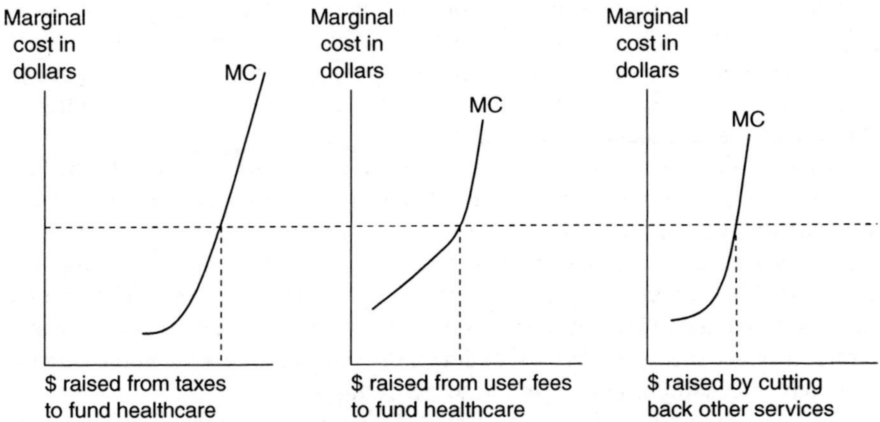

Figure 4.2 Efficient revenue generation.

Proposition 4.4 Efficiency as least burden requires marginal conditions
Least burden is achieved when the marginal cost of a health dollar raised from taxes, the marginal cost of a dollar paid in healthcare fees and the marginal cost of a dollar transferred from alternative uses into healthcare in terms of the value forgone, are equalized (Figure 4.2).

To the extent that distributive concerns and accessibility matter, "optimal sharing of burden" also involves considerations of equity and ability to pay. For the poor paying for the marginal cost of healthcare services may still be too much, *unless there is a transfer that raises their ability to pay*. Otherwise, in order that they have access to healthcare services there is a case to require them to pay less than the marginal cost – in any case pay less than higher-income households.

Proposition 4.5 Subsidizing the poor to ensure accessibility to care
Unless there are sufficient transfers to the poor, there is a case to subsidize healthcare costs expended by the poor in order to ensure accessibility of healthcare to them.

4.3 Equity versus choice

Universal accessibility to healthcare is generally regarded as important and sometimes even paramount, regardless of the form of democracy or the lack of it, anywhere. America until quite recently appeared to be the main exception, but then the passing of the healthcare reform bill under President Obama seems to suggest that after all America also prefers universal accessibility to "choice care," – if choice care is really only affordable for the rich. But as we suggested in Section 4.2, universal accessibility can only mean universal accessibility of "basic care," since society cannot afford to make the very costly kind of care available to all. Given this trade-off that we have to confront in reality, the best we can do is to preserve basic care and make basic care available at an "acceptable quality" (given the resource constraint) while allowing choice at the individual level as far as possible. This is the rationale for the LCS that we proposed earlier on. If each person is given the same supplement in a lifetime, even choice care can be equitable in a substantive sense. Of course, the well-to-do can always further increase their choices by spending more. Unfortunately the bigger subject of income inequality is outside of the scope of this volume

An early paper from the World Health Organization recommended that the highest priority of research be devoted to five general areas[2]: (1) global factors and processes that affect health equity and/or constrain what countries can do to address health inequities within their own borders; (2) societal and political structures and relationships that differentially affect people's chances of being healthy within a given society; (3) interrelationships between factors at the individual level and within the social context that increase or decrease the likelihood of achieving and maintaining good health; (4) characteristics of the healthcare system that influence health equity; and (5) effective policy interventions to reduce health inequity in the first four areas. It is important, however, to realize that two factors stand out as the key factors behind health inequity: excessive reliance on the market and insufficient government input in the publicly provided healthcare sector. Our discussions on mainland China and the United States in the chapters to follow will demonstrate this, and will also hint at the political economy that often becomes the stumbling block to reforms aimed at bringing about greater health equity.

4.4 The validity of cost–benefit analysis in healthcare analysis

It is often held that health and life are not market commodities and should not carry price-tags. It is held by many people that "life is priceless" so that we should not worry about how much we spend as long as lives are saved. It is important to see the flaw in such arguments. Benefit and cost calculations will be necessary as long as resources are scarce and as long as we want to make intelligent choices about the use of resources. As long as choices have to be made ranking of alternatives is unavoidable. Benefit and cost calculations merely represent a way of indexing alternatives in a consistent fashion so that we can rank alternatives and make choices.

Without downplaying the respect for life putting "price tags" on lives saved or risked is necessary because otherwise we may make serious mistakes in our policy decisions. It is important to note that "saving lives" is in fact no more than extending lives. Lives can never be "saved" as if the saved person no longer needed to die. Extending a life for a longer time is presumably worth more than extending a life for a shorter time, other things being equal. A year of higher quality life is presumably worth more than a year of lower quality life. Diverting valuable resources from alternative uses and thereby adversely affecting people's quality of life and life expectancy in the name of "saving" a few lives clearly may not be appropriate.

Economists often value lives in terms of the economic value of the surviving years. Economic value comprises expected productivity and the value of consumption that survival makes possible. But values that enter into cost–benefit comparisons should be comprehensive. That is: they should include non-economic values as well. Non-economic values include such things as the value of being together with one's family, and even simply the subjective value of being alive.

In recent years the concept of QALYs has come into vogue. The concept is a logical derivative from the observation that a year of survival with a high quality of life must be worth more than a year of survival with a lower quality of life. Intelligent comparison will require translating different quality life-years into equivalent common quality (quality-adjusted) life-years. Thus one "quality X" life-year may be worth A times one "quality Y" life-year where "A" is a translation factor or relative worthiness factor to be determined. A unified way of converting dissimilar objects into comparable units is to use *shadow prices* to value or cost those objects. Shadow prices are so called because they cannot be observed in the market price and must be imputed.

To give the concept a more practical context, consider the medical procedures that extend the patient's life while inflicting discomfort, or alternatively medical procedures that shorten the patient's life while reducing discomfort. The concept of QALY is to allow us to evaluate and compare the desirability of such procedures and practices.

We may use the following approach in evaluating the output of a medical procedure.

In the case where life is extended, the value of the procedure can be calculated as:

> $\sum_i$ shadow price of a life-year at quality-after-procedure minus shadow price of life-year at quality-before-procedure for year i for all years of expected remaining life without the procedure (*this represents the change in value of each year of life as a result of the procedure*);

plus

> $\sum_j$ shadow price of a life-year at quality-after procedure for year j up to expected end of life with the procedure (*this represents the value of additional life-years following the procedure*)

In the case where life is shortened, the value of the procedure can be calculated as:

$\sum_i$ shadow price of a life-year at quality-after-procedure minus shadow price of life-year at quality-before-procedure for year i up to expected end of life with the procedure (*this represents the change in value of each year of life as a result of the procedure up to expected end of life with the procedure*);

minus

$\sum_j$ shadow price of a life-year at quality-before procedure for year j up to expected end of life without the procedure (*this represents the value of life wiped out by the procedure*)

In the above it is assumed that we have a shadow price for life-years of a given quality. Clearly this is a simplification used only to illustrate the trade-off between length of life and quality of life. In practice it will be necessary to consider the many dimensions of quality of life (such as mobility, ability to communicate, sense of touch, taste, sight, hearing ability, self-care ability, etc.) and price the separate dimensions separately. Value of a "normal" life-year in principle comprises:

$\sum_i$ normal quantity measure of life faculty i $\times$ unit shadow price of life faculty i at normal quality

Value of a "disease-handicapped life-year" can be represented as:

$\sum_i$ quantity measure of life faculty i under the handicap $\times$ unit shadow price of life faculty i at the reduced quality

Notwithstanding the logic of QALYs, the valuation of quality versus length of life is likely to vary greatly from person to person. Some people may prefer to gain quality at the expense of quantity (length of life), while others may prefer to gain quantity at the expense of quality. With respect to the choice between a life-extending procedure p_i and a quality-enhancing procedure p_j is, optimality would call for (assuming that the scale of each procedure can be adjusted infinitesimally) the following "marginal conditions":

$$\frac{\text{marginal utility of longer life}}{\text{longer life resulting from procedure } p_i} \times \frac{\text{longer life from } p_i}{\text{marginal cost of } p_i}$$

$$= \frac{\text{marginal utility of sweeter life}}{\text{sweeter life from procedure } p_i} \times \frac{\text{sweeter life from } p_i}{\text{marginal cost of } p_i}$$

Without implying that we can actually achieve this optimal condition, a consistent, logically sound way of estimating the benefits of medical procedures or treatment, such as the approach illustrated above, is necessary if we are to evaluate whether medical equipment should be acquired or whether a procedure should be performed.

4.5 Benchmarking and cost–benefit analysis

Thus, any kind of decision in principle can and should be subject to a cost–benefit analysis if the decision is to improve welfare. The decision may be whether or not to acquire equipment (an investment decision), whether or not to buy a package tour (a consumption decision), whether or not to take a course (typically a human capital investment decision), whether or not to extend business hours by an additional hour (a business operation decision), whether or not to undertake a diagnostic test, prescribe a drug, or perform an operation (a medical decision), or whether or not to adopt a new policy (a public policy decision).

To be meaningful, cost–benefit analysis must have a decision that is the object of the analysis and a *benchmark decision* that is the basis for comparison. Benefits and costs of the decision under analysis must be measured against the benchmark decision. Thus, a statement, made before the details of a proposed new airport had been worked out, to the effect that keeping an existing airport would lead to a loss of $X billion by the year 2050 would not make much sense, because there was no identified benchmark for comparison. If the proposed new airport is poorly located or poorly designed, retaining the old airport would have been justified.

Proposition 4.6 Benchmarks for cost–benefit analysis
Cost–benefit analysis needs estimates of costs and benefits relative to some benchmark, which is often the status quo. Advocates of a change from the status quo sometimes make the statement that keeping the status quo would cost society $X. Such statements generally do not make any sense without specific information about the proposed alternative, which then will serve as a benchmark.

4.6 Pitfalls to avoid in cost–benefit analysis

The essence of cost–benefit analysis using the representative individual approach is to translate all costs and benefits into comparable units for comparison and then to compare costs with benefits for the representative individual. The trick is (1) avoid leaving out relevant costs and benefits, (2) avoiding double-counting, (3) translating costs and benefits into common, comparable units and comparing total benefits with total costs, and considering these costs and benefits as they affect the representative individual.

Avoiding leaving out relevant costs and benefits

It is important to note that the comparison between costs and benefits should not be restricted to "economic costs" and "economic benefits." What carries a market price is of course easier to value, but something that does not carry a price tag may still be important. A correct cost–benefit analysis has to take account also of non-economic costs and non-economic benefits. For example, how do we value the benefit of reducing the mortality rate by 1 percent? Or the cost of more air pollution? Because there are no market prices to value these costs and benefits they have to be imputed. The imputations will of course be subject to errors and one can never be sure that the imputed prices are right. However, there is no alternative to imputing such prices. In fact, any decision reflecting our choices would implicitly assume some imputed prices. What we are saying here is that an explicit imputation would be preferred to implicit but ill-considered or even unconsidered assumptions.

Sometimes an implicit price can be estimated on the basis of the behavior of individuals responding to market price signals. For example, if people are observed to be willing to pay higher rent for a quieter environment, the cost of noise may be estimated statistically using a "hedonic price model." If people are willing to take a more dangerous job that carries a known risk of fatal accident in return for a higher wage we can estimate the implicit valuation of life, assuming that the wage premium is a price paid in compensation for the increase in the probability of dying.

Alternatively, one could use the *contingent valuation method* and survey the "willingness to pay" of respondents for a hypothetical benefit or for avoidance of the destruction of some desirable quality. Such survey methods are known to be subject to a number of biases, particularly strategic bias – the bias built in to solicit a policy change by respondents – and information bias or the bias due to the absence of a basis for inferring values for lack of personal experience with the hypothetical or contingent event.

Because shadow prices are subject to a large margin of error, it will be useful to recalculate costs and benefits with alternative assumptions of shadow prices. This is yet another example of the practical use of sensitivity analysis.

Avoiding double counting

The construction of a mass transit system will save the time of commuting for people living in a city. This benefit may be reflected in the rise in land values and in housing price appreciation. But it will be wrong to add the rise in land values on top of the savings in time. The time savings may actually lead to higher rents for flats that directly benefit from the construction. This increase in rents will then allow landlords to capture some of the benefits that otherwise accrue to commuters. But adding the housing valuation on top of the gains from time savings would involve double counting of benefits.

Discounting

Discounting is the translating of future benefits and costs into units that are comparable to present benefits and costs. In general, even in the absence of inflation, \$100 a year from now is normally regarded as being worth less than \$100 today. For one thing we can turn \$100 today into \$100(1+r) a year from now, where r is the market rate of interest or rate of return on investment. For another thing the promised consumption of \$100 a year from now is only a promise. There is always a chance that one does not survive or that one may not be able to consume the said amount a year from now. Finally, it is hypothesized that consumers may have "time preference for present consumption over future consumption."

The discounted values of the yearly benefits into the future are summed together into one number which is called present value or capitalized value of the stream of benefits. Thus:

$$\text{Present Value of Benefits} = \sum_i \text{Benefit in Year i} \times \text{Discount Factor from Year i to the Present}$$

Similarly, we have

$$\text{Present Value of Cost} = \sum_i \text{Cost in Year i} \times \text{Discount Factor from Year i to the present}$$

Instead of separately treating the benefit stream and the cost stream, we can capitalize the *net benefit stream* thus:

$$\text{Present Value of Net Benefits} = \sum_i \text{Net Benefit in Year i} \times \text{Discount Factor from Year i to the Present}$$

In general, a decision can be said to increase welfare *over the benchmark decision* if the present value of net benefits is positive.

If we are to maximize welfare, we would choose that option among all mutually exclusive options which maximize the present value of net benefits compared to the benchmark. If no option is superior to the benchmark, then the benchmark decision would be the best decision.

It is important to note that the choice of the discount rate for calculating the present value will affect the ranking of different projects. A project with a net benefit stream that is "front-loaded" relative to another one will become relatively less desirable if the discount rate is reduced.

The choice of the discount rate has always been controversial in the literature and will always be controversial in practice. The community is unlikely to agree upon a single "social time preference rate" for discounting. When it comes to using the opportunity cost of capital for discounting, it is pointed out that:

> Some economists have proposed that the SDR (Social Discount Rate) should be calculated in terms of the social opportunity cost of the different

> sources weighted according to the relative contribution of each source.... [As a result] the value of weighted social opportunity cost of capital depends on the sources of a project's resources, which may vary from one project to another.
>
> (Boardman *et al.*, pp. 254–255)

Given such difficulties, it is often necessary to perform *sensitivity analysis* to find out how the ranking of alternative decision options may change when the discount rate changes.

The imperative of using the representative individual approach

Traditional cost–benefit analysis would rule out a decision to save a life if it costs $7 million but the statistical value of saving a life is estimated at $5 million. However, once it is realized that $7 million is just $1 per capita per year, and that this can save the loss of one life per year, people may decide that the life should be saved. The *ex ante* cost of one life per year, in terms of worry for everyone, within a population of seven million for the representative individual may well be more than $1, even though the *value of a statistical life* may be estimated only at $5 million. In general estimates of the value of life are either inferred by observed behavior, such as the willingness to take a higher risk to life when offered a wage premium, or from the contingent valuation method. Suppose the risk of fatality is higher in job A over job B by 1 / 10,000 per year, while other conditions are all equal, and the yearly wage premium is $500. Assuming risk neutrality, $500 = value of life * 1/10,000. It may be inferred that life is valued at $500*10,000 = $5,000,000. Under the contingent valuation method, the respondent may be asked how much he is willing to pay to get a specified reduction in the risk of fatality. The value of life is again derived by similar mathematics.[3]

4.7 Cost effectiveness and cost utility analysis

While cost–benefit analysis is preferred whenever possible, the information requirement may sometimes be too demanding for it to be feasible. When this is the case, cost effectiveness analysis and cost utility analysis may be used in its place. While cost–benefit analysis deals with the question of whether one strategy or a decision is desirable by comparing the total costs with the total benefits arising from that strategy or decision, cost effectiveness analysis and cost utility analysis simply assume that the intended result is desired, and the only question left is which of a number of alternatives is the least costly way of achieving the stipulated result.[4] The difference between cost effectiveness analysis and cost utility analysis is that whereas the former does not specify the nature of the outcome to be achieved – which can therefore be anything desirable – such as protection from an infectious disease, reduction in homicides, reduction in high school dropout, etc., the latter assumes that the desired outcome is an extra

QALY.[5] Note that these approaches dispense with the need to put a money value to the outcome.

The main advantage of these approaches, as mentioned above, is that they require less information than cost–benefit analysis but may still be reliable in terms of ranking alternative clinical procedures. The shortcoming is that neither cost-effectiveness analysis nor cost-utility analysis is a substitute for cost–benefit analysis, which will always be needed to tell whether a procedure is worthwhile in the first place.

4.8 Conclusions

Ultimately, health policy is intended to serve the public interest, and that we interpret to be identical with the *ex ante* welfare of the "representative individual." This hypothetical person incorporates the interest of everyone in society. He has no identity, but imagines he could be anyone in the community to be affected – by the introduction or any change in an insurance plan, by the introduction of a new gadget in hospitals, by higher fees, by raising taxes to finance healthcare, by cutting back other public services to fund healthcare, etc. The proposal of this approach is to ask the policymaker to consider the interest of everybody, and yet to detach himself from the interest of anybody in particular.

There are many questions that need to be answered when it comes to health policy, because health policy is indeed complex. But complex as health policy is, there is a logical way to ask the questions.

First is how much resources do we want to devote to healthcare from the public purse? This is the question about how much burden we want to impose on taxpayers for healthcare. But this question cannot really be answered as a lumpy question, because ultimately, spending is always made incrementally. So we need to consider the benefit versus the cost of an incremental allocation to healthcare, given the status quo, *assuming that the money spent can be efficiently utilized.*

Efficient utilization of resources by bureaucrats of course cannot be taken for granted. So there is a need for a good governance mechanism that allows medical professionals sufficient leeway to make their professional decisions, and yet be held accountable for their decisions. As we will see in the chapter on the UK National Health Service, the United Kingdom had opted for "the internal market," but is now trying to replace that or supplement that with an alternative or supplementary governance mechanism. The search for a better governance mechanism is still on.

Once the question about resource allocation has been answered, the next question is how to allocate the money between improving accessibility and improving quality. We argue, once again, that it is cost–benefit comparison that determines the coverage of "basic care" and its quality. While universal accessibility is held to be desirable, there is a large range of possibilities within the general norm of universal accessibility. Universal accessibility can be advanced by improving geographical service points, reducing waiting, lowering fees, extending service hours, etc. Each of these must be considered again using cost–benefit analysis.

Review questions

1 What should be included in “standard care” for a largely publicly funded healthcare plan? Why should an item be included or excluded?
2 What is the “user pays principle”? Would you support it? Why?
3 Why is there cost effectiveness analysis on top of cost–benefit analysis?
4 What is the difference between traditional cost–benefit analysis and *ex ante* cost–benefit analysis?
5 How would you choose whom to save, when the resources permit you to save only one out of two people?

5 Health policy in mainland China, Hong Kong and Taiwan

Settling down to a model?

5.1 Introduction

One common theme among health policy studies is that people respond to incentives as rational beings (Ellis and McGuire, 1996; Yip and Eggleston, 2004; Chalkley and Tilley, 2006: Godager *et al.*, 2009). Indeed, a recent edited volume (Sloan and Kasper, 2008) carries the title "Incentives and Choice in Healthcare." Consumers of healthcare services respond to price signals; suppliers of healthcare services as well as private insurers respond to profit incentives; insurers have invented devices like co-payments and deductibles to control and manage expenses, taking advantage of people's natural incentives. Insurers often rely on the services of designated doctors to serve as gatekeepers to contain escalating costs and to deal with the tendency of patients to over-utilize publicly subsidized services. Insurers also often collaborate with health service providers to form HMO-like organizations to deal with the diverse goals of caregivers as "agents" and insurers as "principal." These responses appear to transcend social situations and political regimes.

The current chapter will examine healthcare systems in three different jurisdictions, namely mainland China, Hong Kong and Taiwan, under one unifying theoretical framework. Paradoxically, mainland China, which is supposed to operate under a socialist system, with public hospitals far outnumbering private ones, is actually the most market-oriented, as underfunded hospitals seek every opportunity they can grab to bolster their revenues. Hong Kong has a mixed system, with public domination for inpatient care and private domination in outpatient care. Healthcare providers in Taiwan are predominantly private,[1] with private providers accounting for 70 percent of all hospital beds and 98 percent of all clinics, but Taiwan runs the most comprehensive national health insurance (NHI) program among the three jurisdictions, and has service purchase contracts with most service providers. Despite the differences in institutions, interestingly, the policy concerns in all three jurisdictions are strikingly similar.

Central to health policy is risk management, and central to risk management are risk pooling, cost sharing and cost containment. Hong Kong, Taiwan and the mainland follow different approaches to risk pooling. In a sense, the tax-financed Hospital Authority is like a giant HMO that offers healthcare to Hong Kong's citizens who, though, instead of directly paying an insurance premium or membership fee, fund it through taxes. Hong Kong permanent residents enjoy very low, even nominal fees for publicly provided healthcare services – if they can afford the time to wait or if there is a real emergency. Taiwan's NHI, launched in 1995, on the other hand, charges insurance premiums, but these premiums vary from person to person according to the ability to pay and may be waived for the poorest. The premiums thus are effectively *an earmarked tax*, i.e., a tax devoted to a designated purpose. Its character as a tax is based on its mandatory nature as well as the principle of ability to pay. Taiwan's annual capping of co-payments for inpatients directly addresses the main concern of a recent working paper by Wagstaff (2008), and effectively limits the financial risk that may follow a major healthcare need. While Hong Kong and Taiwan commit a lot of the fiscal revenue to supporting healthcare, mainland China until quite recently has seriously underfunded its healthcare system. Instead of offering truly affordable services through providing hospitals with adequate public funding, the Chinese mainland, until quite recently, largely depended on government regulations to ensure that workers were protected through the "laobao" or "laodong baoxian tiaoli" (labor insurance regulations). The lack of risk-pooling across enterprises and local governments often prevented individual units from reimbursing the insured patients' beneficiaries for their medical expenses, hence imposing a heavy burden on the patients themselves. Meanwhile the enterprises excessively burdened by healthcare bills may suffer a loss of competitiveness (Dong, 2001, pp. 6–7). With the Social Insurance Law (shehui baoxian fa) put into effect as of July 1, 2011, contributions from different employers and employees are pooled together, but into different funds that pertain to different localities and contribution rates into medical insurance may vary from place to place.[2]

Hong Kong in 2011 committed about 2.2 percent of its GDP in public revenue on healthcare; Taiwan in 2010 committed about 1.7 percent of its GDP in public subsidies on NHI premiums. In 2011 mainland China spent 636.7 billion yuan of its general revenue on healthcare, roughly 1.4 percent of its GDP of 47,156 billion yuan, and up 32.5 percent over the year. "Healthcare spending by the government had risen 2.6 times in the eleventh Five-Year Plan period over the tenth Five-Year Plan period."[3]

Reflecting the realization that effective "financial protection" (Wagstaff, 2008; Wagstaff and Pradhan, 2005) cannot be provided without sufficient public funding, and that this is essential to building a more harmonious society, all three lands have pledged increases in public spending on healthcare. Hong Kong had pledged to increase public spending on healthcare to 17 percent of total government spending, up from around 15 percent that had prevailed for some time through 2010. President Ma Ying-jeou said the Taiwan government would increase spending on healthcare and medical research and development to bringing the national health expenditure up to 7.5 percent of the gross domestic product (*Taiwan Today*, January 20, 2012). Wang Jun, vice minister of finance in China, said that as part of its drive to improve healthcare, the government planned to spend 1.13 trillion yuan ($173 billion) on healthcare between 2009 and the end of 2011. This amount surpassed the previous plan to spend 850 billion yuan on healthcare during that time frame.[4]

The importance of protecting citizens from the adverse financial consequences of catastrophic healthcare spending is underscored by Wagstaff (2008), who found that introducing health insurance reduced worries over financial risks so much in Vietnam that people ate better and consumed more, with the result that height-for-age and weight-for-age among young school children showed a marked improvement. There is little doubt that worries over healthcare expenditures play a role in mainland China's high savings rate (Woo, 2005).

In the next section, using a theoretical framework that assumes that caregivers derive their satisfaction from their professional work and from their financial reward, and that they respond to their different institutional and market environments accordingly, we can predict the different behavior and thus the implications on the quality of care and access to healthcare in the different jurisdictions. Section 5.3 focuses on consumers' behavior. We assume that consumers derive utility from "consumption attributes" generated from a household production function (Becker, 1965; Lancaster, 1966), but these attributes may be physical, such as nutrition and taste, or mental, such as a sense of security and the freedom from anxiety. Section 5.4 considers the subject of anxiety and financial risks, an important subject underscored by the work of Wagstaff (2005, 2008) and Wagstaff and Pradhan (2005). Section 5.5 deals with the subject of preventive care and promoting healthy lifestyles through incentives. Section 5.6 addresses the subject of cost containment and consumer choices under an environment of rapid medical advance, a concern common to mainland China, Taiwan, Hong Kong and indeed all other countries. The concluding section highlights the key findings from the survey of the health systems in the three jurisdictions, whose experiences have been shown to be amenable to analysis under a common, incentive-based theoretical framework.

5.2 Modeling caregivers' behavior

Corresponding to different institutional environments we distinguish four kinds of health service providers: pure public caregivers, pure private caregivers, public caregivers acting like private caregivers, and private caregivers acting like public caregivers. They can all be treated as maximizers of utility that comprises two components: non-pecuniary or professional satisfaction and pecuniary satisfaction.[5]

Purely public sector caregivers

Purely public sector caregivers are paid salaries only, and Hong Kong's Hospital Authority is a prototype of this model. They can increase their professional satisfaction by working harder to provide more and better care, but this is offset by the disutility of effort. Equilibrium is reached when the marginal utility of professional satisfaction is equal to the marginal disutility of effort, but this may be prevented by bureaucrats who may dictate the number of patients that each doctor has to see each day, and when bureaucrats mandate long working hours and shifts, or otherwise interfere with their decision making. Professional satisfaction is assumed to be highest when they are free to make clinical decisions professionally without interference by bureaucrats, and when their professional decisions are not swayed by profit or cost considerations.

Because of the need to contain costs, bureaucrats and administrators in Hong Kong limit the use of certain drugs and procedures, and manpower constraints are also extremely tight. Doctors who work in the Hospital Authority as well as those who work in Department of Health clinics earn salaries. This means that their professional judgments are generally free from profitability concerns.

In the years following the Asian Financial Tsunami, because of budget cuts or funding increases that lag behind demand growth, longer queues have developed in Hong Kong reducing acccss,[6] the quality of care in its public hospitals has been declining, and more and more patients are driven away or forced to turn to private care, while professional autonomy has been decreasing. At the same time, the remunerations of doctors – particularly those of new entrants into the profession, were reduced.[7] All this has led to a rise in the attrition rate in Hong Kong. Although some improvements have been made in the more recent years following improvements in Hong Kong's fiscal position, a serious brain drain from the public healthcare sector has continued. Lo and Yaung (1998) also found that compensation is a key variable behind Taiwan doctors' sense of dissatisfaction and thus the decision to quit. Another complaint in Taiwan is that with a small budget and facing huge demand, doctors work under immense pressure, and usually are expected to see more than 100 patients every day.[8]

Purely private caregivers

Purely private caregivers earn a profit and are entirely independent with regard to pricing and healthcare delivery.[9] Private caregivers in Hong Kong and on the mainland enjoy much autonomy, but have to face the discipline of the market and the competition from public service providers. They are medical professionals as well as entrepreneurs and they reap a profit that is the product of a per-unit service profit and the quantity of services supplied. The fees that they charge may be profit-maximizing, but they may stop short of profit maximizing if professional satisfaction from serving more patients with modest means is important to them. Profitability may also be a positive factor on quality, since it avails the caregiver to more resources, but profit orientation can have negative effects on quality, if it dominates over professional judgments. Under information asymmetry, doctors can boost or create demand, and private hospitals can cut costs at the expense of patients' interests. On the other hand, freedom from bureaucratic influence may benefit patients by enhancing the quality of care.

In general, a public doctor will turn to private practice if his utility from practicing as a private doctor is higher than that from practicing as a public doctor and conversely a private doctor may join a public health service. This may be due to the lure of higher earnings or the perceived freedom from bureaucratic influence.

Proposition 5.1 The motives of private caregivers
Private caregivers may maximize profits or may alternatively maximize professional satisfaction subject to a profit target having been achieved ("satisficing" à la Herbert Simon, 1956).

Proposition 5.2 Profit maximizing in an environment without good public care
Private caregivers are more likely to be pure profit maximizers if patients do not have the alternative of a decent public healthcare sector. Without a decent public healthcare sector the profit maximizing equilibrium may become so attractive that professional satisfaction is rendered secondary.

Public provider acting like private caregivers

Public healthcare is felt to be not sufficiently funded almost anywhere, and mainland China, Hong Kong and Taiwan are not exceptions. In Hong Kong, however, public hospitals are not allowed to boost their incomes by offering more services and charging them at a profitable price. On the mainland, where the degree of under-funding is acute, public hospitals are allowed to do so. In particular, with doctors being paid a small salary, hospitals encourage doctors to make it up through bonuses,[10] and bonuses depend on the profit derived at the end of the year. Doctors also earn extra incomes through the "red packets" offered them by patients' families. While many fees are regulated, public hospitals on the mainland have been allowed to sell drugs and provide various unregulated and expensive services to derive a profit. Ongoing reform aims at changing this.

Profit orientation no doubt has undermined professional and patient satisfaction. As a result many public hospitals are only public in name, and they operate much like for-profit hospitals (Ho, 1995a, 1995b). According to UNICEF, "60 percent of China's healthcare spending goes to drugs, compared with the worldwide average of 15 percent" (*Time Magazine*, May. 12, 2003). While the government does impose strict price regulation on routine services, it does allow hospitals and clinics to earn profits on drugs and on various diagnostic services, which are priced to yield handsome profits. From time to time there have been reports of outrageous prices being charged by public hospitals, [11] and periodically there have been reports of high fees leading to tragedies on the mainland such as the case of the death of a pregnant woman in Beijing whose husband worried over the cost of the operation and refused to sign consent for caesarian section (*Mingpao*, December 26, 2007). Quite apart from the adverse effects on accessibility, profit orientation may affect clinical decisions and undermine quality through unnecessary services and inferior supplies. These considerations suggest that profit orientation in the publicly provided healthcare sector should be avoided. A professionally run and adequately funded public healthcare system that runs alongside the private system will serve as a benchmark for the latter and will enhance its quality. A decent "public option" of healthcare offers people the possibility of turning away from private care, meaning that private care has to be good in order to keep its customers. If the public system is also profit-oriented, patients have no alternative and may be exploited by profit-oriented caregivers.

A persistent complaint about mainland China's healthcare is that it relies too much on the sale of drugs for financing (yi yao yang yi 以藥養医) and an important direction of reform is to move away from this to relying on user charges on services to finance medical services (yi yi yang yi 以医養医). A recent article in *Jinan Daily* (濟南日報) (January 13, 2012) observed that ultimately more public funding is necessary. Without adequate public funding, hospitals have to raise funds from patients one way or the other, and patients may simply not be able to afford it. In 2011, public funding for healthcare went up 32.5 percent year on year, and reached 636.7 billion yuan. This figure, however, remained a mere 1.35 percent of the GDP.

Private caregivers given public caregiver duties

Price regulation is one way to manage the degree of profit orientation, and may be necessary under a third party reimbursement system, such as NHI. Thus Taiwan's Bureau of National Health Insurance (BNHI) used its monopsony position to control healthcare costs (Foreman, 1999; Laupacis *et al.*, 2002). As Lu and Hsiao (2003) point out, a key factor behind the success of Taiwan's NHI program is that it was able to avoid the "overcharges, duplication and overuse of health services and tests, transaction costs, and other costs" normally expected with third party health insurance.[12] Taiwan's experience shows that private caregivers can be given public caregiving duties: to provide basic care for the general public under the terms and conditions as specified by the public health insurer. Although most caregivers in Taiwan are private, they are constrained by the reimbursement formula as specified by the BNHI when they deliver services on behalf of the BNHI, and cannot set prices independently. The Hong Kong Hospital Authority's Cataract Surgeries Program, launched in 2008 to reduce the queues in the public sector, pays surgeons a set fee for operations performed, but allows doctors some leeway to charge additional fees up to HK$8,000.

In general, a private doctor may do contracted work alongside his private work, or devote himself solely to contracted work, or decide not to take up any contracted work at all. In Hong Kong, contracted work is still not very popular among private doctors, probably because of the constraints as specified for such work. In Taiwan, however, contracted work represents the bulk of the work for most private healthcare providers.

Proposition 5.3 Government-regulated fees for private care
A precondition for private providers to provide basic care acting like public providers is that the charges collected by the private providers must not be excessively lucrative. Otherwise they will have the incentive to over provide services.

5.3 Patient behavior: prevention, healthcare, utilization of services

Following Becker (1965) and Lancaster (1966), we can see households as purchasing market goods as inputs to produce "consumption attributes" or "characteristics" that are the "final objects of consumption" determining utility. These include *physical* consumption attributes and *mental* consumption attributes. Physical attributes refer to such attributes as taste, sound and nutrition. Mental attributes refer to such attributes as a sense of security, confidence and self-esteem. It is further assumed that uncertainty gives rise to anxiety and is a negative mental good or "mental bad." The accumulation of savings, as well as a sound healthcare system, fosters a sense of security and thus contributes to a "mental good." Health is assumed to have an independent, direct, effect on utility as well as an indirect effect as an input in the household production process. For example one has to be in relatively good health to join a tour and enjoy it.

As explained in Chapter 1, "functional health" is a flow, measured in EHDs in a year, which is associated with the "health stock." Depreciation of the health stock will depend on lifestyle variables and random factors such as disease-bearing mosquitoes or accidents and may be slowed down by healthcare.

Households face a lifetime budget constraint but are assumed to make decisions over a shorter time horizon, such as a year, when the situation is more comprehensible and certain. For each decision horizon the consumer has to decide the split between total spending and savings, and the split between different kinds of spending. Healthcare costs are uncertain so there is just no telling how much one needs to save. This means that households potentially face considerable financial risk. Different public healthcare regimes will have different implications on such risks and thus on the welfare of households.

Figure 5.1 shows that a rational consumer would carry his consumption to the point where the marginal utility from consumption, net of out-of-pocket costs, is equal to the marginal disutility (inclusive of healthcare cost) due to a loss of health resulting from that consumption. Part of this disutility arises from the need to spend more on healthcare consequent upon a loss of health. Since marginal disutility due to a loss of health will be greater if the treatment cost is greater, if the price of healthcare services understates cost, there will be an excessive spending on goods that undermine health. The marginal disutility line shifts to the broken line, and the equilibrium spending is increased. Thus under-pricing healthcare tends to lead to a less healthy lifestyle.

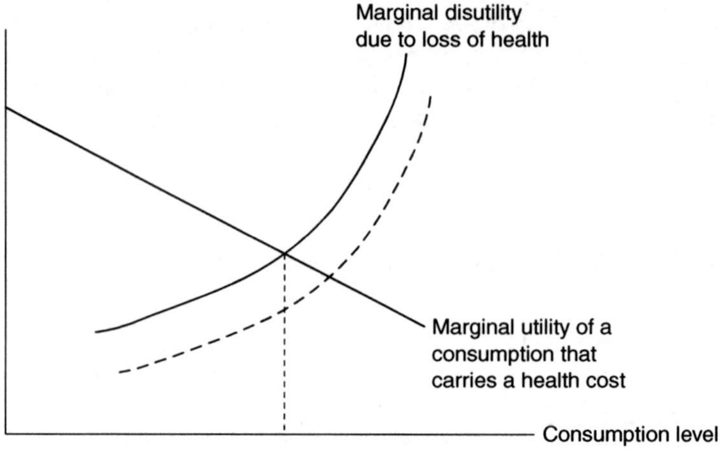

Figure 5.1 Spending on an unhealthy consumption (underpricing of healthcare costs reduces the marginal disutility due to loss of health).

Figure 5.2 shows that a rational consumer would also tend to overutilize medical resources quite independently of his actual health conditions if the healthcare services are priced below marginal social cost. Equilibrium consumption of medical services goes up from Q* to Q*'.

Proposition 5.4 Effects of underpricing of medical services
Underpricing healthcare not only leads to a less healthy lifestyle but also directly encourages an overutilization of medical resources. To the extent that the patient often depends on the advice of his doctor as to what services and how much of each medical service is needed, underpricing of medical services will make patients less resistant to his doctor's recommendations for services.

Proposition 5.5 Co-payments
Insurers depend on co-payments as a means of reducing moral hazard. If co-payments are too low, moral hazard will result.

In Taiwan as well as in Hong Kong, publicly provided healthcare services are charged at very low rates. This is especially the case with outpatient care in Taiwan and inpatient care in Hong Kong. Table 5.1 shows some of the charges prevailing in Taiwan as of 2011, which have not changed since 2005. Table 5.2 shows some of the Hospital Authority fees and charges for eligible Hong Kong residents (in US dollars, HK$7.8=US$1):

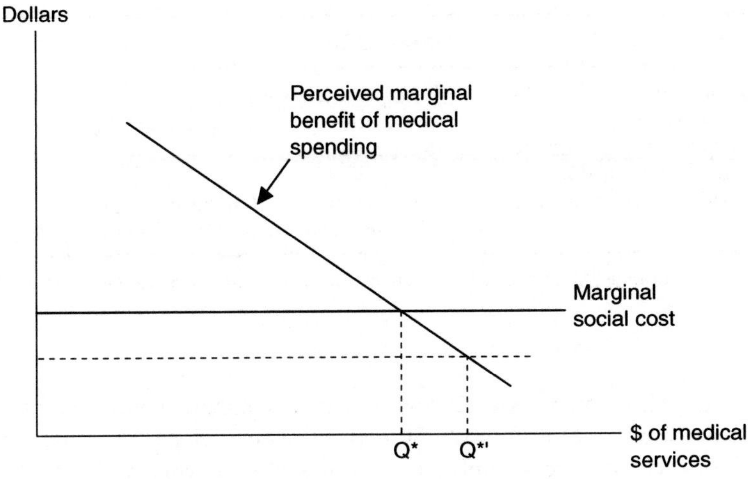

Figure 5.2 Underpricing leads to over consumption.

Table 5.1 Co-payments for outpatient care in Taiwan

Institution class	*Co-payments*				
Type of institution	*Western medicine outpatient centre*		*Emergency care*	*Dental care*	*Traditional Chinese medicine*
	With referral	*Direct visit*			
Medical centers	210	360	450	50	50
Regional Hospitals	140	240	300	50	50
District hospitals	50	80	150	50	50
Clinics		50	150	50	50

Source: National Health Insurance in Taiwan Report 2011.

Notes

Individuals classified as disabled pay co-payments of NT$50 for any medical care regardless of type of medical institution they visit.

Patients who return for their first checkup after an outpatient procedure or within 30 days after being discharged from the hospital pay the same co-payment as if they were given a referral as long as they have a hospital certificate confirming the need for a follow-up visit.

This co-payment schedule took effect on July 15, 2005.

In Hong Kong the Hospital Authority inpatient fee "covers general nursing, core pathology investigations, catering and domestic services."[13] There are no separate doctor's fees or surgery fees. So these are very low charges indeed. Yet in Hong Kong people benefiting from comprehensive social security allowance as well as others who plead to be too poor to pay and whose applications for waiving of fees are approved do not have to pay anything at all. Over-utilization, especially among this group, has been a serious problem in Hong Kong.

Table 5.2 Hong Kong Hospital Authority fees for eligible residents, 2012

Service	*Fees (US$)*
Accident and emergency	12.8 per attendance
In-patient (general acute beds)	6.4 admission fee, plus 12.8 per day
In-patient (convalescent, rehabilitation, infirmary & psychiatric beds)	8.7 per day
Specialist out-patient (including allied health services)	12.8 for the first attendance, 7.7 per subsequent attendance, 1.3 per drug item

Source: Hong Kong Hospital Authority. HK$ amounts converted to US$ at exchange rate of HK$7.8=US$1.

In contrast to such nominal fees, Taiwan presently requires a co-payment for inpatient care at 10 percent rising up to 30 percent of total costs depending on the length of stay. There were a number of revisions of co-payments during the first ten years of the NHI. Interestingly, there was hardly any resistance from the public, and overall satisfaction with the NHI actually climbed. The annual ceiling on co-payments ensures that despite the co-payments, people can afford healthcare. According to Chu Tzer-ming, president of the BNIH, "While hiking co-payments somewhat shifts the burden of healthcare costs to patients, the main savings come from reduced hospital visits," (*Taiwan Review*, 02/01/2008) In contrast, on the mainland, excessive utilization has never been a problem. If anything, patients delay visits to hospitals and discharge themselves prematurely.

As predicted, Taiwan's very low outpatient charges have led to one of the world's highest outpatient visit rates (Wang and Cheng, 2006) while Hong Kong's non-existent inpatient charges for Comprehensive Social Security Allowance (CSSA) recipients and other low income groups have similarly attracted a disproportionate number of non-fee-paying inpatients.[14]

In contrast to Taiwan and Hong Kong, most patients on the mainland have to face relatively high medical fees when everything is added together. Many would avoid using medical services even though such services are needed. This sometimes leads to delays in getting the necessary care with irreversible, often tragic consequences.

This discussion suggests that reimbursement to caregivers under the NHI system should not be so remunerative as to generate supply-side moral hazard, but should be high enough cover direct costs. Co-payments charged to patients should reflect the marginal cost of the service and avoid demand-side moral hazard. This could, however, lead to anxiety and has to be dealt with using another instrument, such as a high cost ceiling that caps healthcare expenditures.

5.4 Household anxiety and health insurance

Since medically advised healthcare expenditures are uncertain, they are a source of much anxiety, and anxiety and stress constitute a "mental bad." Mental bads not only reduce happiness but may also indirectly cause other illnesses. Failing to receive timely medical attention may lead to rapid depreciation in the health stock, and this will cause a significant decline in utility and possibly premature death.

Given that uncertainty over healthcare spending is a major source of anxiety, any institutional arrangement that reduces this uncertainty will immediately raise welfare. Just as Sweden imposes a high cost ceiling, so Taiwan implements a "coinsurance ceiling" of US$788 per stay and US$1,333 cumulative for the calendar year (US$1 = NT$33).[15] This is an "annual deductible" within which patients need to come up with co-payments and beyond which the co-payments are waived.

The idea of an annual spending threshold is also adopted on the mainland, but unlike that in Taiwan it is not an expenditure ceiling. In Beijing, which implemented a new and fully fledged health insurance system[16] on July 1, 2008, there is an annual spending threshold of 1,800 yuan per year. Patients have to pay full fees within the threshold, generally out of their own personalized Medisave account, and then be responsible for a co-payment beyond it. Covering some 11.71 million people, a reimbursement rate at 70 percent of outpatient healthcare costs beyond the annual deductible usually applies. For inpatient care, full fees are payable up till the threshold. From then on up to 30,000 yuan a co-payment at 15 percent of expenses is payable; from 30,001 to 40,000 yuan, 10 percent of expenses are payable; from 40,001 to 70,000 yuan 5 percent of expenses are payable. Beyond 70,001 yuan, however, the patient has to pay 30 percent and then full cost for anything above 170,000 yuan (*Xinjing Bao* or New Beijing News, June 24, 2008).

Perhaps surprisingly, the protection for the elderly is smaller. For the elderly inpatient, personal responsibility is 40 percent for expenses beyond the annual threshold amount up to 70,000 yuan and is 100 percent above this level (i.e., there is no more benefit). For children and students, personal responsibility for inpatient care is 30 percent for expenses above the annual threshold and below 170,000 yuan (*Xinjing Bao*, June 24, 2008). There is moreover a deductible amount for the elderly that stands at 1,300 yuan for the first hospitalization, and at 650 yuan each time from then on. For children and students the deductible amount is 650 yuan for each hospital admission.

The EBP system in Taiwan, with an annual deductible beyond which no further co-payment is required, is very attractive to people, because of the assurance that they will never have to pay more than a certain amount on inpatient healthcare in any year. The "deductible plus co-payment beyond the threshold" system, as practiced in Beijing, is less attractive and rather complicated, but nevertheless provides a great relief to those suffering from worries over an unknown cost of care and whether or not they can get the necessary medical care when they need it.

Hong Kong has struggled with the idea of mandatory contribution, which the Special Administrative Region government has leaned toward in the past, and which combined an insurance element with a Medisave account element, but Donald Tsang in his last term as chief executive of the Hong Kong SAR decided that there was not enough public support and finally gave up the idea, and instead opted for a regulated inpatient care insurance program called the Health Protection Scheme that promises to divert those who can afford it to private hospitals and thus offer some relief to the public hospitals. One central idea is that patients should have the benefit of more transparent fees through the preannouncement of service package fees based on *Diagnosis Related Groups* (DRGs).[17] HK$50 billion was set aside from the public coffers to kick start the program as a subsidy for the high risk enrollees.[18] Ho (2011a, 2011b) has criticized the proposal as untenable because if the public hospitals are reasonably good there is little reason for people to spend money to enroll in such health insurance schemes, which do not really offer much beyond basic care. A precondition for the proposed policy to fly is that the public hospitals do not offer people adequate protection, and that would be failing their most basic mission.

Ho (2011a) paints a rather depressing picture for Hong Kong's healthcare system if the government continues with the "patient diversion strategy":

> the market will find its way out, given whatever constraints prescribed by the government. As market participants adapt to the regulatory constraints, price increases and insurance premium increases will take place, and the market participants will find a way to survive and derive a profit. In order to do this the private sector's best way out is to drain the public sector of its resources, in particular to attract doctors and nurses to an extent that quality becomes increasingly unacceptable.
>
> This is not too difficult to do, and indeed should become easier over time, as the staff left in the Hospital Authority hospitals become increasingly demoralized, having to work understaffed and in an unfriendly environment that does not allow much professional autonomy.
>
> In the end, therefore, it can be predicted that basic care in the Hospital Authority hospitals will deteriorate so much that anyone who can afford it will buy "voluntary" private insurance rather involuntarily. Healthcare costs will continue to rise, and the burden on citizens will continue to escalate.

5.5 Sustainability and preventive care and promotion of a healthy lifestyle

One of the central concerns of any publicly funded healthcare system is financial sustainability. In order to achieve sustainability, wasteful spending needs to be contained, so that the revenue requirement will not keep rising. The Taiwan NHI premium rate was 4.25 percent when the system was launched in 1995; it was increased to 4.55 percent in September 2002. It was further increased to 5.17 percent in April 2010. While these increases cannot be said to be big, they are worrying.

One of these mechanisms that Taiwan introduced to contain cost increases is co-payments. In general, for inpatients, the longer the stay in the hospital the higher the co-payments will be. The idea is to encourage the patient to leave the hospital once conditions have stabilized. But there is a cap on cumulative co-payments paid: at NT$29,000 for a single hospital stay for a particular condition and NT$48,000 cumulatively for the entire calendar year. For outpatient visits, the typical co-payment is NT$50, but visits to better equipped medical centers and hospitals can require co-payments of NT$210 with referrals or NT$360 without referrals.

Another mechanism to contain costs is the Global Budget Payment Scheme (GBPS), introduced in 1998, under which payments to a caregiver are capped for the year under a complex formula and subject to negotiation. A different cap may apply to each medical field such as hospitals, western medicine, Chinese medicine, etc. Once the total services performed exceed the specified quota, the reimbursement ratio declines drastically, thus exposing caregivers to financial risks. This can be seen as a form of bureaucratic control, and it leads directly to a change in behavior. According to Cheng and Chang (2007), hospitals will avoid treating costly patients in areas where the global budget is perceived to be binding, and will provide excessive services in areas where there is still room to reach the global budget, since there is a surplus from the services rendered still below the global budget over costs. Caregivers may also deny treatment altogether. Concern over the GBPS came to a head with the case of a four-year-old who was refused treatment for severe injury by a Taipei hospital in 2005, the city government investigated the incident. In the end a pricing committee comprising medical, academic, and other experts reached an agreement to guarantee that the reimbursement rates will not be reduced for surgery and anesthesia, and for 25 hospitals designated for accidents and emergencies (*United Daily*, June 16, 2005).

Another mechanism, gate-keeping, is used in both Hong Kong and Taiwan. Taiwan encourages referrals through lower co-payment charges on specialist visits. Hong Kong relies on nurses to differentiate between emergency and non-emergency cases in accident and emergency departments, and on doctor recommendations for admission A related mechanism is "casemix-based capitation" financing, such as implemented in Hong Kong. Another related method is the prospective payment that Yip and Eggleston (2004) report as in place for six Hainan hospitals, which have to bear a percentage of expenditures over the prospective payments. Still another method, used by the Hong Kong Hospital Authority, is the delisting of expensive medications from the publicly funded drugs that can be prescribed by doctors.

One superficial attraction of the Hong Kong system is that fees and charges at Hong Kong's public hospitals are extremely low. Indeed, inpatient care is virtually free, as patients' payment of HK$100 per day is probably not even sufficient to pay for their meals. As was pointed out by several consultancy reports (Hong Kong SAR Government, 1999, 2001, 2008), such a system is not sustainable. Indeed, the long queues mean that many patients are effectively denied care or timely care.

But there is even one greater concern, which is related to population aging. With population aging, it is becoming even more important that the younger generation adopt a healthy lifestyle that will reduce the chances for the "health threatening events" and slow down the depreciation of the health stock. When patients pay only a fraction of their healthcare costs, there will be less attention to preventive care, and indeed the figures provided by the government suggest that lifestyle-related illnesses, such as hypertension and colon cancer, are now affecting more and more of the younger population.[19]

Accordingly, to prompt young people to adopt a healthier lifestyle at an early age, the annual deductible on healthcare expenditures should probably rise with age beyond 50. Since older people on average use healthcare that costs several times that of prime age adults, increasing the annual deductible with age reflects the age profile of healthcare costs, and allows better quality care. The financial motive will then motivate people to adopt a healthier lifestyle. Moreover, and equally important, increasing the ceiling for the elderly will also help procure more resources for quality care.

One other central concern of the Hong Kong government is to ensure affordability of healthcare for low income groups. Indeed, in Taiwan as well as the mainland this is a major concern. As pointed out earlier, Taiwan now exempts the poor from insurance premiums and often even the co-payments. Similarly, in Hong Kong people on the comprehensive social security allowance are automatically exempted from Hospital Authority fees. To the extent that professionally advised healthcare is a merit good,[20] there is a case for reducing, though not exempting, the co-payments for the poor, as well as reducing the annual cap on co-payments for them. Co-payments and annual caps can go hand in hand with transfers to the poor. This will be far more efficient than totally exempting the poor from co-payments altogether.

There is, however, a need to distinguish between premiums and co-payments. From the efficiency point of view, exempting co-payments will cause serious moral hazard problems; but exempting the poor from premiums need not distort behavior at all. Exempting the poor from premiums is like giving them a lump-sum grant. Giving the poor fixed stipends on redistributive grounds will not distort relative prices and thus will not generate inefficiency. Exempting co-payments, on the other hand, will lead to over-utilization of services, and will hurt the quality of care for other patients.

Proposition 5.6 Importance of anticipating behavioral responses
Financial sustainability of a healthcare system requires anticipating the behavioral responses of the people to different incentives associated with the healthcare system, and building in features that take advantage of such responses.

5.6 Medisave, pricing, budget caps and patients' choices

For a decade the Hong Kong SAR government has been expressly fond of a medical savings (Medisave) scheme modeled after Singapore (Hong Kong SAR

Government, 1999, 2001, 2008). One dominant proposal in the 2008 consultation document is for mandatory contributions toward a "personal healthcare reserve," with savings left after health insurance premiums have been paid to be reserved for future medical care purposes. There are certainly merits in a Medisave plan. If people have savings in the Medisave accounts they will have some ability to pay the charges required. The number of non-paying patients in public hospitals will be reduced, and some may even choose to seek care in the private sector, thus releasing resources for others less able to afford private healthcare.

Beginning from an experiment from 1994 documented by Yip and Hsiao (1997), a number of cities in mainland China have already set up Medisave arrangements, requiring contributions from both employers and employees to a personalized Medisave account on a monthly basis. Zhenjiang and Jiujiang are two of the pioneering cities that adopted a Singapore style Medisave system. By 2008, it was reported that personal Medisave balance on average reached 1,000 yuan in Zhenjiang, and around 800 yuan throughout the province of Jiangsu. From July 1, 2009 the personal Medisave account was separated into two tiers: with funds in excess of 3,000 yuan being put into a second tier account, out of which withdrawals can be made to meet health insurance expenses, the Medicare needs of one's family members, as well as specified items under prevention. The first tier balance is strictly for meeting one's own healthcare expenses, which could be outpatient or inpatient. In general, after paying from personal accounts up to a limit, funds from social healthcare funds will be drawn to reduce the burden on the individual.[21]

Medical savings accounts by themselves are, however, ineffective in checking the escalation of healthcare expenditures (Hsiao, 2001). Indeed, the fact that the money in the Medisave account has essentially no alternative use means that consumers are more ready to spend it. Profit-oriented healthcare givers are likely to encounter less resistance when they recommend services. This underscores the importance of basic care pricing regulation, so caregivers will not find it financially attractive to render services excessively. Thus in its first experimentation with an MSA, China coupled the use of MSAs with supply-side payment controls (Yip and Hsiao, 1997).

Hong Kong does not have a reimbursement system like that of Taiwan. Instead, hospitals are given annual capitation budgets based on the number of cases in each DRG treated in the past ("casemix-based financing"). Given such constraints each hospital is under considerable pressure to contain costs, which may translate into great efficiency but may also imply a sacrifice of doctors' autonomy. Some Hospital Authority doctors have expressed regrets over not being permitted to prescribe medications that are known to be of value, and many complain of excessively long hours and having to see too many patients each day. Loss of professional autonomy is one of the reasons behind the loss of doctors to private practice.

Admittedly, keeping healthcare costs under control is not easy. Given the need to preserve the pharmaceutical companies' incentives for research and development, having patents to protect the interest of these companies and thus to keep new drug prices high is unavoidable. The cost of treating a health problem knows no limits. In contrast, government budgets have limits, and there are competing uses for public funds.

Accordingly, some kind of bureaucratic constraint on professional decisions will be unavoidable. One less intrusive kind of constraint is to divide services into two kinds: basic and optional. Doctors will be given a free hand in regard to heavily subsidized basic care, whose prices are regulated and will not be overly costly to provide. Regarding non-basic or optional care, there should be no pricing regulation, but a *cost-sharing* arrangement can be set up and can be shown to be welfare-enhancing. An example is a government-provided LHS which is a personal account of contingent funds. Fixed for each patient over the lifetime, it may be withdrawn only with matching payments by the patient. There are two built-in mechanisms against abuse. One is that the patient has to come up with his own share of spending. The other is that if his lifetime quota of the public subsidy is used early in his life he will have less or nothing at all later. Since the LHS can be capped at any level that is comfortable to the government, it will increase patients' choices without overburdening the government.

5.7 Conclusions

While most countries have been trying very hard to control the percentage of the GDP devoted to healthcare Hong Kong, Taiwan and mainland China have all explicitly raised spending on healthcare. This reflects a sensitivity to the needs of the public and should be applauded.

While Hong Kong is struggling with its healthcare reform, and is putting more emphasis on private insurance and private hospital care, Taiwan has consolidated its widely acclaimed NHI scheme, and the mainland has made significant progress along similar lines. According to Vice-Premier Li Keqiang, "the funding of public hospitals through medicinal drug sales will be scrapped in some county-level hospitals" as of 2012, while efforts would be made to "expedite the development of the medical insurance system, expand the coverage of the basic healthcare network and raise healthcare subsidies." According to the report, "300 county-level hospitals will see a change in their funding." Li pledged to separate medical services from drug management and increase doctors' income.[22] A more recent report summarized the achievements in the following:[23]

- 1,295 people Chinese now are under Basic Health Insurance. This includes nearly eight million former employees and retirees of closed enterprises and workers of struggling enterprises.
- Personal healthcare expenses as a percentage of total healthcare expenses have fallen 4.8 percent
- Basic drug prices have fallen some 30 percent, ten categories and 41 items of basic public health services are all provided free or with subsidy.
- Government subsidies for the new cooperative and town and city residents' health insurance rose from 80 yuan per person per year to 200 yuan per person per year.

- The reimbursement rate for inpatient care for included services rose from 40 percent to 50 percent in 2008, to about 70 percent in 2011

The experiences in Taiwan, Hong Kong and mainland China all show that defining what constitutes basic care and covering basic care for all is very important. Indeed, this holds the key to public satisfaction with the healthcare system.

We have seen that appropriate pricing and capping of co-payment expenditures are both important components of a sustainable and high performance healthcare system. It is not surprising that Taiwan, which practices such a system and which maintains universal accessibility, enjoys truly high public satisfaction. Indeed, the public satisfaction rating hovers around an all time high of 88.2 percent in 2010.

The central mission of the public healthcare system is to serve as a safety net for people who cannot afford private healthcare and to provide a benchmark and alternative to private caregivers whoever not satisfied with private care can turn to the public sector for treatment. The benchmark will keep private healthcare-givers on their toes, as a "professionally run" rather than profit-oriented public healthcare system sets a standard against which private healthcare providers have to compete. With such an alternative in place, private healthcare providers will need to provide good value for money before they have business. In the absence of such competition, patients will have little choice, and the quality of the private healthcare sector cannot be assured.[24]

Taiwan's experience with co-payments and annual capping of co-payments is very positive[25]. The approval rating of the NHI was only 39 percent in the very

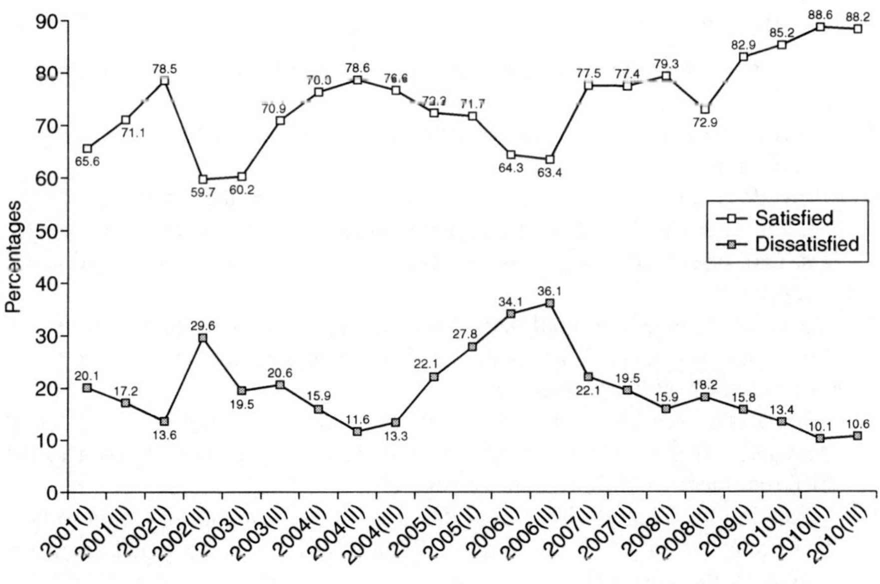

Figure 5.3 NHI public satisfaction ratings.

beginning. It rose above 70 percent in the early 2000s, notwithstanding the multiple increases of co-payments from 1997. Hong Kong's public healthcare system, in contrast, has for a long time suffered from excessively low charges. The system has come under increasing stress, with effective rationing through long queues. Until quite recently, mainland China had been at the other extreme, often allowing healthcare providers to charge heavy fees, effectively denying services from the poor.

Perhaps the central message from a review of their experiences and the theory of provider and patient behavior is that prices hold a central place in the healthcare market, and rightly so. For basic care, prices have to be set right: not too high as to cause supply-side moral hazard, and not too low as to result in overuse or under-provision. For "frontier care," i.e., care that is at the forefront of research and development, the cost of regulating prices is probably too high as it could stifle innovation. Here the discipline of the market, jettisoned by the scrutinizing eyes of the discriminating consumer, may help strike an optimal balance between consumer and supplier interests. In a recent State Council Meeting on healthcare reform, it was pointed out that in the twelfth Five-Year Plan healthcare reform will proceed in three directions: first is to consolidate the universal health insurance scheme and to raise the medical benefits for all citizens, with in-patient care costs covered up to 75 percent; second is to consolidate the basic drug plan and care delivery system; third is to reform the public hospital management and incentive system particularly scrapping the practice of financing healthcare with drug prescriptions.[26] These general directions are consistent with the analysis of this chapter.

Review questions

1 What is the officially announced imperative behind Hong Kong's healthcare reform? Is that justified?
2 What is the role of political economy that shapes the course of healthcare reform in Hong Kong?
3 How does the pricing of healthcare services affect the efficiency of the healthcare system? Is there a distinction between prices received by providers and prices paid by users of the services? Why is this distinction important?
4 Consider the idea of annual budget caps as applied to users and providers of healthcare services. What does the Taiwan experience tell us about the direction of healthcare reform?
5 "China is a very big country with diverse economic conditions in different provinces. It therefore needs different healthcare systems that adapt to the different local conditions." Do you agree?
6 Financing healthcare with sale of drugs is now considered in China to be a bad policy. What is wrong with it? What may be done to guard against it and as an alternative?

6 Publicly funded healthcare systems

United Kingdom and Canada

6.1 Introduction

Economists are well aware of the positive functions of the market in promoting efficiency and consumer choice. The market system is based on decentralized decision making, with consumers seeking out the suppliers that will offer them the best deal and suppliers competing among themselves for consumers' dollars. Suppliers need to minimize costs in order to stay competitive ("production efficiency"). They also have to offer products that meet the demands of the market ("consumers' sovereignty"). At the same time, consumers compete among themselves for the available services. If they are keen on a product, they pay more, thus preempting those other consumers who are less willing to pay for the product. As a result, produced goods will go to those who value them the most ("consumption efficiency").

However, the healthcare market is a rather special kind of market. In order for markets to be efficient, it is necessary for consumers to be well informed, so that they will buy from the cheapest supplier of any given product and so that they will buy the products which best meet their needs. But healthcare is not a homogeneous product. The healthcare supplied by caregiver A may be quite different from that supplied by caregiver B, and the consumer has difficulty telling if A or B is providing a better service. With high information costs, and in particular with *asymmetric information* – consumers having to rely on doctors to tell them what they need – the market cannot be expected to function very well.

Moreover, healthcare is a service that is often needed when the patient is in trouble, and sometimes when he is in deep trouble. He often cannot afford to shop around for a better deal. Even though he may consider a treatment or a recommended diagnostic test very expensive, he may have little choice but to do as his doctor advises. When the patient is desperate, such as when death is threatening and nothing seems to be working, he may even pay a lot for something that may not work at all. He is typically not in the position to tell if what was prescribed for him is in his best interest.

Clearly, the healthcare market is not a "perfectly competitive" market, which would require (a) product homogeneity; (b) perfect information flow; (c) a large number of suppliers selling the same product. In a perfectly competitive market, buyers and sellers are both "price-takers." Participants in such a market have little say over at what price to buy or to sell a product, and have to take whatever price prevails as his relevant price. In the healthcare market, however, such fair balance of power between buyers and sellers does not exist. Instead, the caregiver is the expert and the patient is often completely dependent on him. Against this background emerges the British "fund holding" system whereby a GP fund holder will champion the interests of the patient and buy services for him. In Canada, the provincial insurers will ensure that the doctors follow the rules of pricing and practice before reimbursing them for the services rendered.

6.2 The market discipline

In a free market in which consumers can easily switch from one supplier to another, suppliers are constrained by the market to produce efficiently. In a competitive market, the inefficient producer who produces at a higher cost than industry will be eliminated. If the producer ignores market signals, and continues to produce something that the market has signaled is no longer wanted, he will be punished.

Because of these desirable functions that the market may perform, some healthcare reforms tried to mimic the market. In 1990, the Thatcher administration performed surgery on the National Health Service and split the purchase (GP fund holders) function from the provision function (NHS trusts) in order to promote competition between providers. The "internal market" aims at providing a way whereby "money follows the patient" – hospitals have to attract patients to get funding and to reduce costs in order to stay in the black. Several studies, however, suggest that such competition hurts quality. Propper and Burgess (2003), both of the University of Bristol, found that introducing more competition into the NHS could lead to higher death rates among patients. When hospitals are more concerned with saving money than about saving lives, quality can suffer. Comparing the rate of deaths from emergency admissions for heart attacks, a common indicator of the quality care, in those hospitals with no local competition – some one in three among trusts – with those that had to compete for business, they found death rates from acute myocardial infarction highest in hospitals which had to compete for business. The Labour government briefly scrapped the internal market when it came to power in 1997. A White Paper issued on December 9, 1997 announced

> This White Paper sets out how the internal market will be replaced by a system we have called "integrated care," based on partnership and driven by performance. It forms the basis for a ten year programme to renew and improve the NHS through evolutionary change rather than organisational upheaval. These changes will build on what has worked, but discard what has failed.
>
> The needs of patients will be central to the new system. Abolishing the internal market will enable health professionals to focus on patients, making

> the NHS better every year. Individual patients, who too often have been passed from pillar to post between competing agencies, will get access to an integrated system of care that is quick and reliable.
>
> (Department of Health, 1997)

The British Medical Association, which represented the views of professional doctors, concluded:[1]

> Evidence shows that competition and market incentives do not lead to better or more positive outcomes in healthcare. The purchaser–provider split is expensive, divisive and creates artificial divisions between different parts of the health service. The opposing policies of PbR (payment by results) – which encourages hospitals to treat more – and PBC (practice-based commissioning) – which encourages GPs to use secondary care less – establish inherently adversarial relations and the potential to strain relationships between primary care doctors and their secondary care colleagues...
>
> In the long run, the promotion of markets in the NHS and the lack of incentives both for providers, and providers and commissioners to work together, are creating a more fragmented service, which is likely to have an adverse effect on the quality of care for patients – particularly those with long-term conditions. Seamless care pathways and better co-ordination between the different sectors within healthcare are unlikely to be achieved when providers are in competition, rather than collaborating, with one another. The BMA strongly supports an alternative approach, one encouraging co-operation and collaboration between providers.

Apart from the erosion of cooperation and collaboration between providers as pointed out in the BMA document, a money-follows-patient model may even bring about supply-side moral hazard, if payment to the provider depends on the services rendered. If payment is instead based on prospective payments and a DRG, on the other hand, there is another kind of moral hazard, as the provider may be tempted to under-provide services that the patient may need.

That there is little conclusive evidence so far for the positive effects of the purchaser–provider split was also the conclusion of a recent study based on a large-scale 20-year literature review:[2] the reforms have not been proven to bring about the beneficial outcomes that classical economic theory predicts of markets, including provider responsiveness to patients and purchasers; large-scale cost reduction; and innovation in service provision (p. 10).

Proposition 6.1 Limits of the market under high information cost
When services are heterogeneous and the quality of the services is not readily known to consumers, the market may not be efficient.

Proposition 6.2 Unverified benefits of the purchaser–provider split
The principle that a fund holder who is better informed about the services of providers and knows the needs of patients might work well for his patients in choosing providers and championing their interests is sound, but there could be side effects like erosion of cooperation and collaboration between providers, difficulty of planning ahead on account of uncertainty of funding and even moral hazard, and there has been no conclusive evidence about the benefits, notwithstanding over two decades of experimentation with the internal market.

6.3 Professional–bureaucratic governance mechanism

The NHS in the United Kingdom was established in 1948, with the aim of directly funding and providing a comprehensive range of health services to its citizens through general taxation free of charge. Medicare in Canada, similarly, is a government-funded healthcare program. But instead of directly providing healthcare to its citizens, Canada in 1957[3] opted for a universal health insurance program, which reimburses doctors when they see patients and hospitals when the latter provide inpatient services. Canada is a federal state and provincial funding is supplemented by federal funding under the specific requirements of the Canada Health Act. Canada's healthcare system is "unique in the world in that it bans coverage of [physician and hospital] core services by private insurance companies."[4] While Canada's primary care is dominated by private practitioners, hospital care is almost entirely public. The Cambie Surgery Centre prides itself as "the most modern and only free standing private hospital of its type in Canada." This private hospital was featured in a *New York Times* story in 2006, which described the public insurance system as "slowly breaking down" as "private clinics are opening around the country by an estimated one a week" (*New York Times*, February 26, 2006).

Neither the NHS nor Canada's Medicare is in any danger of falling apart, as public support for them remains very strong, and politicians are unlikely to materially bring them to demise. Just as the NHS is considered central to the United Kingdom's core values, so Medicare is considered central to Canada's core characteristics. Still, both are subject to worries about sustainability as cost soars and about excessively long waiting times and the lack of choice.

Both financial sustainability and queuing time are related to efficiency and cost awareness, while choices are obviously related to whether there is sufficient diversity of providers. Healthcare reformers in the United Kingdom have sought to improve on these fronts by the internal market, which so far has not proven to work. Healthcare reformers in Canada comprise official reformers and market reformers. The former have brought about various improvements through streamlining the Canada Health Act, reducing queuing time through a Wait Time Guarantee, more effective prevention, and a national pharmaceutical strategy, among others. They remain, however, committed to maintaining the predominant role of public health insurance. Private reformers on the other hand advocate a more flexible system that would allow greater room for private insurers to operate in Canada's healthcare market, including topping up the public insurance benefits for a service delivered. Canada has so far taken the position that a doctor gets all the payments from the provincial insurers, or opts out and gets paid entirely by private insurance, and this position has attracted the support of such organizations as the Canadian Union of Public Employees that claims to have 615,000 members across Canada.[5] Referring to studies in Australia and Britain, CUPE is also of the view that contracting out work to for-profit providers will not shorten the waiting list for services:

> One of the reasons given for the longer waits was that there aren't enough medical professionals to go around. With a finite pool of human resources to complete various procedures, trying to relieve the demand on the public sector by removing precious health professionals from it doesn't make much sense.
>
> Another reason is that when doctors work in both private and public clinics they have a perverse incentive to keep public wait lists long. By doing so they justify the need for the private clinic and benefit themselves.[6]

As was explained in the earlier chapters, under specific conditions markets will produce desirable results in terms of greater efficiency, but it will be wrong to assume that market forces are the only forces that can bring about desirable outcomes. There are many professionals who are devoted to service and who exercise their professional autonomy to achieve satisfaction as professionals. And there are alternatives to the market in the form of public accountability and governance that can keep service standards improving and punish poor service. The Canada Health Act, for example, maintains that five principles have to be followed before a province will get federal funding under the Canada Health Transfer (CHT):[7]

Public Administration: The provincial and territorial plans must be administered and operated on a nonprofit basis by a public authority accountable to the provincial or territorial government.

Comprehensiveness: The provincial and territorial plans must insure all medically necessary services provided by hospitals, medical practitioners and dentists working within a hospital setting.

Universality: The provincial and territorial plans must entitle all insured persons to health insurance coverage on uniform terms and conditions.[8]

Accessibility: The provincial and territorial plans must provide all insured persons reasonable access to medically necessary hospital and physician services without financial or other barriers.

Portability: The provincial and territorial plans must cover all insured persons when they move to another province or territory within Canada and when they travel abroad. The provinces and territories have some limits on coverage for services provided outside Canada, and may require prior approval for non-emergency services delivered outside their jurisdiction.

That non-market mechanisms work rather well in Canada has been suggested by Angell (2008) (and as indicated also in the United Kingdom) who found that against many criteria Canadian patients fare better against their American counterparts even though overall Canadian Medicare costs far less, as shown in Table 6.1, which is an updated and expanded version of table 1 in Angell, 2008. There is reason to believe that the absence of universal health insurance is what underlies the markedly lower doctor consultation rate in the United States.

In the United Kingdom, the Health and Social Care (Community Health and Standards) Act 2003 established "*NHS foundation trusts*" to provide and develop services for NHS patients according to NHS principles and standards. They are independently accountable entities subject to NHS inspection and reporting to Parliament. NHS foundation trusts are designed so that they can better tailor their services to best meet the needs of the local population and tackle health inequalities more effectively. NHS foundation trusts have greater freedoms to manage their own affairs and improve services. The purpose in establishing NHS foundation trusts is to:

1 Devolve more power and responsibility to the local level so that NHS hospitals are better able to respond to the needs of patients. The establishment

Table 6.1 Differences in healthcare between Canada, United Kingdom and the United States

	Canada	*United Kingdom*	*United States*
Total healthcare spending per capita (PPP dollars, 2009)	4,363	3,487	7,960
Public spending per capita on health (PPP dollars, 2009)	2,836.5	2,701.6	3,554.2
Life expectancy, year (2011)	81.48	80.17	78.49
Infant mortality rate per 1,000 births (2012)	4.85	4.56	5.98
Hospital beds per 1,000 (2008)	3.4	3.4	3.1
Discharge rates, all causes, per 100,000 population (2008)	8,403	13,762	13,086
Physicians per 1,000 (2009)	2.4	2.7	2.4
Doctor consultations, number per capita per year (2008)	5.5	5.9	3.9
Nurses per 1,000 (2009)	9.4	9.7	10.8
Magnetic resonance imaging units per million population (2007)	6.7	5.6 (2008)	25.9
MRI exams, total, per 1,000 population (2006)	33.3 (43 in 2009)	59 (2008) 67.2 (2009)	89.1 (91.2 in 2007)

Sources: OECD Health Data 2011; CIA World Factbook; International Profile of Healthcare Systems, the Commonwealth Fund 2010.

of NHS foundation trusts aims to bring about improved access to higher quality services for NHS patients by incentivizing innovation and entrepreneurialism.

2 Devolve accountability to local stakeholders including NHS patients and staff. NHS foundation trusts set up governance arrangements that give local stakeholders and the public opportunities to influence the overall stewardship of the organization and its strategic development.
3 Support patient choice by increasing the plurality and diversity of providers within the NHS.

NHS foundation trusts are inspected by the Healthcare Commission for compliance with healthcare standards and targets in the same way as all other NHS trusts. NHS foundation trusts are also overseen by an independent regulator called Monitor. Monitor has statutory powers to authorize NHS trusts as NHS foundation trusts, oversee compliance by NHS foundation trusts with their terms of authorization (like a 'license' to operate) and intervene in the event of significant non-compliance with the terms of authorization and other statutory obligations. NHS foundation trusts have members drawn from patients, the public and staff and are governed by a board of governors comprising people elected from and by the membership base.

With so many things in a state of flux it is not easy to keep abreast of what is shaping up in the United Kingdom. In 2005 there was a consolidation and therefore a reduction in the number of primary care trusts, each of which would take care of an average population just falling short of 330,000. It was held that these streamlined primary care trusts would work better with local authorities in social and health planning. Then the coalition government under Cameron announced its intention to abolish PCTs altogether by 2013, with commissioning to be taken up by general practitioner consortia. Service providers were supposed to be financially more independent and to be capable of going bankrupt. But widespread objections eventually forced Health Minister Andrew Lansley to step back rather than taking the 2011 Health and Social Care Bill forward.

As discussed in the 2010 review by Laura Brereton and Vilashiny Vasoodaven for the Institute for the Study of Civil Society, there have been numerous studies on the different aspects of the NHS as it was evolving from the 1990s through the 2000s. In a democratic society with sufficient transparency of information, public bodies are constantly under the scrutiny of the public eye. Alternatives to the market as a governance mechanism to ensure accountability are available and do work, and they may actually outperform the market in terms of promoting efficiency.

As Angell (2008) observed: in the United States where the market dominates in healthcare "People who are wealthy or well insured may get an MRI they do not need, whereas those without insurance may not get an MRI they do need." Table 6.1 shows that the utilization rate of MRI is markedly higher in the United States than in either Canada or the United Kingdom.[9]

Proposition 6.3 Professional–bureaucratic–public accountability
Accountability and efficiency may still be maintained to ensure the efficiency of a public healthcare system through professional–bureaucratic–public governance mechanisms. Whether this or the market works better is an empirical question.

6.4 Public–private interface in healthcare

A central concern of any healthcare insurance program is moral hazard and escalating costs. Since the United Kingdom and Canada do not charge co-payments when covered patients use covered services, overutilization of services due to moral hazard is a big concern. In Canada, demand-side moral hazard for outpatient care is held in check because drugs are not covered except for the elderly and the indigenous population. In the past, some doctors were found filing claims with the provincial insurer for consultations that never happened, but random checks keep claims generally honest. Drug prices in Canada are typically lower than those in the United States as the federal government control costs through negotiations with suppliers. In the United Kingdom medications administered in hospitals and NHS walk-in clinics are free, but most patients – except those who are on the government's target assisted lists, such as young children and the elderly – have to pay for prescription drugs.[10] In both the United Kingdom and in Canada, private health insurance thus serves only a supplementary role, and is not commonly sought after. Private health insurance typically is offered as an employee benefit in both countries, and may cover private hospital care, drugs and dental services, and may require deductibles.

Public doctors accepting private patients

NHS foundation trusts are allowed to take in private patients who are charged higher fees to supplement their incomes. The private patient cap was introduced by the Health and Social Care Act 2003 (which established NHS foundation trusts) and, by limiting the income NHS foundation trusts can earn from private patient activity, serves "to ensure that NHS foundation trusts focus their efforts primarily on the needs of NHS service users" (Department of Health, Gateway Reference Number: 12871). Such incomes from private patients supplement public funding and may benefit the NHS patients. But many people worry that this would encourage doctors to take on private patients, leading to longer queues for NHS patients. However, if this actually allows the healthcare system to have more resources, including manpower, over the longer run NHS patients may also benefit. The important thing is that NHS must not be grossly underfunded and that doctors must not have a private interest in the matter, i.e., any income derived should not be pocketed. Gross underfunding could lead to neglect of NHS patients. Doctors having a private interest in admitting private patients could give priority to caring for private patients in order to earn more for themselves. In any case, it is important that the resources derived from private patients be used to hire more hands to provide more timely care to NHS patients.

With a huge government budget deficit, the Cameron government proposed to significantly raise the cap significantly so that NHS hospitals in England will be free to use almost half their hospital beds and theatre time for private patients. According to a BBC report, a recent revision to the ongoing health bill will allow foundation hospitals to raise 49 percent of funds through non-NHS work if the bill gets through Parliament, up from an average of about 2 percent.[11] The health secretary says the move will benefit NHS patients. This could be true if public funding is so slim that the NHS has to raise funds to operate, but a better alternative perhaps is to levy affordable charges to patients so that the NHS can remain accessible and can continue to function. The price and cap or EBP proposal discussed in earlier chapters can help avoid the scenario of longer waiting lists that could result from the revised private patient caps.

Proposition 6.4 Excessive private patient caps and inadequate public funding

When public funding is inadequate, and services are free to regular NHS patients, NHS trusts and foundation trusts may need to supplement their incomes from admitting private patients, and this may lead to two classes of patients: those who pay may enjoy priority over those who do not. Charging all patients a fee and capping their annual healthcare expenses may alleviate this problem.

Private doctors working part time in public hospitals or to fill public care duties

There is an acute shortage of healthcare professionals in the public sector in many countries, and the NHS is no exception. In order to alleviate the manpower shortage, some healthcare authorities have tried to engage private doctors to work on a part time basis in public hospitals to perform specific duties. Some have also tried to contract out specific assignments to private doctors and private hospitals. In a 2006 document of the British Medical Association, it is stated that "The BMA, the Department of Health and the NHS Confederation are keen to encourage flexible ways of working to improve recruitment and retention of consultants in the health service."[12] It is important to ensure that these part time private doctors do not take advantage of their contacts with NHS patients to procure more clients for their private practices.

Standard, publicly provided care

Every publicly funded healthcare system has to define the limits of care to be provided by public funding. Evidently it will be impossible to provide all kinds of care, regardless of cost. We have already explained in Chapter 4 how cost–benefit considerations should determine what is to be covered by publicly provided healthcare (Figure 4.1). If a service is to be covered, there is the possibility that a care delivery unit may be short of funds in any given period, simply because the demand in that period is bigger than expected. In some jurisdictions, like Taiwan, services are subject to some budget cap in any given year and caregivers have to work within the budget. This gives rise to financial pressures, and the quality of care may suffer. On the other hand, without some kind of budget limit, there is the worry that doctors may ignore cost–benefit consideration completely, and simply recommend a service as long as it has expected positive marginal benefit, however small. Thus, the notional cost of every service should be taken account of, and every unit should report the total cost. Its performance should be assessed in relation to the total cost, and the yearly assessment should produce feedback to the unit to help improve cost–benefit performance over the longer term. In principle, while the cost of the service should be made known to the doctors and other professional staff who should be reminded of this cost when they provide the service, imposing a rigid budget cap to the unit offering the service may not be consistent with the public interest.

For greater sustainability instead of completely free services patients should be charged an affordable cost when they receive standard services in hospitals. However, private caregivers should also be allowed to provide better-than-basic care to patients who prefer such. Canada has so far insisted that a doctor either collects the payment from the official provincial insurer or collects all payment from the patient or his private insurer. No caregiver should collect payments on top of the reimbursement from the official insurer. But if there are sufficient public healthcare givers (hospital or clinic) already offering the standard basic service at an acceptable quality, and patients are not forced to consult a private doctor or use a private hospital for lack of an alternative, then the private doctor or hospital can be counted upon as offering a preferred alternative.

In *Chaoulli* v. *Quebec*, the Canadian Supreme Court ruled that Quebec's ban on private health insurance for publicly-insured services violated Quebec's charter of human rights and freedoms *when there are lengthy waiting times for treatment in the public system*. The ruling was politically very contentious, as many worried that it would eventually lead to the dismantling of the Medicare system, despite its conditional nature. In this case Dr. Jacques Chaoulli claimed that his patient had encountered a year-long wait for hip surgery and it would not make sense to disallow him to buy private insurance that would pay for privately delivered care.

This case shows how private insurers and private caregivers can potentially enhance the public interest. To protect the public from health and associated financial risk a reliable non-profit backbone of care provision is indeed necessary. Failing to provide timely care and still prohibiting patients from getting private care through private insurance would certainly hurt the interests of patients and therefore the public interest.

This backbone is based on the professional model to prevent supply-side moral hazard, but patients need to be charged the direct cost as far as possible to prevent demand-side moral hazard. An annual ceiling for out-of-pocket eligible healthcare expenses is set in order to protect patients from excessive burden. These features are designed in light of human nature – worry about excessive burden, and propensity for excessive supply under the profit motive or excessive demand when services are priced below their true marginal costs.

Public healthcare and private healthcare can and should coexist, because they complement each other. Public healthcare provides a benchmark against which private caregivers have to compete. Private caregivers have to offer value before they can attract patients who have the public care option. If they can survive and can attract patients notwithstanding the availability of public care, both the private caregivers and their patients should benefit. On the other hand, if reliable and timely public healthcare is not available, people will be forced to use private services even if their quality is not very good. Private healthcare can also provide services not covered by public care.

Proposition 6.5 Public healthcare as backbone; private health insurance as supplement
When the public healthcare system is functioning well and is able to provide reliable, timely care to patients, private healthcare givers will need to compete with this system in order to get patients. Patients will then not be forced into private healthcare, and "revealed preference" suggests that the private healthcare system is providing a valuable alternative and is enhancing welfare. Private health insurance to provide such supplementary care should not be banned.

6.5 Single payer insurance versus pluralistic private insurance

In the Supreme Court debate leading to the *Chaoulli* v. *Quebec* decision, dissenting opinions were expressed by Binnie and LeBel, who referred to

> an overly optimistic view of the benefits offered by private health insurance, an oversimplified view of the adverse effects on the public health system of permitting private sector health services to flourish and an overly interventionist view of the role the courts should play in trying to supply a "fix" to the failings, real or perceived, of major social programs.
>
> (Para. 169)

They also noted that:

> Not all Canadian provinces prohibit private health insurance, but all of them take steps to protect the public health system by discouraging the private

> sector . . . the mixture of deterrents differs from province to province, but the underlying policies flow from the Canada Health Act and are the same: i.e., as a matter of principle, healthcare should be based on need, not wealth, and as a matter of practicality the provinces judge that growth of the private sector will undermine the strength of the Canada Health Act.
>
> (Para. 174)

A key advantage of single payer insurance is that it saves administration costs and that the single payer can set the standards of reimbursement. In Canada, doctors are not allowed to charge patients anything on top of the reimbursement that they get from their provincial insurers. This has proved to be an effective control on healthcare costs, even though some doctors may consider this unfair. These doctors argue: if I can provide better service and patients are willing to pay, why should I not be paid what I deserve?

The counter argument is that in the healthcare market patients may not be able to tell who is giving them better service. They might even consider higher charges as an indicator of better service, thus leading to a competition for higher charges. A central concern is also that if charges escalate, patients who cannot afford the extra payment may not be able to get the services that they need.

Proposition 6.6 Primary care in Canada and single payer insurance
Canada has insisted on single payer health insurance. This makes sense if there is no public healthcare as an alternative to private doctors. In Canada primary care is almost entirely provided by private practitioners. There is no benchmark care provided publicly. The single payer insurance sets reimbursement standards and controls costs.

Proposition 6.7 Public primary care and private insurance
A country that provides publicly funded primary care that is of good quality, widely accessible, and that charges standard fees should allow private insurance plans that pay for better than basic care. This will allow more choice without impinging on the availability of affordable basic care.

6.5 Conclusions

Public healthcare and private healthcare should play different roles. Public healthcare is to provide basic and reliable protection to all. Private healthcare is to provide more choice and care when individuals opt for such care of their own accord. If someone can afford it, and some provider can satisfy the demand, the government should not intervene, except to ensure that the transaction is truly voluntary, that no one is misleading the other party into the transaction, and that the caregivers are professionals well qualified to perform the work.

We have argued that public healthcare should serve as the backbone of care because without it, patients have little choice but to follow the advice of their doctors and to pay for the services as recommended. In the healthcare market, competition alone cannot protect the interests of patients, as information cost is high and patients often cannot wait and shop around. If all caregivers are market-driven, patients have reasons to worry that the same profit incentives may be distorting the professional decisions whoever they turn to. On the other hand, the availability of a viable public care option means that a private doctor has to somehow convince a patient that he provides better service and good value for money, before he can attract the patient.

Many attempts have been made to introduce competition within the public healthcare sector through some "internal market" mechanism. Essentially the idea is to bring in some form of "money follows the patient." The NHS experience in the United Kingdom suggests that this experiment with internal markets has not been very successful. At least there are many skeptics. The Labour Party when it came into power in 1997 wanted to scrap the internal market, but some form of internal market competition was still maintained. In a statement made as recently as 2009, then Health Minister Edwina Hart of the Labor administration announced that the NHS was to enter a "new dawn as the last vestiges of the internal market were to be removed from the health service in Wales." She promised seven new health boards would signal the start of a more "streamlined" and "citizen-focused" NHS, one that promises to return the NHS to its founding principle – namely to "put the welfare of the sick in front of every other consideration," as Aneurin Bevan the father of the NHS put it in 1948.

According to the *Western Mail*, Mrs. Hart was reported as having said that

> We have to be more citizen-focused in the NHS, we've got to recognize that our job is to the patient. It's not about bureaucracy but [about] how patients get through the system.... I think we are on the doorstep of a new dawn – this is a massive reorganization.... The traditional split between community-based health services and hospital care will be consigned to the dustbin of history today as NHS trusts and local health boards are scrapped. They will be replaced by seven new health boards responsible for providing all NHS services.[13]

With the Labour administration replaced by the coalition government, all this is gone, but even Cameron will not dare to touch the spirit of the NHS, which is to provide free care at the point of service. This really makes the problem a lot more complicated, because certainly affordable service of an acceptable quality is far more important than free care of an unacceptable quality.

It should be understood that competition provides just one form of discipline or governance mechanism. There are alternative governance or accountability mechanisms that have proved to work. Defining clearly lines of accountability and professional monitoring is one way. Ensuring transparency of information and press freedom is another. In principle, both the market and the bureaucracy will affect professional decisions, and it is a challenge to find out what works better. The NHS has come full circle. It is time to re-examine the internal market and compare it with the professional–bureaucratic–public scrutiny system of governance.

It is no accident that Peter Black, the Welsh Liberal Democrat health spokesman, remarked that the new health boards faced a huge challenge in delivering a first class health service for Wales in the face of an accumulated structural deficit across the country of £200 million. Indeed, it was in part the financial pressures on the healthcare system that drove healthcare reform along the "internal market route" – with the presumption that the internal market would improve efficiency and help reduce costs. That brings us back to the subject of collecting user fees. From our earlier discussion, user fees reflecting direct marginal costs provide the best instrument against supply-side and demand-side moral hazard. Instead of trying to provide "premium" or "superior" services and charging "private patient" fees to make up for the shortage of funds, more reasonable charges with annual capping of out-of-pocket costs will better tackle the budget constraint problem. Informing doctors about the notional costs of the various services is yet another way of facilitating the comparison of costs and benefits of the various medical interventions and diagnostic services when they recommend such services.

Review questions

1. What are the weaknesses and strengths of the Canadian and the British systems of healthcare?
2. How are doctors in primary care in Canada and in the United Kingdom paid? Would you worry about supply-side moral hazard given the operating environment? GPs in the United Kingdom were reported to be given extra incomes by the NHS for reducing referrals to hospitals.[14] In what sense does this undermine professional judgment?
3. Compare the advantages and disadvantages of the single payer health insurance versus the pluralistic health insurance schemes offered in the marketplace.
4. What is the rationale for the purchaser–provider split? Did it work in the United Kingdom? What are the potential problems associated with the money-follows-patient model of healthcare financing?

7 Singapore

Medisave, Medishield, Medifund and ElderShield

7.1 Introduction

Singapore prides itself for its efficiency and spirit of self-reliance. Singapore spends less than 2 percent of its GDP on public healthcare expenditure. This is even less than the approximately 3 percent that Hong Kong spends. Yet Singapore's health indicators are very good. Its life expectancy and infant mortality rates are generally superior to those of the United States, and are comparable to Hong Kong. The main reason for this is that the philosophy of relying on citizens' own resources for healthcare promotes prevention. But Singapore also understands the need for risk pooling and so very much relies on the insurance principle to manage catastrophic financial risks.

As of 2011 Singapore had a population close to 5–2 million, of which only 4.3 million are permanent residents. Its population is relatively young, with a median age at 38.0 as of 2011, as compared to 41.7 for Hong Kong, but somewhat older than that of the United States, whose median age stands at 36.9 (C.I.A). Singapore's life expectancy at birth in 2010 was 79.3 for males and 84.1 for females, which compares very favorably with those of the United States, which stood at 75.7 and 80.8 for males and females respectively.[1]

What appears remarkable about Singapore is that while achieving very impressive health indicators, public healthcare expenditure has remained very low as a percentage of the GDP, in fact barely over 1 percent in 2009. Total healthcare expenditure is also very low, at 3.9 percent of the GDP. This is in sharp contrast with the United States, as shown in Table 7.1.

Healthcare in Singapore is regulated by the Ministry of Health and its statutory boards. The Singapore healthcare system is unique in that it is administered by an efficient bureaucracy and follows a consistent philosophy combining self-reliance, professional self-regulation, and government regulation that is guided by a strong sense of serving the public interest. All hospitals, clinics, clinical laboratories and nursing homes are licensed by the ministry. Self-regulation is performed by various professional bodies, including the Singapore Medical Council, Singapore Dental Council, Singapore Nursing Board and the Singapore Pharmacy Board. In addition, health-related products such as medicines, medical devices, nutrition supplements, etc. are regulated by the Health Sciences Authority.

Table 7.1 Overall and public expenditure on health in 2009 (percentage of GDP)*

	Over all (%)	*Public (%)*
Australia	8.7	5.9
Austria	11.0	8.5
Belgium	11.4	8.6
Canada	11.4	8.0
France	11.8	9.2
Germany	11.6	8.9
Hong Kong	5.5	2.6
Japan	8.5	6.9
Korea	6.9	4.0
New Zealand	10.3	8.3
Singapore	3.9	1.0
Sweden	10.0	8.2
Switzerland	11.4	6.8
United Kingdom	9.8	8.2
United States	17.4	8.3

Source: Calculated from OECD Health Data, Statistical Yearbook of Singapore, Hong Kong Annual Digest of Statistics.

Note
* Japan and Australia data refer to 2008.

7.2 Philosophy

The Singapore system encourages prevention to a greater extent than most other healthcare systems. It does this by a multi-pronged approach to encourage self-reliance and prevention:

a Public healthcare is provided at a fee that discriminates against the well-off; so that well-off people receive relatively minor subsidies. Well-off people should not count on the government to give them much assistance at all in terms of healthcare. This differential support for people with different means has been reinforced with a means test since 2009.

b People are forced to put money in their "Medisave" accounts, which are personal accounts that constitute part of the central provident fund system; except for specified specialist services, they cannot generally draw on these funds even for most outpatient visits, and must pay out-of-pocket or from their private health insurance policies.

c Very active public education exists about self-reliance and prevention through a healthy lifestyle.

d Strong public hygiene is maintained by an efficient administration, with punishment against offences.

The Singapore system is sensitive to the needs of the poor, and promises never to "withhold help to a Singaporean because of financial limitations."

The government considers its role is to serve as the dominant healthcare provider and the leader in terms of introducing modern care practices and technology. Pricing in the public hospitals serves as a benchmark which private hospitals need to take note of when they compete for patients.

Starting on January 1, 2009, Singapore has introduced means testing for public hospital patients. Subsidies for class B2 and class C wards are no longer automatic, but are based on patients' tax-declared incomes or, for non-working patients, the value of their homes. The subsidy rates are higher for citizens than for non-citizen permanent residents. Patients belonging to the highest earning group, as well as those who refuse to disclose their incomes, will still enjoy some subsidies, which stand at 50 percent for class B2 and 65 percent for class C wards. Non-citizens who have the right to permanent residency in Singapore enjoy 10 percent less subsidy than Singaporeans. Foreigners are not entitled to any subsidies. Outpatient visits to government medical facilities. such as accident and emergency, specialist outpatient and polyclinic visits do not require means testing.

For patients with no income, who include retirees, full-time housewives and children, the value of their homes will be used to determine their subsidy level entitlements. The threshold is based on a "property annual value" (AV) or in other words the annual rental value (net of the rental values of any extras such as furnishings and additional services provided). Patients with home AVs below or equal to S$11,000 enjoy the maximum subsidy levels whereas above this, they receive the minimum levels (50 percent for class B2, and 65 percent for class C).

Considering the administrative side of such arrangements, one cannot help but admire how Singapore overcomes what could be an administrative nightmare for others. To most people running a means test on all inpatients would appear to be very cumbersome. It does appear that Singapore has an unusually efficient civil service that can deal with all the complexities arising from micromanagement. What works in Singapore may therefore not work elsewhere.

Table 7.3a and Table 7.3b show the daily ward charges for selected public and private hospitals in Singapore. As can be seen in Table 7.3a, even among public hospitals costs vary from hospital to hospital, suggesting that the bureaucracy tries to mimic the market in differential pricing based on the quality of the hospitals. Means-testing is required for the heavily subsidized wards in public hospitals.

It should be noted that the baseline charges are quite similar in public and private hospitals in Singapore. A1 wards in public hospitals are not subsidized and in principle should be market prices. Singapore makes sure that public medical services are available to Singaporeans who want them. It is their choice to visit a private facility.

It is interesting to note that prior to 2009 anyone could in principle choose any ward when admitted to a hospital. Singapore relied then on self-selection to extend subsidies to deserving people. Usually, human nature would encourage a well-off patient to opt for a more comfortable ward, one that is more private and

Table 7.2 Subsidy schedule for different wards in Singapore's public hospitals

Average monthly income of patient (S$)	*Class C subsidy (citizens) (%)*	*Class B2 subsidy (citizens) (%)*	*Class C subsidy (permanent residents) (%)*	*Class B2 subsidy (permanent residents) (%)*
3,200 and below	80	65	70	55
3,201–3,350	79	64	69	54
3,351–3,500	78	63	68	53
3,501–3,650	77	62	67	52
3,651–3,800	76	61	66	51
3,801–3,950	75	60	65	50
3,951–4,100	74	59	64	49
4,101–4,250	73	58	63	48
4,251–4,400	72	57	62	47
4,401–4,550	71	56	61	46
4,551–4,700	70	55	60	45
4,701–4,850	69	54	59	44
4,851–5,000	68	53	58	43
5,001–5,100	67	52	57	42
5,101–5,200	66	51	56	41
5,201 and above	65	50	55	40

Source: "Singapore Starts Means Testing in Hospitals," posted Thursday, January 8, 2009 online, available at: www.hospitals.sg/singapore-starts-means-testing-hospitals.

Table 7.3a Daily ward charges in Singapore (public hospitals) (as of January 1, 2012, in S$; S$1 = US$0.8 approximately in January 2012)

Restructured hospitals#	*Single-bed room A1*	*2-bed room A2*	*4-bed room B1*	*5-bed room B2+*	*6-bed room B2*	*Open Ward C*
Alexandra Hospital (rates inclusive of 7 percent GST)						
Singapore citizen	275	n.a.	176	n.a.	52	27
Permanent resident	275	n.a.	207	n.a.	90	63
Foreign resident*	275	n.a.	207	n.a.	187	171
Non-resident**	275	n.a.	207	n.a.	187	171
KK Women's and Children's Hospital						
Singapore citizen	345	n.a.	198	130	60	31
Permanent resident	345	n.a.	250	179	109	80
Foreign resident*	345	n.a.	276	n.a.	n.a.	n.a.
Non-resident**	349	n.a.	304	n.a.	n.a.	n.a.
National University Hospital						
Singapore citizen	428	257	From 205.44	n.a.	From 71	From 41
Permanent resident	428	257	234	n.a.	112	482
Foreign resident*	428	257	257	n.a.	257	257
Non-resident**	428	257	257	n.a.	n.a.	n.a.
Singapore General Hospital						
Singapore citizen	From 344.54	n.a.	From 202.23	From 128	From 64	From 32
Permanent resident	From 344.54	n.a.	228	From 174	From 114	From 72
Foreign resident*	From 344.54	n.a.	270	258	240	223
Non-resident**	380	n.a.	270	n.a.	n.a.	n.a.

Source: online, available at: www.income.com.sg/insurance/wardcharges.pdf.

Notes

Rates shown above for B2+, B2 and C class wards in restructured hospitals for Singapore citizens/permanent residents are based on maximum subsidy level.

* Foreign resident refers to Employment Pass holders, S pass and work permit holders.

** Non-resident refers to international patients.

Above rates are rounded up to the nearest dollar and before 7 percent GST unless otherwise stated.

\# Public hospitals in Singapore were restructured as financially independent and accountable entities separate from the Government in 1989.

Table 7.3b Daily ward charges in Singapore (private hospitals) (as of January 1, 2012, in S$; S$=US$0.8 approximately in January 2012)

Hospital	*Single-bed room A1*	*2-bed room A2*	*4-bed room B1*	*6-bed room C*
Gleneagles Hospital	528	288	218	n.a.
Mount Alvernia Hospital	400	230	170	120
Mount Elizabeth Hospital	578	295	238	n.a.
Parkway East Hospital	435	230	198	n.a.
Ruffles Hospital	460	281	208	158
Thomson Medical Centre	480	258	195	n.a.

Source: online, available at: www.income.com.sg/insurance/wardcharges.pdf.

is air-conditioned. So means testing was considered not necessary in order to save administrative costs. The change in 2009 reflects either a belief that reliance on self- selection to sort out who is more deserving of greater subsidies was not working as well as expected, or an increase in the confidence of the bureaucracy to handle the means testing, or a combination of these factors. Over the years, without knowing it, the Singapore healthcare system has become more and more complex and administratively more and more demanding. It is possible that Singapore had underestimated the administrative cost and under-reported the real social cost of publicly provided healthcare. But generally the increased complexities have reflected a civil service that was able to cope with such increased complexities.

Proposition 7.1 Singapore style regulation
Singapore-style regulation reflects a bureaucracy that shows attention to detail that requires strong administrative support and a philosophy combining self reliance and professional self-regulation.

7.3 The infrastructure

Primary healthcare

Primary healthcare includes preventive healthcare and health education. Private practitioners provide 80 percent of primary healthcare services while government polyclinics provide the remaining 20 percent.

Singapore maintains a network of 18 outpatient polyclinics, while some 2,000 private medical practitioners' clinics provide additional primary healthcare services. "Each polyclinic is an affordable subsidized one-stop health centre, providing outpatient medical care, follow-up of patients discharged from hospitals, immunization, health screening and education, investigative

Table 7.4 Fees at Singapore's polyclinics: medical consultations

Description	*Singapore citizen*	*Child/elderly (citizen)*	*Permanent resident*	*Non-resident*
Consultation	10.20	5.60	15.50	37.50
Family physician clinic	20.00	20.00	30.00	49.30
Nurse clinician service	6.00	6.00	9.00	12.00

Source: online, available at: http://polyclinic.singhealth.com.sg/PatientCare/Fees/Pages/Home.aspx.

Note
Units in Singapore dollars.

facilities and pharmacy services." The needy elderly receive further help through the Primary Care Partnership Scheme (PCPS), which provides access to those who have difficulty traveling to the polyclinics. Fees for outpatient visits to Singapore's polyclinics are listed in Table 7.4 and are quite affordable. Outpatient visits to public hospitals generally costs more. Concessionary fees are given to Singaporean citizens aged 65 and above, children up to 18 years of age and students.

Hospitals

The market shares between public hospitals and private hospitals are roughly 8:2. In 2006, there were 29 hospitals and specialty centers in Singapore, giving a ratio of 2.6 beds per 1,000 total population. Out of the 29, 16 are private hospitals, seven are public hospitals comprising five acute general hospitals, a women's hospital, a children's hospital and a psychiatric hospital. The remaining eight are specialty centers that provide cancer, cardiac, eye, skin, neuroscience and dental care. The government's role as the dominant healthcare provider allows the government to influence the supply of hospital beds, the introduction of high-tech/high-cost medicine, and the rate of cost increases in the public sector which sets the benchmark in terms of pricing for the private sector.

Five acute hospitals and eight specialty centers operate independently as non-profit corporations wholly-owned by the government. This means that they use commercial accounting systems, are subject to financial discipline and accountability, and enjoy greater flexibility in management than if they were run within the civil service. All receive an annual subvention from the government, and are subject to broad policy guidelines as set by the Ministry of Health.

The 13 does not include community hospitals that provide services to the convalescent sick and aged who do not require the care of the general hospitals. Community hospitals are a cost saver, as accommodating these patients in general hospitals would be much more costly to society.

7.4 The key schemes: Medisave, Medishield, Medifund, ElderShield

The Central Provident Fund (CPF) of Singapore dates from 1955, well before Singapore's independence in 1963. It currently operates three types of individual accounts: an *ordinary account*, which can be spent on the purchase of a home, approved investments, CPF insurance and education; a *special account*, principally for old-age provisions; and finally a *Medisave account* designated for expenses on hospital treatment, medical benefits and approved medical insurance. CPF contribution and allocation rates are revised from time to time. The latest, applicable from September 1, 2011, for specific employee categories as indicated in the notes to the Table 7.5, is illustrative and are set out in Table 7.5.

Medisave

Medisave was introduced in April 1984. It is a mandatory medical savings scheme under which individuals put aside part of their incomes into a personal Medisave account to meet their future personal or immediate family's hospitalization, day surgery and certain outpatient expenses. Contributions used to lie within the range of 6–8 percent of monthly wages up to a set limit, depending on age, the contributions rates have been revised several times and now stand at 7–9.5 percent, as indicated in Table 7.5. Contributions to the Medisave account are subject to a Medisave contribution ceiling (MCC) beyond which further contribution into Medisave is not required. The MCC stands at S$41,000 as at July 1, 2011. The excess is transferred to the special account for members below 55 years and to the retirement account for members aged 55 years and above to top-up any minimum sum shortfall. Once the required amount has been topped up to cover any minimum sum shortfall, Medisave account overflows will go into their ordinary account. When a member withdraws his Medisave at or after age 55, he needs to set aside at least the minimum Medisave sum (MMS) in his account, which is S$36,000 (wef July 1, 2011).

Funds in the Medisave scheme can be drawn upon to pay for specific hospitalization expenses incurred in Class B2/C wards in public hospitals as well as certain outpatient treatments like chemotherapy, radiotherapy and dialysis. Medisave savings may also pay for one's immediate family members' hospitalization expenses, day surgery and selected outpatient treatments. "Immediate family members" refers to spouse, children, parents and grandparents. Grandparents must be Singapore citizens or permanent residents. Withdrawals are subject to specific limits under the different categories of services paid for. Specifically, Medisave may cover:

- S$450 per day for daily hospital charges which includes a maximum of S$50 for doctor's daily attendance fees.
- A fixed limit for each surgical operation.

Table 7.5 CPF contribution and allocation rates effective September 1, 2011

Employee age (years)	*Contribution rate (for monthly wages exceeding $1,500)*			*Credited into*		
	Contribution by employer (% of wage)	*Contribution by employee (% of wage)*	*Total contribution (% of wage)*	*Ordinary account (% of wage)*	*Special account (% of wage)*	*Medisave account (% of wage)*
35 and below	16	20	36	23	6	7
35–45	16	20	36	21	7	8
45–50	16	20	36	19	8	9
50–55	12	18	30	13	8	9
55–60	9	12.5	21.5	11.5	1	9
60–65	6.5	7.5	14	3.5	1	9.5
Above 65	6.5	5	11.5	1	1	9.5

Source: online, available at: CPF Board: http://mycpf.cpf.gov.sg/Members/Gen-Info/Con-Rates/ContriRa.htm.

Notes
These rates apply only for private sector employees and for non-pensionable employees who work in statutory bodies and aided schools and ministries, and who are Singapore citizen, SPR in the third year and onwards of obtaining SPR status. Contribution rates apply for wages up to S$5,000. If the monthly wages are less than S$1,500, lower contribution rates apply For (1) pensionable employees (statutory bodies) (2) pensionable employees (ministries), other contribution rates apply.

- Approved day surgeries, up to S$300 per day for daily hospital charges including a maximum of S$30 for the doctor's daily attendance fees, as well as a fixed limit per table of surgical operation.
- Psychiatric treatment, up to S$150 per day for the daily hospital charges including a maximum of S$50 for the doctor's daily attendance fees, subject to a maximum of S$5,000 a year.
- Approved community hospitals, up to S$150 per day for the daily hospital charges before June 1, 2010 or S$250 per day for daily hospital charges for admission on or after June 1, 2010, including a maximum of S$30 for the doctor's daily attendance fees, subject to a maximum of S$3,500 a year before June 1, 2010 or S$5,000 a year for admission on or after June 1, 2010.
- Approved convalescent hospitals, up to S$50 a day for the daily hospital charges, including a maximum of S$30 for the doctor's daily attendance fees, subject to a maximum of S$3,000 a year.
- Approved hospices, up to S$160 per day for the daily hospital charges, including a maximum of S$30 for the doctor's daily attendance fees.
- Day rehabilitation at day rehabilitation centers, up to S$20 per day before June 1, 2010 or S$25 per day on or after June 1, 2010, subject to a maximum of S$1,500 a year.

For a hospitalization claim, the patient must have stayed in the hospital for at least 8 hours (unless the patient is admitted for day surgery) or died within 8 hours of being hospitalized. This and various withdrawal restrictions are "meant to help members avoid over-using their Medisave savings, so that they have sufficient Medisave savings for their own future healthcare needs."

Medishield

A problem with any personalized Medisave account is that there is no telling if the amount saved will be enough. If a serious illness strikes, it could be easily wiped out. The Singapore government realized that Medisave cannot by itself deal with the problem of bigger risks, and introduced a catastrophic health insurance scheme called the Medishield in 1990. This is designed as a low cost scheme that controls moral hazard problems through co-payments and deductibles. Premiums for Medishield can be paid with funds in the Medisave account. From December 1, 2008, Medishield benefits were enhanced and now cover up to 80 percent of inpatient care charges at the Class B2/C level. Singaporeans have the option of purchasing Medisave-approved private integrated shield plans to cover inpatient care for the more expensive wards.

Medifund

Medifund was set up in April 1993 to help needy Singaporeans. This fund acts as a safety net for those who cannot afford the subsidized bill charges despite

Medisave and Medishield coverage. Medifund was established with an initial capital of S$200 million and capital injections are made from time to time when the government's fiscal position is strong. The scheme is financed by the interest incomes from the endowment fund.

ElderShield

ElderShield, introduced in 2002, is an affordable severe disability insurance scheme that helps Singaporeans pay for the expenses of care associated with severe disability or age-related morbidity. It provides a monthly cash payout to help pay the out-of-pocket expenses for the care of a severely-disabled person. The Ministry of Health has appointed three private insurers to run ElderShield. Premiums are determined at the age of entry and will not increase with age. Premiums are payable annually up to the age of 65, and the coverage will be good for life. Singapore citizens and permanent residents with Medisave accounts are automatically covered under ElderShield at the age of 40 and may pay with cash or from their Medisave accounts. In 2007 ElderShield was enhanced. For those who join after 2007, the enhanced scheme applies, and the monthly payout is S$400 instead of S$300 per month and is payable for a maximum of 72 months instead of the earlier 60 months. Moreover, an optional ElderShield supplement became available that pays even higher benefits and for a longer period.

Proposition 7.2 Evolution of the Singapore healthcare system
As Singapore builds up its healthcare system from Medisave to Medishield to Medifund to ElderShield, reflecting in part lessons learnt on the way, and in part changes in the make-up of the Singapore society, the system has become more and more complex, but Singapore civil servants appear ready to take on the administrative challenge of an increasingly complex system, which is likely to be too complex to administer in other jurisdictions.

7.5 Evaluations and conclusions

Singapore's system of healthcare financing has been built up over time along the principle of self-reliance combined with social insurance, both of which are clearly good general principles. But the extent of centralized bureaucratic control stretches the imagination of many observers. Although the government arguably has succeeded in achieving efficiency in terms of the health outcome versus the amount of government-committed resources in healthcare, the burden to the community is actually quite considerable. Singaporeans generally have to put aside 7–9.5 percent of their monthly incomes for their Medisave accounts, and yet must depend on themselves for out-of-pocket expenses for most outpatient visits to clinics. The funds in the Medisave accounts are in their names, but they are not allowed to have much discretion over their use. It is not clear if the cost of the bureaucracy that administers the Medisave, Medishield, Medifund and ElderShield schemes has been counted in the government-funded cost of healthcare, which is reported to be merely around 1 percent of the GDP. Moreover, the loss of the freedom of choice over consumption versus savings should also be counted as a cost.

The Singapore system provides strong incentives for people to adopt a healthy lifestyle. The system of government-run hospitals and the role of the government in controlling the prices of healthcare services are conducive to cost control. However, when funds accumulated in Medisave accounts have little alternative use people may well over-spend on such items as specialist outpatient care.

Unlike the American system, Singapore's system provides universal coverage and is sensitive to the needs of the poor.[2] Whereas the American system allows plenty of room for abuse, including in particular Medicare fraud, which was recently highlighted in a *60 Minutes* story, the Singapore system is tightly controlled, and does not easily allow fraudulent medical claims on public coffers.

However attractive on the surface the Singapore system may appear, given the extreme loss of choice for citizens and the extreme demands on the bureaucracy to manage the complex schemes, it is unlikely that it can easily be duplicated elsewhere.

Review questions

1. How is Singapore able to achieve its fame in running a lean but efficient healthcare system? Would you recommend the Singapore system to your country? Why or why not?
2. Look at Table 7.4 for the contribution rates to the Central Provident Fund. What do you notice? Can you explain the rationale behind what you notice?
3. Is it correct to say that Singapore has a universal healthcare system?

8 Universal publicly funded basic healthcare in Australia and New Zealand

8.1 Introduction

Compared to Singapore, both Australia and New Zealand rely much more on public funding, and both provide universal access to healthcare. In this respect Australia and New Zealand appear closer to the UK than the Singapore model. However, like Singapore, Australia and New Zealand depend very much on the private healthcare market to provide primary healthcare services. Australia has both public and private hospitals, with the former accounting for more than twice as many inpatient days as the latter.

Australia even extends coverage to visitors from countries that offer similar treatment to its citizens.[1] The coverage is quite broad and includes both inpatient and outpatient care, as well as many prescription drugs. Inpatient care in public hospitals in both countries is essentially free. Still, both Australia and New Zealand allow and actually encourage patients to buy private insurance plans to top up the standard coverage under the public system (such as dental, optometry and podiatry, and elective surgery in private hospitals). About one-third of New Zealanders have some form of private health insurance, which accounts for less than 6 percent of total healthcare expenditures, and about half or more than 11 million Australians in 2012 have private insurance.[2] Private insurance contributes 7.6 percent of total health expenditure in Australia. Since 1999, the government has subsidized private health insurance premiums. The subsidy rate is 30 percent for those below 65, 35 percent for people aged 65 to 69 years, and 40 percent for those aged 70 and above. The Australia and New Zealand experience shows that when affordable public healthcare is available and readily accessible, private insurance and private healthcare can serve as supplements and are welcomed by the people. The fear of "rip-off" would be valid if patients have no viable public healthcare alternative, and had to use private services even at unreasonably high costs.

One interesting approach undertaken by Australia to reduce the time of waiting for elective surgery, which is common among countries offering universal public healthcare, is to provide extra funding specifically targeted at reducing the time of waiting. The Elective Surgery Waiting List Reduction Plan was given a budget of A$600 million through the four-year (2008–2011) aims to reduce the number of people waiting longer than clinically recommended for elective surgery, and has proved immensely successful.[3]

Proposition 8.1 Private healthcare and health insurance supplements public healthcare
Rather than relying on private health insurance and private healthcare, the sensible response to unduly long waiting lists is to directly fund and strengthen the public healthcare sector so that affordable public healthcare is readily available and considered adequate. When this happens private caregivers cannot overcharge patients without turning them away. We can then be assured that private caregiver and private insurance will serve a valuable supplementary role.

Since 1984 Australia has imposed a Medicare levy (an earmarked tax for healthcare that was originally set at 1 percent of taxable income but was later revised to 1.5 percent), but this is not enough, and much of the health-related expenditures comes from the general revenue. In 2007–2008, this levy only accounted for 18.2 percent of total health funding by the Australian government. Since October 1997, a further surcharge of 1.0 percent was payable by 'high-income' earners. In 2008, high income earners were defined as those individuals earning more than A$70,000 for individuals and couples earning more than A$140,000.

In New Zealand public funding accounted for about 81 percent of healthcare expenditures in 2010/2011. Of this general taxation accounts for 87.7 percent, the accident compensation scheme 11.3 percent, and local government 0.9 percent. The government sets an annual global budget for most publicly funded health services. Funding is distributed to district health boards (DHBs) using a weighted, population-based formula. DHBs provide services both directly through their own facilities and indirectly though private providers such as GPs most of whom are grouped as primary health organizations (PHOs) and private surgical hospitals. Accident and injury care is financed by a separate, quasi-governmental agency, the Accident Compensation Corporation (ACC), funded by employer and employee levies.

8.2 Pricing, mandatory social insurance and private insurance

In Australia "schedule fees" are stipulated over a range of healthcare services, but doctors are free to charge above the schedule fee, provided that patients are willing to pay the excess. In mid-2009, 74 percent of all medical services and 80 percent of general practitioner visits were provided at schedule fees with no excess billing. When charges are at the schedule fees, patients will pay a 15 percent co-payment. In New Zealand patients also enjoy significant subsidies funded by general taxes when they use medical services. The share of these out-of-pocket payments paid by private households stood at 14 percent of total national health expenditures in 2007.

Both Australia and New Zealand offer drug plans that require a standard co-payment, with concessionary rates for the poor. Alternative medicines and therapies are normally not covered, though some allied health services are covered in Australia with proper referral.

As noted earlier, Australian healthcare providers are allowed to charge beyond the schedule fees, with the extra amounts paid by patients or their insurers on an out-of-pocket basis. In order to facilitate insurance pricing comparison, the Department of Health and Aging also launched a new website in 2010 (Privatehealth.gov.au) that allows consumers to easily compare policies. Perhaps unique to Australia, Medicare provides "provider percentile charts" that show the number of services billed by the providers for selected MBS (Medicare Benefit Schedule) items.[4] The patient can look at his own billing data and read from the item percentile chart to decide whether his service provider is claiming more or fewer services than other providers for that MBS item.

Proposition 8.2 Transparency of pricing and schedule fees
Australia believes that transparency of pricing and the setting of schedule fees will help contain cost escalation, as the schedule fees provide a benchmark for pricing and transparent cost comparison increases the effectiveness of price competition.

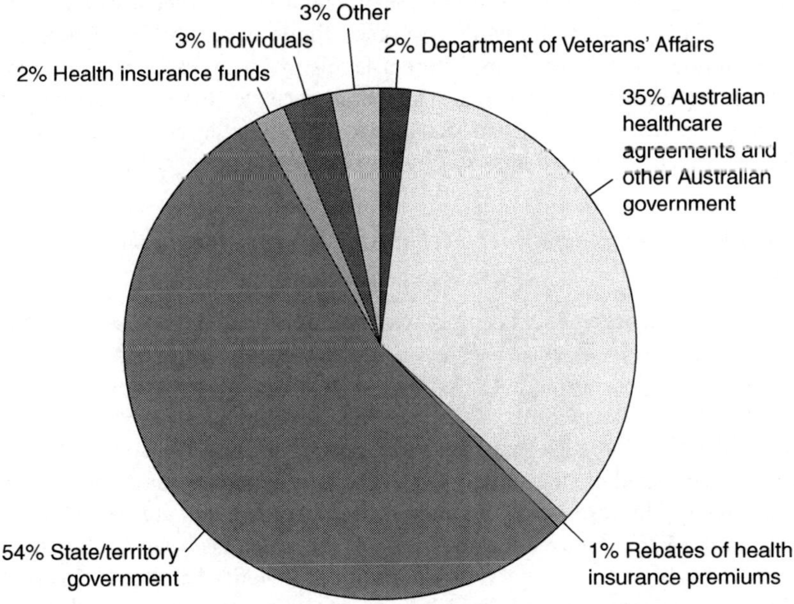

Figure 8.1 Financing of Australia's public hospitals, 2008–2009 (source: online, available at: www.aihw.gov.au/hospitals-funding/ accessed February 10, 2012).

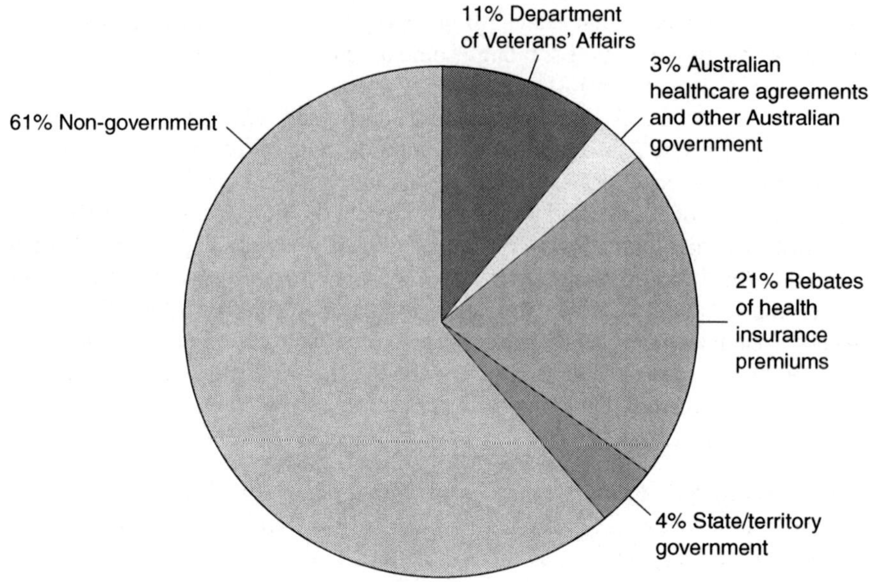

Figure 8.2 Financing of Australia's private hospitals, 2008–2009 (source: online, available at: www.aihw.gov.au/hospitals-funding/ accessed February 10, 2012).

As indicated in the above charts individuals pay about 3 percent of the costs of public hospitals in Australia while insurance funds cover another 2 percent. All the remaining costs come from different levels of government and different government departments. For private hospitals, private funds consisting of private health insurance funds and out-of-pocket payments cover 61 percent while 39 percent can be traced back to government sources.

Social health insurance: safety net mechanisms and caps for eligible expenses

Australia does not charge patients any co-payment for inpatient care. Australians are further protected from excessive out-of-pocket healthcare expenses arising from outpatient services through a safety net mechanism known as the Medicare Safety Net. The Medicare Safety Net provides families and individuals with financial assistance for high out-of-pocket costs for out-of-hospital eligible expenses as stipulated in the MBS. Once eligible expenses reach an annual "Medicare Safety Net threshold," additional Medicare benefits are available for out-of-hospital MBS services for the rest of the calendar year (Table 8.1). Further, to cover high cost drugs, a Pharmaceutical Benefits Scheme (PBS) provides that once a Safety Net threshold is reached, an Australian can apply for a PBS Safety Net card, which will entitle the bearer "less expensive or free" drugs for the rest of the calendar year.

Table 8.1 Medicare safety net thresholds as at January 1, 2012 (Australian dollars)

	Threshold amount (A$)	*Who it is for*	*How it is calculated*	*What the benefit is*
Original	413.50	All Medicare cardholders	Based on gap amount	100 percent of schedule fee for out-of-hospital services beyond the threshold.
Extended concession and FTB(A)	598.80	Concession cardholders and families eligible for FTB(A)	Out-of-pocket costs	80 percent of out-of-pocket costs or the EMSN benefit cap for out-of-hospital services
Extended general	1198.00	All Medicare cardholders	Out-of-pocket costs	80 percent of out-of-pocket costs or the EMSN benefit cap for out-of-hospital services

Notes

Out-of-pocket costs is the difference between the Medicare benefit and the doctor's fees charged.

Schedule fee is a fee for service set by the Australian Government. Medicare Safety Net Benefits are based on the schedule fee, and apart from GP consultation, usually leave a "gap amount" equal to 15 percent of the schedule fee, unless the threshold amount has been reached, in which case benefits = 100 percent of the schedule fee.

FTB(A) = Family Tax Benefit (Part A). The Family Tax Benefit is an annual tax benefit to help families with the cost of raising children.

Table 8.2 Example of an FTB(A) family benefiting from EMSN

EMSN threshold met	*Doctor's fee (A$)*	*MBS rebate (at 100% schedule fee *) (A$)*	*Out-of-pocket cost before EMSN rebate (A$)*	*EMSN rebate (80%) (A$)*	*Out-of-pocket cost (A$)*
Initial specialist consultation	124.00	83.95	40.05	32.04	8.01

Australia uses an EBP model to limit risk exposures for its citizens. Under the Original Medicare Safety Net, once "gap expenses" (i.e., out-of-hospital Medicare services that exceed the schedule fee) have reached a threshold, the Medicare payment is increased to 100 percent (up from 85 percent) of the Medicare schedule fee for out-of-hospital services for the remainder of the calendar year. The Medicare Safety Net covers essential diagnostic and consultation costs such as GP and specialist consultations, blood tests, CT scans, MRIs, pap smears, psychiatry, radiotherapy, tissue biopsies, ultrasounds, x-rays. Patients will still have to be responsible for payments over and above the schedule fees. From 2004, however, they also get assistance to cover these excess payments under the Extended Medicare Safety Net (EMSN).

Extended Medicare Safety Net

Through the EMSN, introduced in 2004, Australia will cover 80 percent of the out-of-pocket costs for MBS services provided out-of-hospital after a threshold of $578.60 (as at January 1, 2011) per family that qualifies for Family Tax Benefit (FTB) A.[5] For all other Medicare cardholders the threshold is $1,157.50 (as at January 1, 2011). Note that the smaller the threshold, the faster will a family enjoy the bigger benefit that falls under the EMSN. Table 8.2 shows how this works.

Proposition 8.3 EBP in Australia
Australia adopts the EBP principle to keep healthcare affordable. However out-of-pocket charges are exclusively for out-of-hospital care, which is rendered free and which tends to produce excessive burden on the public purse.

The mandatory NHI called Medicare is funded mostly from general revenue and partly by a 1.5 percent levy on taxable income, though some low-income individuals are exempt or pay a reduced levy. This levy can be considered a health insurance premium. For those enjoying incomes higher than certain specified levels,[6] an additional Medicare levy surcharge of 1 percent of taxable income is payable unless they have an appropriate level of private hospital coverage. This surcharge covers the spouse and children under 21 as well as student children below 25. It aims to encourage people to get private hospital coverage so they will likely use the private system and thus reduce the burden on the public system. In 2007–2008, the revenue raised from the Medicare levy (including the surcharge) funded 18 percent of total federal government health expenditure.

Other federal, state and territory government health expenditure is funded from general tax revenue, including the goods and services tax (GST), with some revenue raised from patient fees and other nongovernment sources. In 2007–2008, governments funded 69 percent of total health expenditures, with 43 percent funded by the Australian federal government and 26 percent funded by state and territory governments.

Private health insurance

About one-third of New Zealanders and one-half of Australians[7] subscribe to some form of private insurance, largely as a supplement to the social health insurance that they already enjoy, covering part of the out-of-pocket costs that patients are responsible for as well as extra services not covered by the public schemes. Private insurance contributes 6 percent and 7.6 percent of total health expenditure in New Zealand and in Australia respectively.[8] Since 1999, the Australian government has subsidized private health insurance through a private health insurance rebate at 30 percent of the premiums. This was later enhanced so that enrollees after April 1, 2005 enjoy a higher rebate, at 35 percent for people aged from 65 to 69 years, and at 40 percent for people aged 70 years and older. Considering the number of enrollees in private insurance and the magnitude of the subsidy, the total revenue involved is quite substantial. This had led many, especially those who choose not to or who cannot afford to buy private insurance, to believe that the amount of subsidies may be better spent if directly allocated to beef up the quality of public hospital healthcare. This is one notable finding of the 2010 Menzies-Nous Group Survey.

Unlike Canada, the Australian government has always considered private insurers a partner that helps build a more viable healthcare system. But without the government's indirect control over claims through making services widely available at schedule fees, moral hazard may result, as private doctors and hospitals are tempted to make more and larger claims, leading to a rise in premiums. Although Australia does not directly control caregivers' fees and charges, to the extent that Australians can turn to the public caregivers who charge only the schedule fees, private healthcare givers cannot overcharge without turning away patients. Here overcharging means charging a premium price without commensurate, superior services.

Apart from indirectly containing premium inflation and the private insurance rebate, Australia also encourages people to take up private insurance by instilling confidence in the security and fairness of the insurance industry. The Private Health Insurance Ombudsman's office maintains a website that makes comparison of premiums easy. Under the Private Health Insurance Act 2007 private insurers have to be registered with and be monitored by the Private Health Insurance Administration Council (PHIAC), an independent Australian government body that ensures solvency and capital adequacy requirements are met. Moreover, incentive is given for early enrolment in private health insurance. Once enrolled, premiums will not rise. However, the later one enrolls, the higher will be the premium, which rises 2 percent for every year after the age of 30 enrolment in private health insurance is delayed. Premiums are based on community rating and are unaffected by the health status or other risk factors of individual members.[9]

Proposition 8.4 Private insurance as a supplement to social insurance
While everyone is protected by public health insurance private insurance serves a useful supplementary role in both Australia and New Zealand. However, according to the Menzies-Nous Group Survey 2010, "when given a choice, the uninsured (in Australia) thought that subsidies for private insurance would be better spent on improving public hospitals" (p. 3).

8.3 The healthcare infrastructure and cost control

In both Australia and New Zealand, primary care is dominated by private practitioners. They generally charge a fee for service, which is not regulated, but Medicare in Australia pay GPs only the schedule fee payment (inclusive of the 15 percent paid by patients before they reach the yearly threshold and 100 percent thereafter). Although Australian doctors are allowed to extra-bill, with the government's encouragement, most have chosen to charge according to the schedule fees.[10] In New Zealand people are enrolled in their local PHOs, and GPs are, as in Australia, paid through fee-for-service and co-payments with partial government subsidy. Since 2001, a new strategy based on capitation payments through PHOs has been adopted to promote better cost control and prevention, as well as to reduce out-of-pocket costs for patients (Cumming and Mays, 2011).

Physicians in Australian public hospitals are typically paid a salary though they may also be paid on a per-session basis for treating public patients. They are permitted to keep their private practice.

In both Australia and New Zealand, public hospitals dominate inpatient care. Under Medicare the Australian public hospital system provides free hospital care for patients. Public hospitals are jointly funded by the federal government and state and territory governments through five-yearly agreements. Like NHS hospitals in the United Kingdom, public hospitals in Australia also admit private patients and this constitutes a supplementary revenue source. In New Zealand, public hospitals are run and owned by DHBs which are responsible for the healthcare needs of the local population. Funding to hospitals in Australia is jointly provided by various levels of government on the basis of casemix, which represent a classification system that bundles patient care episodes into clinically coherent groups each considered as requiring similar resources. For example, in the State of Victoria, "casemix models are used to monitor, manage and administer the funding of healthcare provided by public hospitals."[11]

Public healthcare in New Zealand is financed in the most part by taxes collected by different levels of government (93 percent), and in part by levies on employers (7 percent). The funds are distributed to DHBs which either directly provide services at government-owned facilities (about one-half, by value, of all health services) or purchase them from private providers, including doctors, private hospitals and community caregivers.

Australia is mindful about possible cost explosion in healthcare. Any expansion in the scope of medical services must be justified through careful cost–benefit comparison. Similarly, new drugs have to meet cost-effectiveness criteria and are subject to nationally negotiated pricing before inclusion in the formulary of publicly subsidized medicines. Australia is well aware of the impact of technology driving up costs, and makes an effort to contain growth in the cost of expensive diagnostic services (pathology and radiology). GPs are given a gate-keeping role in referring patients to specialists. In New Zealand, a sophisticated booking system rations elective surgery services based on needs evaluation, while a greater use of capitation, i.e. prior funding ahead of utilization, promotes cost awareness among service providers, at the same time reducing user fees for patients and enhancing service accessibility. Australia offers a PBS, which offers coverage for a comprehensive and evolving list of drugs purchased at a negotiated fixed price while patients make a small co-payment set by the federal government. New Zealand adopts a central buying mechanism through tendering to keep drug costs down. New Zealanders have to pay the extra cost for pharmaceutical products beyond the lowest-priced generic products available. Both Australia and New Zealand consciously and actively promote prevention in containing healthcare cost increases.[12]

Salaried specialist doctors in public hospitals in Australia may be allowed to treat some private patients in those hospitals under an income sharing arrangement. Private hospitals derive their incomes mainly from patients with private health insurance. Private hospitals provide one-third of all hospital beds and almost 40 percent of total hospital separations. Most emergency surgery is provided in public hospitals, while the majority of elective surgery procedures are provided in private hospitals and day surgeries. Ongoing reform aims at improving management for public hospitals and their responsiveness to local needs and increasing the federal government's support.

Proposition 8.5 Backbone nature of publicly provided healthcare
Public hospitals in New Zealand and Australia take care of inpatient needs of the majority of the population and almost all emergency needs for their respective populations. Access to primary care in both countries is assured by keeping user fees affordable.

8.4 Quality assurance

The Australian government conducts periodic surveys to gauge the satisfaction of Australians with their healthcare system. As a country that follows the EBI model, it commands a high level of confidence among the public, averaging just short of 70 percent depending on the age group, according to the Menzies-Nous 2010 survey (Figure 8.4).[13] Interestingly, older people who need and use services

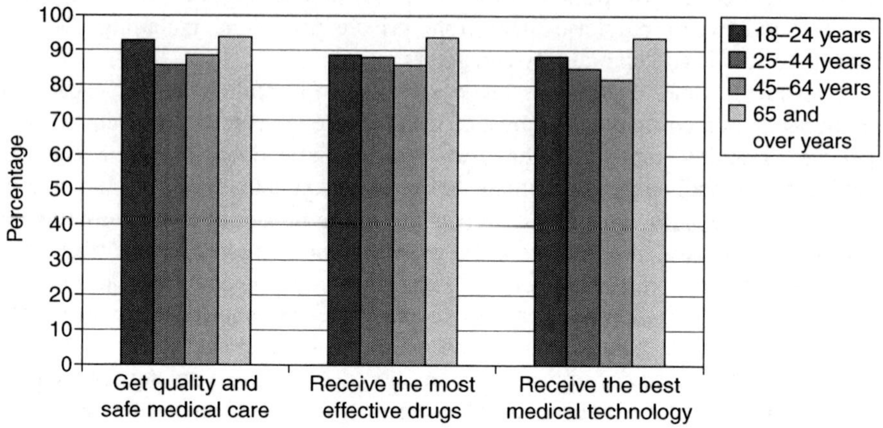

Figure 8.3 Confidence in healthcare system access by age group of population in Australia (source: Menzies-Nous 2010 survey).

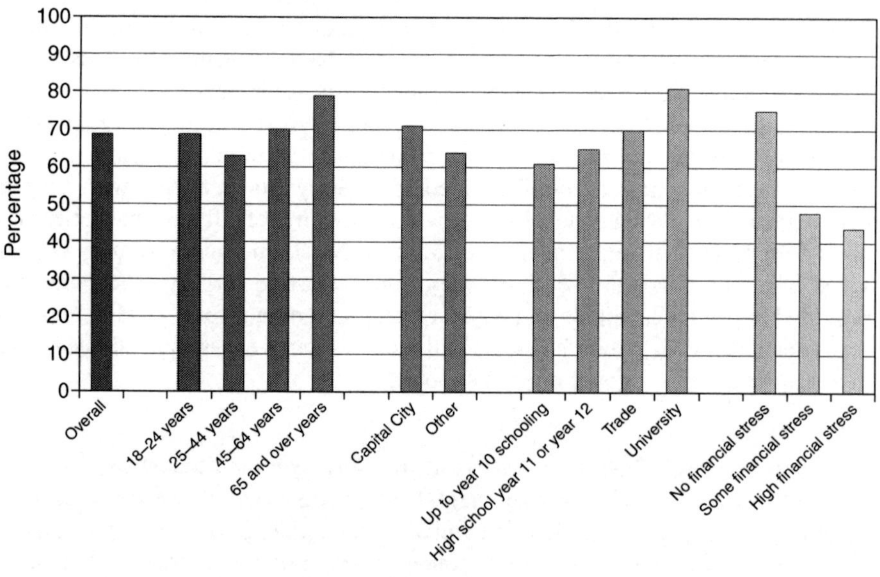

Figure 8.4 Percentage of Australians reporting confidence in the healthcare system, 2010 (source: Menzies-Nous 2010 survey).

more have indicated greater confidence. This probably suggests that they have gained greater confidence through their personal experience, while younger people have yet to realize the benefits. Confidence in access to quality care is stronger, averaging around 90 percent across the entire population.

Surveys, transparent reporting and public accountability are indirect mechanisms to assure the quality of the healthcare system. Both Australia and New Zealand have established effective internal and professional accountability through an Australian Commission on Safety and Quality in Healthcare, which sets standards and conducts accreditation to service providers, as well as spearheads various quality improvement efforts. Since 2008 a single national registration and accreditation system has been in place for nine health professions: medical practitioners; nurses and midwives; pharmacists; physiotherapists; psychologists; osteopaths; chiropractors; optometrists; and dentists.

In New Zealand, a quarterly hospital benchmark information report is distributed by the Ministry of Health to the DHBs providing them with information on quality and outcome indicators including patient satisfaction. DHB performance is rated regularly against different aspects of performance including waiting times, access to primary care services and mental illness outcomes. All health service providers like hospitals and facilities for the disabled receive third-party certification audits and accreditation. There is also a quality improvement committee that works with public participation to improve performance in New Zealand's public hospitals and achieve identified health targets.

Notwithstanding these efforts to promote quality, there is a limit to how much quality can be achieved and maintained when resources are limited and demands are rising. In both Australia and New Zealand, inpatient services in public hospitals are essentially free, but public satisfaction with public hospitals is rather low. One rating of Australian public hospitals stood at only 39 percent as compared with 71 percent for private hospitals.[14] An inpatient service that is entirely free may not be sustainable over the long run.

Proposition 8.6 Quality of public hospitals
To serve effectively as the backbone for healthcare, public hospitals must achieve a satisfactory quality, which must be funded adequately. Such quality care must be available on a timely basis before subscriptions to private insurance plans and the use of private hospitals are truly optional.

8.5 Conclusions

The systems in Australia and New Zealand in many ways are like the UK system, but in other ways deviate from it. Like the United Kingdom, theirs are essentially tax-funded systems, and both countries similarly take universal accessibility to quality care as central. Australia has taken the EBP approach, while

New Zealand achieves this by keeping fees and charges low. Sustainability of the systems, however, is an ongoing concern, especially because the most expensive services, namely inpatient services, are essentially free. A commentator on the Australian parliament's blog wrote:[15]

> The harsh reality is that we cannot afford to do everything that we want or need to do to improve people's health, at least not without finding new revenue sources (for example from taxes, the private sector and individuals). As Minister Roxon explained last week, the constraints on public sector financing mean that governments will need to play a more active role in determining what will, and will not, be funded in healthcare. In health circles, this exercise is known as priority setting.

Unlike the United Kingdom, however, they have been less keen on the internal market and the purchaser–provider split, even though the New Zealand DHBs do purchase about half of the services for the population within their jurisdictions. Generally, Australia and New Zealand have accommodated a greater degree of private participation in the healthcare market than the United Kingdom, and have done so without endangering accessibility, as Canada had feared.

Review questions

1. Compare and contrast New Zealand and Australia's healthcare systems in terms of access, choice, quality and sustainability.
2. Compare the EBP framework of Australia's system with the EBI model discussed in Chapter 4. What are the advantages and disadvantages?
3. Would you recommend public subsidization of private insurance plans? Why?
4. According to PrivateHealth.com, in 2009–2010 benefits paid to members were around 86 percent of total premiums paid by members. This is quite low by international standards, and Australians appear to get a good deal. How did Australia achieve this?

9 Three European countries

France, Switzerland and Sweden

9.1 Introduction

France, Switzerland and Sweden, like all the other developed nations which we have reviewed so far, provide universal healthcare coverage to their entire populations. This universal coverage, as we have seen, sometimes is offered through publicly funded and operated healthcare facilities (as in the United Kingdom, Australia and Hong Kong) with hospitals and public clinics open to all citizens and permanent residents at nominal or no charges. Sometimes it is offered in part through a network of private or semi-private providers (as in Taiwan and Canada), who work under contract with the national or provincial insurers. We will see that in the three European countries that we are going to review, government-provided or government-supported health insurance may work alongside private insurers and that the shares of public and private insurance may vary greatly from one country to another. As indicated in Table 7.1, however, government funding for healthcare is in each case quite substantial, ranging from 6.8 of the GDP in the case of Switzerland to 9.2 percent of the GDP in the case of France in 2009, suggesting that publicly funded healthcare is the backbone of the healthcare systems in all these countries, while private healthcare takes on largely a supplementary role.

9.2 Public healthcare as the backbone of the healthcare system, supplemented by high cost ceilings and private for-profit healthcare plans

France avails all its residents with publicly financed healthcare. Citizens are automatically covered under the statutory health insurance scheme. Others are covered either through *Couverture Maladie Universelle* (CMU) or, in the case of illegal aliens, the *L'Aide Médicale d'Etat* (AME). The public health insurance scheme provides comprehensive but basic coverage over outpatient and inpatient services, ambulatory care, as well as prescription drugs. Supplementary private insurance is available for most French people through employers or voluntary subscription – with subsidies if they are qualified.

France recognizes the need to contain moral hazard and to raise funds to finance the healthcare program. For inpatient care, 20 percent co-payment plus a daily maintenance charge of €16–€20 is imposed. For doctor visits and dental care a 30 percent co-payment is payable. France encourages patients to visit the same primary care doctor who serves as gatekeeper for inpatient and specialist services by charging a lower 30 percent co-payment rate, as compared with a 50 percent rate for visits all other GPs. Subsidies on prescription drugs vary from 0 percent to 100 percent, depending on the cost-effectiveness of the drug.

While most co-payments can be paid by one's private insurer, if a patient visits a doctor other than the GP whom he has designated as his primary caregiver, he will need to pay a higher co-payment and the extra charges cannot be reimbursed by the insurer. This system of gatekeeping (called the *médecin traitant*, in place since 2004) reflects a good understanding of human nature, and combines that understanding with the recognition that the cause of preventive care and efficient utilization of healthcare services are best served by a professional doctor who really knows the patient and his needs. France is unique in maintaining that certain minimal non-reimbursable co-payments must be paid by a patient even if he has private insurance, although there is an annual ceiling of €50 for such non-reimbursable out-of-pocket expenses. The minimal patient-borne charges are €1.00 per doctor visit, €0.50 per prescription drug, €2.00 per ambulance and €18.00 per expensive hospital treatment.

France recognizes the different abilities to pay of different people, and exempts patients suffering from chronic conditions and poorer patients from cost-sharing as long as the services are within the package of standard benefits covered by the public insurance plan.

Although there is no annual spending limit as required under EBP as described in Chapter 4, France exempts chronic patients from coinsurance payments and lifts co-payments from patients after 31 days when they are hospitalized. This is certainly in the spirit of EBP.

Sweden is more explicit about EBP as it provides for a high cost ceiling for medical consultation charges and another one for prescription drug costs. After a patient has paid a total of SEK900 in doctors' fees over any 12-month period, further visits to doctors' clinics within those 12 months will be free of charge. Similarly, nobody needs to pay more than SEK1,800 in drug costs over a 12-month period. These annual spending thresholds have been in place for quite a number of years and have not been changed.

The drug costs with a high cost ceiling of SEK1,800 refer only to outpatient drug costs, since patients do not have to pay for drugs administered while they are hospitalized. Outpatients pay the full costs up to SEK900 per year, and enjoy progressively lower charges until SEK1,800 have been paid up, beyond which no more payment will be due.

What is perhaps debatable about the Swedish cost-sharing and the cost capping mechanism is the appropriateness for keeping inpatient fees and "high cost ceilings" so low. Inpatient charges amount to only SEK80 a day which is not much more than US$10. Outpatient visits are, contrary to expectation based on cost considerations, much higher, with fees ranging from SEK100 to SEK200. Specialist visits are subject to a maximum fee of SEK300. Perhaps for this reason – although the fees are still considered low by international standards – Sweden has a remarkably low consultation rate among all the OECD countries. The lower cost for inpatient charges may be due to a belief that inpatient services are less subject to moral hazard, since patient admissions are generally at the recommendation of a doctor and being hospitalized is not in itself an attractive experience. However, charges are not just for containing moral hazard but they also provide a source of financing that can help maintain the quality of the services. To serve as a meaningful source of financing, the out-of-pocket charges will need a higher ceiling. The sum of the caps for doctor visits and the drug charges at SEK2,700 is just about US$400, and that is for a 12-month period. A higher cap, say at US$1,000 and even US$2,000 for an advanced country, is not too much especially if it helps avail the healthcare system of much needed resources to meet the high demands and expectations of the public. Moreover, there is really little point in providing different high cost ceilings for drugs and for consultations.

Interestingly, even though Switzerland relies on the private sector to supply basic health insurance it also practices the EBP principle. It puts a cap on co-payments paid by the patient over the year at CHF700.

Proposition 9.1 Cost sharing, moral hazard and sustainability
Meaningful cost sharing not only helps contain moral hazard but also offers a source of financing that allows a healthcare system to be maintained without deterioration in the quality of services.

Proposition 9.2 High cost ceilings need to be set right
It is important that each citizen not be overly burdened, but it is also important that the state not be overly burdened. The higher the quality of care demanded, the higher will be the annual cap on out-of-pocket charges needed, which will enable the healthcare system to have the resources to provide the services needed.

9.3 Pricing, insurance and cost containment

Whereas everyone in Sweden is automatically entitled to healthcare coverage that is typically provided (i.e., run) and always financed by the state, France and Switzerland make sure that everyone is covered by health insurance. France offers a public health insurance scheme and allows a relatively minor, supplementary role for private insurers, while Switzerland requires everybody to purchase a health insurance plan from a private provider.

Unlike the United States though, Switzerland's private health insurers are heavily regulated. Although different insurers may charge differently, each must offer the same basic coverage to everybody at the same premium regardless of his health record, and they must not derive a profit from the basic coverage, even though they can profit from additional supplementary insurance should their clients opt to buy such. Basic coverage is defined by the government, presumably with reference to the social benefit of covering the service as compared to the cost. Such an approach corresponds with the discussion in Chapters 1–4, even though reference to a comparison between social cost and social benefit is not explicit. In regard to long-term care Switzerland makes reference to "medical necessity" (Squires, 2010, p. 51).

One of the key worries about insurance plans is the problem of moral hazard boosting costs. To contain the problem notwithstanding the statutory health insurance out-of-pocket expenditures are quite high and account for 30.6 percent of total health expenditure according to Squires (2010), First of all, the statutory health insurance plans are subject to a minimum annual deductible of CHF300. Beyond the deductible, enrollees in the Swiss statutory health insurance plan must pay CHF10 for each inpatient day, a co-payment at 10 percent for all services and 20 percent for brand-name drugs when a generic alternative is available. Since as much as 75 percent of acute inpatient services are provided by public or publicly subsidized, non-profit hospitals, supply-side moral hazard for inpatient care is not serious.

In France, the health authority or Haute Autorité de Santé defines the benefit package to be covered as basic care, and sets reference prices for various medical services. Doctors in France are allowed to charge above the reference price, just as doctors in Australia are allowed to charge above the schedule fees. Because reimbursements are based on the reference price, any extra charges above the reference prices will come from the patient or his supplementary insurer, and will not burden the public purse.

As was mentioned earlier, in Sweden patients pay SEK100–150 for a visit to a primary care doctor, and SEK200–300 for a visit to a specialist or to access emergency care – provided such payments have not yet reached the relevant high cost ceilings. Most health centers in Sweden are run by county councils, and most doctors earn salaries. Most private providers work under contract with county councils and payments to these providers are treated the same as payments to public facilities. All these arrangements help contain costs because doctors under contract cannot charge any price they like and have a third party insurance company foot the bill.

Proposition 9.3 Basic care and reference prices

By making patients pay for any excess over the reference prices, reference prices in France effectively motivate patients to help limit the demands by doctors and thus contain medical cost inflation, while saving money for the public purse. By fixing the prices for standard services in public and private healthcare providers Sweden also effectively contains medical cost inflation. These initiatives help make a publicly funded healthcare system sustainable.

9.4 Financing, compensation and the rise of capitation plans

Most countries in Europe, and in particular the three countries discussed in this chapter, provide comprehensive tax-financed healthcare services that are run by the government. In Sweden, for example, almost all hospitals are owned and operated by the county councils, while in both France and Switzerland, over two-thirds of hospital beds are either government-owned or publicly subsidized non-profit hospitals. Staff working in these facilities are typically paid salaries,[1] and this serves to contain the problem of supply-side moral hazard.

Private healthcare givers usually receive compensation based on fee-for-service,[2] which tends to promote supply-side moral hazard, but the extra billing is generally borne either by the patient or his supplementary insurer. These extra bills then are subject to patients' willingness to pay and supplementary insurers' scrutiny. Since they do not burden the public purse, there is no worry that this may affect sustainability of the system. As long as the basic coverage provides reasonably sufficient protection for citizens, so that the supplementary care is truly voluntary, we can assume that the optional care will enhance welfare.

Hospitals that receive public funding generally are funded based on prospective payments ("capitation") that are variations of the DRG framework.[3] It is well established that prospective payments will promote efficiency because hospitals will be incentivized to achieve savings whenever possible. However, according to Squires, any deficits of public and subsidized hospitals in Switzerland are covered by the canton. This arrangement, if unqualified, will lead to inefficiency, as hospitals will then have little incentive to save costs. Perhaps this is one reason why Switzerland has the longest average hospital stay for acute care at 7.8 days (as compared with 5.5 in the United States, 2007 data) and why Swiss healthcare is among the most costly in the world, though still significantly lower than that in the United States. According to Squires (2010), a resolution passed in the federal parliament in 2007 and to be implemented in 2012 will limit reimbursements to hospitals only to services that adhere to cantonal hospital planning. If such planning is based on cost–benefit comparisons of each service coverage to be considered, this will reduce waste.

According to Santesuisse, the association of health insurers in Switzerland, more and more Swiss are opting for managed care, which is based on capitation. In 2010, only 56.4 percent had health insurance of the traditional type (down from 75.4 percent in 2008). All the rest had managed care plans of one kind or another. This is understandable in view of managed care's lower cost and higher efficiency, and is welcome because managed care tends to promote prevention at the same time as it minimizes cost.

Proposition 9.4 Prospective payments or capitation promote efficiency
Prospective payments to caregivers encourage caregivers to save costs, as failing to avoid avoidable costs will undermine their financial positions. Prospective payment schemes include DRG-based payments to publicly funded hospitals and managed care plans that are run by private caregivers.

Proposition 9.5 Blanket coverage and global budgets for public healthcare plans
Public healthcare plans that offer blanket coverage of services regardless of cost and needs, and global budgets that cap funding for specified care areas are polar cases that represent, at one extreme, offering a blank check to publicly funded caregivers that could offer any service as requested and whose deficits would be covered by taxpayers, and at another extreme, withholding necessary services from citizens because the caregiver does not have the resources to offer them.

9.5 Efficiency

Even though Switzerland relies on private health insurers to provide for all health insurance, and all countries are experiencing an increase in the number of private suppliers in the healthcare market, publicly provided healthcare continues to dominate in all three countries. It is a common belief that publicly provided services are generally less efficient than privately provided services. Whether healthcare is provided efficiently in these countries, therefore, deserves study.

Efficiency, as was pointed out earlier, is essentially a concept based on an output–input ratio. All three countries have populations that are much more aged than that of the United States. The percentages of population over 65 for the three countries are all over 16 percent, and stood at 17.4 percent in the case of Sweden in 2007, as compared with 12.6 percent for the United States. In 2009, none of the three countries spent more than 12 percent of their GDP on healthcare, whereas the United States spent 17.4 percent on healthcare. Given that crude health outcomes for the three countries are all far better than those for the United States, and that far less resources are employed to take care of healthcare, the prima facie evidence is for these countries to be all more efficient than the market-oriented healthcare system. This conclusion should be valid, notwithstanding the observation made earlier that health outcomes are the results of a multitude of factors, and healthcare is only one factor among many, because the differences are just too big to be explained by these other factors.

One common factor that distinguishes the three European countries from the United States is that they all make sure that not only is basic healthcare available to all, but also that basic healthcare, including private basic healthcare insurance, is not for profit. At the same time, they all try to contain healthcare cost through co-payments, fixing of reference prices for reimbursement, and control of drug costs. Both the French and the Swedish are asked to designate a doctor as their primary care provider and this should always be the first point of contact, so that higher co-payments are payable for visits to hospitals and specialists without a referral.

There are good epidemiological reasons for decentralizing some of the health policy management functions and management to the local level. In Switzerland

Table 9.1 Health outcome indicators, selected OECD countries, 2007–2009

	Infant mortality rate per 1,000				*Life expectancy at birth all population*		
	2007	*2008*	*2009*		*2007*	*2008*	*2009*
Australia	4.2	4.1	4.3	Australia	81.3	81.5	81.6
Austria	3.7	3.7	3.8	Austria	80.2	80.5	80.4
Canada	5.1	5.0	5.0	Canada	80.7	81.0	81.0
Denmark	4.0	4.0	3.1	Denmark	78.4	78.8	79.0
France	3.8	3.8	3.9	France	80.9	81.0	81.0
Germany	3.9	3.5	3.5	Germany	80.0	80.2	80.3
Japan	2.6	2.6	2.4	Japan	82.6	82.7	83.0
Netherlands	4.1	3.8	3.8	Netherlands	80.2	80.3	80.6
New Zealand	4.8	5.0	4.7	New Zealand	80.2	80.4	80.8
Norway	3.1	2.7	3.1	Norway	80.6	80.8	81.0
Sweden	2.5	2.5	2.5	Sweden	81.0	81.2	81.4
Switzerland	3.9	4.0	4.3	Switzerland	82.0	82.2	82.3
United Kingdom	4.8	4.7	4.6	United Kingdom	79.7	79.8	80.4
United States	6.8	6.5	6.0*	United States	77.9	78.0	78.2

Sources: OECD Health Data 2011; *estimate by CIA for 2012; World Bank, online, available at: http://data.worldbank.org/indicator/SP.DYN.IMRT.IN; http://data.worldbank.org/indicator/SP.DYN.LE00.IN/countries.

Table 9.2 Differences in healthcare between France, Sweden and Switzerland

	France	*Sweden*	*Switzerland*	*United States*
Total healthcare spending per capita (PPP dollars, 2009)	3,978	3,722	5,144	7,960
Public spending per capita on health (PPP dollars, 2009)	3,100.2	3,032.7	3,071.9	3,554.2
Life expectancy, year (2012)	81.46	81.18	81.17	78.49
Infant mortality rate per 1,000 births (2012)	3.37	2.74	4.03	5.98
Hospital beds per 1,000 (2009)	6.6	2.8	5.1	3.1
Discharge rates, all causes, per 100,000 population (2009)	26,251	16,589	16,837	13,086
Physicians per 1,000 (2009)	3.3	3.7 (2008)	3.8	2.4
Doctor consultations, number per capita per year (2009)	6.9	2.9	4.0 (2007)	3.9
Nurses per 1,000 (2009)	8.2	11 (2008)	15.2	10.8
Magnetic resonance imaging units per million population (2007)	7	Not available	14.4	25.9
MRI exams, total, per 1,000 population (2009)	55.2	Not available	Not available	91.2 in (2007)

Sources: OECD Health Data 2011; International Profile of Healthcare Systems, the Commonwealth Fund 2010; CIA World Fact Book.

the 26 cantons finance public acute care hospitals, and are responsible for the licensing of providers and hospital planning. In Sweden while the central government determines the health system's overall objectives and regulations, county councils and municipalities are given funding through a capitation formula based on demographic and other characteristics of the community and are directly responsible for providing care at the local level.

Of the three European countries examined here, Sweden is the only country that has introduced the concept of purchaser–provider split. Although a recent study shows that there may be economic efficiency gains, the authors noted that the observed improvement in efficiency may well be due to factors other than competition as such, and that there seems to be other unintended costs including a possible decline in quality – which was proxied by the 28-day mortality rate after suffering a stroke (Rudholm *et.al.*, 2011, p. 89). Overall, the benefits of the purchaser–provider split are still far from certain. Another recent study of the subject which uses Dutch data also found evidence about the benefits of the purchaser–provider split inconclusive (Schut and Van de Ven, 2011).

9.6 Conclusions

The 1982 Health and Medical Services Act of Sweden says "people shall be offered health services of good quality on equal terms and easily accessible to all." This pretty much summarizes the spirit of European healthcare systems.

Our review of the healthcare systems of France, Sweden and Switzerland shows the importance of distinguishing between basic care and supplementary care. Because healthcare is costly, it is very important to have the right perspective on priorities. The state, obviously, cannot afford to fund everything in the name of healthcare. Defining what comprises basic care that the state should cover is crucial to sustainability.

In most European countries and particularly for all the three countries that we have reviewed, the government assumes the dominant role in providing healthcare, and the profit motive is in each case take out of basic care. In France and in Switzerland, any insurance plan that covers basic care must be run on non-profit principles. In Sweden, private health insurance is practically non-existent for basic care. In all three countries, supplementary, for-profit insurance is allowed, but people can rest assured that they do not really need to subscribe to such plans, as the basic coverage is comprehensive enough to protect the individual against practically all the medical conditions that are essential.

Both Sweden and Switzerland provide for EBP, as out-of-pocket payments are capped over a 12-month period. In France, out-of-pocket payments amount to a very small fraction of total healthcare expenditures, and will in any case not constitute a serious burden on any patient. As Table 9.1 and Table 9.2 indicate, the healthcare systems in Europe, based on healthcare costs and health indicators, appear superior to that in the United States. Although one could refer to differences in lifestyle and other variables as factors other than the quality of the healthcare system in explaining differences in the health indicators, this does not absolve the United States from the failure of educating its people to live more healthily. Indeed, this underscores the fact that health policy is not just about financing healthcare and delivering healthcare services. Everything from food safety and driving habits to workplace safety and crime prevention has a place in health policy.

In the World Health Statistics is a section on "health inequities." In the opening is the following passage:

> In general, the global reporting of health indicators focuses on national averages. However, data on the distribution of health and health services within countries and between population subgroups are equally important. Such data help to identify health inequities – unfair and avoidable differences in health and health service provision – that arise for example from socio-economic factors (such as level of education, occupation and household wealth or income), from geographical location, and from ethnicity and gender.

Regrettably the United States, whose experience will be reviewed in the next chapter, appears to be the single country surveyed in this book that has really failed to deliver "equal access to healthcare." Sweden does not charge citizens a health insurance premium. For France and for Switzerland, subsidies are given to the poor or the premiums are completely waived altogether. In France, co-payments are waived for the chronically sick and the disabled and for the poor. There is, clearly, sensitivity to the needs of the low income, and a common, paramount concern for ensuring the accessibility of basic healthcare in all these European countries.

Review questions

1. How do the three countries deal with the problem of covering the healthcare needs of the poor?
2. How do the three countries maintain sustainability of their healthcare systems?
3. In France, some nominal co-payments must be made by patients themselves and they must not be covered by insurance. What is the rationale for this and is this effective?
4. Switzerland insists that insurance for basic healthcare must be non-profit, and it also plays a big role in providing basic healthcare. What would happen if for-profit basic healthcare operates alongside non-profit basic healthcare, and for-profit basic healthcare insurers operate alongside non-profit basic healthcare insurers?
5. What does each of the countries do to enhance efficiency and promote prevention?

10 The American market-based system

10.1 Introduction

To say that the American healthcare system is market-based is likely to raise many objections, because the United States spends heavily on Medicare and Medicaid, and it also runs a number of public hospitals, as well as many preventive programs including the federal Center for Disease Control and Prevention (CDC) and the Drug and Food Administration (DFA). But the American healthcare system remains the most market-based system in the world, *because public healthcare is essentially a supplement to the dominant market-based system.* This is true, notwithstanding the fact that total government spending per capita in the United States on healthcare was 25.3 percent higher than that in Canada and 31.6 percent higher than that in the United Kingdom (2008 figures, PPP dollars, source: OECD Health Data 2011).

In the United States, apart from self-employed clinicians operating independently or sharing an office, for-profit private healthcare providers include for-profit hospitals, for-profit health insurers, HMOs and preferred provider organizations (PPOs). They operate alongside not-for-profit healthcare providers, HMOs and non-profit insurers.[1] OECD data indicate that the United States spent $7,960 on healthcare for each person in 2009, 87 percent more than Canada's $4,363, on a purchasing power parity basis. In 2010 per capita healthcare spending went up to $8,402. Total healthcare expenditures reached $2.6 trillion, or 17.9 percent of the GDP on healthcare in 2010, as compared with only 11.3 percent in Canada.[2]

Medicare is a federal government-run healthcare plan for the elderly at 65 or over; Medicaid is run by the states, though with partial federal funding, and caters to the needs of the poor who meet specific eligibility criteria. Together with the Children's Health Insurance Program (CHIP), a state-based program, and insurance for Veteran Affairs/and Department of Defense, government-provided insurance amounts to 67 percent of the healthcare expenditures paid by insurance. In addition, the three levels of governments run public hospitals and provide partial funding for some non-profit ones. All public hospitals, including the subsidized ones, may charge Medicaid, Medicare and private insurers for the care of patients. Poor uninsured patients receive their care from public hospitals for free, subject to availability and availability has steadily fallen over the years, with many closed for good. Non-profit rural hospitals care for a disproportionate share of needy patients.

Proposition 10.1 US healthcare as a market based system
Notwithstanding huge public spending, the US healthcare system is market-based, because the public healthcare system serves as a supplement to the private system.

10.2 Efficiency, fairness and quality

It is well known that markets serve useful functions and can often be relied upon to provide efficient allocation of resources. However, the healthcare market and the health insurance market are characterized by high information cost and agency problems, and healthcare is also a matter of life and death that people can ill afford to be denied care on account of cost. While competition is believed to promote efficiency it may also engender waste.[3] In the United States, health insurers compete for survival and need to spend money on marketing. They also try to minimize cost by denying claims whenever possible. As a result, doctors who file claims find themselves often challenged by the insurers and have to spend time documenting and proving that a claim is justified.[4] There is now an industry specializing in medical insurance billing to alleviate doctors' burden of filing a claim, but this also attests to the extent of the burden.

Given that worries undermine mental health and happiness a well functioning healthcare system benefits not just those who are currently sick, but also all the others who can rest assured that should they get sick they will be well cared for. This means that a healthcare system that fails to assure people that timely and adequate healthcare is available and affordable may be considered less efficient than another that can provide such assurance, other things being equal.

What is even more lamentable in the case of the United States is that many of those working class people who are not covered by Medicare or Medicaid actually pay taxes that finance these programs. They are the ones who pay, but get no benefits – at least not until they become old enough to benefit. Another source of unfairness is that various parties in the healthcare market collect the "economic rent" generated by the lack of effective competition due to a lack of information, by the imbalance in bargaining power between buyers and sellers in various markets, including the insurance market, the pharmaceutical market and medical specialist market, etc.

In the United States, given that it is a market-driven system, people who can afford it can get any services that they pay for without much waiting. But they may also be getting services that they do not need. As pointed out by Baicker and Goldman (2011), numerous studies have found that greater utilization is not associated with better health outcomes, while spending can vary substantially across regions ("*small area variations*") (p. 65).

In America, as employers continue to cut down the healthcare benefits of their employees over the years, the ranks of the uninsured and underinsured have risen. These uninsured and underinsured suffer what is called an *ex ante* welfare loss due to worries over the possible prospect of falling sick and failing to get needed care. Such welfare losses are real even if they voluntarily opted not to buy health insurance. Not buying the protection simply means that the cost is considered higher than the *ex ante* welfare benefit of obtaining coverage. If the market price (value) of health insurance is higher than the social cost of a better managed but equally effective health protection plan, then there is an efficiency loss.

Proposition 10.2 Efficiency
Efficiency refers to an output–input ratio. The better the outcome, given the resources committed, the higher is efficiency. The outcome from a healthcare system is not only how well it delivers services to those who use it, but also includes the *ex ante* perception of being protected.

Proposition 10.3 Fairness
Fairness includes a sense of getting a fair return for payments made. The American working class pay the taxes that finance Medicare and Medicaid but need to pay extra to protect themselves. This leads to a sense of unfairness.

Proposition 10.4 Quality
The quality of healthcare must include appropriate care for patients. "Small area variations" suggests that many patients may not get appropriate care.

10.3 Financial risks and health risks

Admittedly, health outcomes are the results of many factors, and the quality of healthcare is only one of them. Many observers consider waiting time and presence of rationing important indicators of quality, although arguably these are quantity indicators more than quality indicators, as they represent the availability of the services and not necessarily the appropriateness of the services. But price rationing may hurt as much as queues. If people are priced out of healthcare, their health stock will depreciate faster, and they will suffer lower quality of life, and may die earlier than otherwise.

According to a 2008 survey by the Commonwealth Fund, 54 percent of chronically ill Americans skipped a test or treatment, failed to visit a doctor when sick, or failed to fill a prescription because of the cost.[5] Worries over the cost of medical bills have eroded the happiness of Americans. Indeed an NBER study indicates that happiness in the United States is declining from one cohort to another. A June 2009 study by the University of Michigan in Ann Arbor reported that 43 percent of those polled indicated that they worried they might not be able to afford care, even with insurance. Table 10.1 from the NBER study indicates that cohorts of males born after 1950–1959 carry negative coefficients in the equation with subjective well-being as the dependent variable.[6] Results for females are similar though less significant. One possible reason for these results is increasing insecurity suffered by younger cohorts.

A recent article in *Health Affairs* concluded that half of personal bankruptcies involved medical bills (Himmelstein *et al.*, 2005). This conclusion was later challenged by Dranove and Millenson (2006), but Dranove and Millenson themselves still concluded that medical bills were a contributing factor in 17 percent of personal bankruptcies: 17 percent is not a small number, and people not declaring personal bankruptcy may still be under considerable stress. If the American healthcare system sets out to provide people with protection against the odds posed by health hazards, then the American system cannot be considered "policy efficient,"[7] since it is committing a lot more resources and still leaving many people unprotected and allowing people to fall into considerable financial stress on account of health risks.

According to the US Census, the number of people with health insurance increased from 253.4 million in 2007 to 256.2 million in 2010. The number of people without health insurance coverage, however, also rose from 45.7 million in 2007 to 50.7 million in 2010, leaving the uninsured rate at 16.7 percent, higher than the 15.4 percent of the previous year.[8] (See Figure 10.1) This is in part due to people losing jobs in the recession of 2008–2009, and thus losing the coverage from policies paid by their employers, in part due to fewer employers offering health insurance benefits – a direct result of the rapid increase in the cost of premiums in recent years. According to a Kaiser Family Foundation report, workers in 2010 paid 47 percent more than they did in 2005 for family health coverage, while employers paid 20 percent more.[9]

Proposition 10.5 Plight of the uninsured and the underinsured in the United States

Americans without health insurance may not get the healthcare needed at the time when they need it, may suffer a decline in functional health that undermines the quality of life and a decline in their life expectancy. Even when they are well they live in constant worry about this and about the financial strains that may arise should they need it. Such worries undermine happiness and health. Medical care costs have led to a significant number of personal bankruptcies in the United States.

Table 10.1 Happiness equations for men in the United States: pooled data 1974–2004

Age	0.0096* (11.36)	0.0066* (4.83)	−0.0254* (4.24)	−0.0171* (2.34)	−0.0552* (4.03)
Age^2			0.00035* (5.48)	0.00026* (3.49)	0.00056* (4.00)
Born <1900				0.6851* (2.05)	2.3501* (1.96)
Born 1900–1909				0.8175* (3.09)	0.6585 (1.45)
Born 1910–1919				0.5418* (2.58)	0.7133* (2.41)
Born 1920–1929				0.4122* (2.57)	0.3769 (1.75)
Born 1930–1939				0.2416* (2.14)	0.2324 (1.57)
Born 1940–1949				0.0441 (0.66)	0.0685 (0.81)
Born 1960–1969				0.0087 (0.12)	−0.0222 (0.26)
Born 1970–1979				−0.0709 (0.58)	−0.2038 (1.34)
Born 1980+				−0.1983 (0.89)	−0.3137 (1.08)
Log of household income					0.1727* (6.83)
Personal controls	No	Yes	Yes	Yes	Yes
Cut1	−1.5040	−0.9830	−1.5561	−1.5089	−1.2807
Cut2	1.3120	2.0188	1.4489	1.4995	1.9392
Sample size	19.027	18.914	18.914	18.914	11.404
Pseudo R^2	0.0066	0.0476	0.0476	0.0484	0.0490
Log likelihood ratio	−17,725	−16,891	−16,891	−16,878	−9,823
Age of happiness minimum			36.8	34.4	49.5

Source: table taken from: NBER working paper No. 12935, 2007; Data based on General Social Survey, 1974–2004.

Notes

The dependent variable is a measure of subjective well-being. The numbers in parentheses are t-statistics against the null hypothesis of a coefficient being zero.

* Denotes statistical significance at 5 percent level. All five regression equations are to be read vertically. They are ordered logits and include 24 year-dummies and nine region-dummies. 'Personal controls' are the number of years of education, two race-dummies, eight number-of-children dummies, seven workforce-status dummies, a dummy for parents divorced when respondent was 16, and four marital-status dummies. The excluded cohorts are those born 1950–1959. The data set excludes 1979, 1981, 1992, 1995, 1997, 1999, 2001 and 2003. The exact wording of the well-being question is: "Taken all together, how would you say things are these days – would you say that you are very happy, pretty happy, or not too happy?"

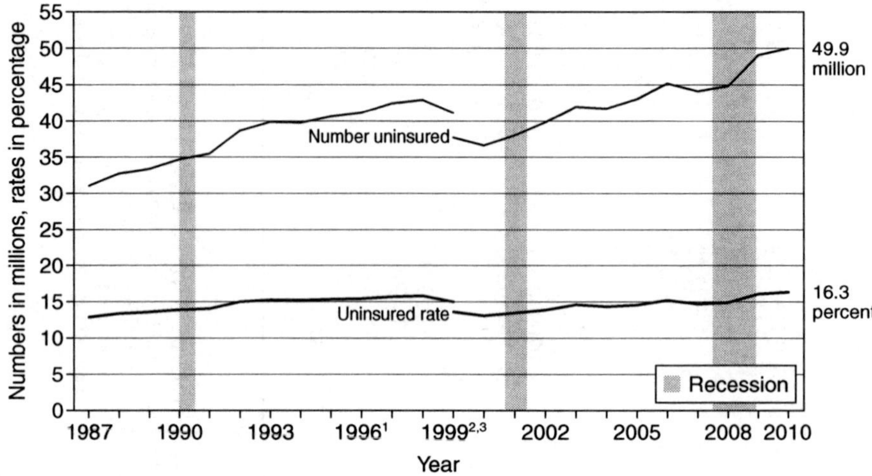

Figure 10.1 Number uninsured and uninsured rate in the United States (1987 to 2010) (source: US Census Bureau, Current Population Survey, 1988 to 2011 ASEC).

Notes

1 The data for 1996 through 1999 were revised using an approximation method for consistency with the revision to the 2004 and 2005 estimates.

2 Implementation of Census 2000-based population controls occurred for the 2000 Annual Social and Economic Supplement (ASEC), which collected data for 1999. These estimates also reflect the results of follow-up verification questions, which were asked of people who responded "no" to all questions about specific types of health insurance coverage in order to verify whether they were actually uninsured. This change increased the number and percentage of people covered by health insurance, bringing the CPS more in line with estimates from other national surveys.

3 The data for 1999 through 2009 were revised to reflect the results of enhancements to the editing process. Note: Respondents were not asked detailed health insurance questions before the 1988 Current Population Survey. The data points are placed at the midpoints of the respective years.

Proposition 10.6 Low policy efficiency of the US health system
The United States commits huge resources on healthcare, both from the public sector and from the private sector, but hardly achieves the main goals of a healthcare system in terms of protecting Americans from health risks, which translate often into risks of loss of functional health and the health stock and financial risks.

10.4 Role of the private insurers and providers in the United States

In the United States, the market for managed care has been on the rise (Table 10.2). Managed care is a concept of health insurance that deals squarely with the

Table 10.2 Rise of managed care in the United States (%)

Year	*Traditional insurance plans*	*HMOs*	*PPOs*	*POS plans*	*HDHP/SOs*
1998	14	27	35	24	~
1999	10	28	39	24	~
2000	8	29	42	21	~
2001	7	24	46	23	~
2002	4	27	52	18	~
2003	5	24	54	17	~
2004	5	25	55	15	~
2005	3	21	61	15	~
2006	3	20	60	13	4
2007	3	21	57	15	5
2008	2	20	58	12	8

Source: online, available at: http://en.wikipedia.org/wiki/Health_insurance_in_the_United_States.

Notes
HMO = Health maintenance organization.
PPO = Preferred provider organization.
POS = Point of service plans.
HDHP/SOs = High deductible health plans with savings option.

principal–agent problem between the insurer and the caregiver, usually by merging the insurance function with the caregiving function, so that the caregiver has an incentive to cut costs and to promote prevention. The two most popular kinds of managed care are the HMO and the PPO. Point-of-service plans follow the family doctor model and require patients to first see the pre-specified primary care doctor, who will make referrals as appropriate. The high deductible health plans with savings options combine catastrophic insurance with a Medisave plan, and may be complemented by health reimbursement arrangements (HRAs) or health savings accounts (HSAs) as authorized by the Internal Revenue Service. They typically work under a managed care mode too.

The Health Maintenance Organization Act of 1973 provides for the certification of HMOs at the state level, whereby these HMOs would allow subscribers access to a network of doctors and healthcare facilities. Although HMOs are insurers they do not operate under an insurance license and may receive federal funds if they meet specific criteria.

As can be seen in Table 10.2, PPOs are gaining popularity. This is largely because PPOs provide cheaper insurance than HMOs or other kinds of healthcare insurance. Typically, PPOs charge a deductible and require a significant degree of cost-sharing. Patients are charged preferred, discounted, rates if they visit facilities within the PPO network with which they have enrolled. Caregivers pay the PPO in order to join a network.

Point-of-service or place-of-service plans require members in the first instance to consult a primary care physician within the network. This primary care physician may then make referrals within or outside the network. The patient will need to pay more using a specialist outside the network. This kind of plans is conceptually very sound, as there are clear advantages for one primary care doctor to keep track of the health changes and needs of a patient, particularly in prevention. It is fast rising in popularity and looks set to overtake PPOs in the not too distant future, probably reflecting its cost-effectiveness.

In the United States, roughly two-thirds of all urban hospitals are non-profit, and they often receive subsidies from the governments. About one in six urban hospitals are public, being financed by the federal, state and/or local governments. Public hospitals include teaching hospitals of major universities. Hospitals, public or otherwise, charge Medicaid, Medicare and private insurers for services provided, though poor uninsured patients receive their care for free. Public hospitals, especially in urban areas, have been under considerable financial pressures, since their patients include many who will not pay. The number of public hospitals has been declining over the years. Naturally, for-profit hospitals generally pick up patients who are in the position to pay, leaving public hospitals and not-for-profit ones caring for those who cannot.

The Obama Administration has attempted to champion "a public health insurance option," "to keep private insurers honest" and to "compete with them" without subsidies from the general revenue. However, because the government does not regulate insurance premiums, private insurers can easily drive away undesirable applicants who will end up in the public plan. It can be expected that the public option is going to be burdened with a load of costly patients to care for but cannot raise premiums because of political pressures. From this perspective the public option appears to be not financially viable.

Instead of trying to offer a public health insurance option as an alternative to private plans, perhaps Obama should aim at rebuilding the public and non-profit hospitals so that they become a viable option for all patients when they need inpatient services. That would make the United States more like Australia in defining the roles for public and private hospitals. But instead of making services free in these hospitals as in Australia, fees and charges should be imposed. EBP should be adopted by capping annual eligible healthcare expenditures.

Proposition 10.7 Role of private and public insurance options
Guaranteeing a minimal acceptable standard of protection for all, and leaving private options to supplement the public backbone of care as is the case in Australia works far better than relying on private insurance to serve as the backbone for protecting citizens and offering a public option to patients rejected by private insurers.

10.5 Fraud

Moral hazard is associated with insurance, which the insurers can contain using co-payments and deductibles. But the insurance market is also a fertile ground for fraud, which is more difficult to deal with. Both in the United States and in Canada, fraudulent claims have been reported, and in the United States the problem is truly alarming, and may be costing taxpayers $60 billion a year, according to a *60 Minutes* investigation.[10] Other estimates put the figure in excess of $47 billion.[11] Senior Agent Waterman in the Miami office in charge of Medicare fraud said

> There's a healthcare fraud industry where people do nothing but recruit patients, get patient lists, find doctors, look on the Internet, find different scams. There are entire groups and entire organizations of people that are dedicated to nothing but committing fraud, finding a better way to steal from Medicare.[12]

In Canada, too, there have been reports of fraudulent claims made by medical doctors. Some are made against the provincial insurer.[13] Others are made against private insurers. In one study, it was found that drug benefit claims continued to be submitted more than a year after the death of 113 people, who were among 335,563 elderly who died between January 1, 1991 and January 1, 1997.[14] But the scale of fraud was much smaller than that in the United States.

Proposition 10.8 Fraud and loopholes in insurance systems
Human nature is such that when there are loopholes in an insurance system, some people will abuse the system. Private insurers can be counted upon to plug these loopholes because their survival is at stake. Publicly funded health insurance is the fertile ground for fraud when bureaucrats are not accountable for losses arising from fraud and leave loopholes unplugged.

10.6 The political economy of healthcare reform

In March 2010, President Obama was able to push the Affordable Health Care for America Act – H.R. 3962 through Congress, and signed it into law.[15] Healthcare reform in the United States has always been very difficult for two reasons. First is the prevalence of vested interests. Second is the need to overcome very challenging party politics. In practice, politics and vested interests are intertwined. Insurers and especially pharmaceutical companies are known to be the biggest lobbyist groups in the United States. According to CBS news, there are 3,000 registered healthcare lobbyists in Washington, an average of six for every member of the Congress. As noted in a CBS story, "in many cases, those lobbyists are former members of Congress who shaped laws that benefited the industry they joined."[16] In 2003, the Bush Administration offered the pharmaceutical industry a multi-billion dollar windfall with Medicare Part D prescription drug coverage for seniors. This greatly boosted the cost of Medicare, but a benefit once enacted is very difficult to abolish. This is posing great difficulty for the Obama Administration as the country is under great pressures to contain the budget deficit after the global financial tsunami in 2008.

Introducing a mandatory NHI plan that effectively takes away the businesses from the hundreds of health insurers is considered politically infeasible in America. Requiring all those who can afford it to buy a minimal coverage health insurance from private insurers[17] is called the "individual mandate," but this requirement has been challenged as unconstitutional by many Republicans for going beyond Congress' Commerce Clause authority. In August 2011, this individual health insurance mandate was struck down by the federal appeals Court.[18] The controversy will have to be resolved in the Supreme Court.

Of particular interest in the Obama plan is a provision for a cap on insurance premiums as a percentage of income. This bears some resemblance to the annual spending thresholds on healthcare expenditures that were discussed in Chapter 2. Both a cap on premiums and a cap on out-of-pocket, eligible healthcare expenditures provide caps on expenditures and both are intended to enhance *ex ante* welfare, protecting anyone, whoever he is, from having to spend too much on healthcare. The difference only lies on the type of expenditure that is capped. The commonality lies in the spirit of protecting citizens from excessive burden. Under the Patient Protection and Affordable Care Act, premium subsidies decline as incomes increase, and vanish when household income reaches four times the federal poverty line.

One proposal of the Obama healthcare reform, somewhat similar to the platform created in Australia to facilitate the comparison of alternative policies available in the marketplace, is the establishment of state-based "insurance exchanges," which will increase the transparency of alternative insurance plans and will avail low income individuals and families with subsidies on premiums, provided that they do not enjoy Medicare, Medicaid, or employer-paid health insurance. Funds will be made available to states to establish exchanges within one year of enactment and until January 1, 2015. Additional taxes, in particular a 3.8 percent tax on investment income for families making more than $250,000 per year ($200,000 for individuals), will be imposed as of 2012. Beginning in 2018, insurance companies will pay a 40 percent excise tax on so-called "Cadillac" high-end insurance plans worth over $27,500 for families ($10,200 for individuals). Clearly this is tantamount to a redistribution to help the poor to procure health insurance.

In proposing a "public health insurance option," President Obama explained in 2009:[19]

> I have no interest in putting insurance companies out of business ... I've insisted that like any private insurance company, the public insurance option would have to be self-sufficient and rely on the premiums it collects. But by avoiding some of the overhead that gets eaten up at private companies by profits and excessive administrative costs and executive salaries, it could provide a good deal for consumers, and would also keep pressure on private insurers to keep their policies affordable and treat their customers better.

No one should doubt President Obama's good intentions. But how will he not put insurance companies out of business if the public option runs parallel to the private plans and is cheaper and better? It appears that a more convincing approach is to offer the "public option" not really as an option or alternative to private plans but as a basic minimum coverage that allows room for private plans to supplement it. This public basic coverage will not be a commercial product and so requiring everyone financially capable to purchase it cannot be ruled unconstitutional. Otherwise it is difficult to see how it will not lead to one of two results: (a) it becomes so successful that it drives out the private plans from health insurance altogether; and (b) the public option becomes the dumping ground for bad risks for the private insurers, eventually becoming financially unsustainable without huge subsidies from taxpayers. Although the law is supposed to require private insurers to take any enrollee regardless of his medical history, the law does not require private insurers to charge affordable premiums. Any private insurer can therefore easily drive away a costly enrollee by charging a sufficiently high premium. Such costly enrollees will therefore end up with the public insurance option.[20]

Proposition 10.9 Politics of healthcare reform
Healthcare reform in America is rendered very difficult because policies that serve the public interest may be considered alien to the private interests of certain groups and may be politically infeasible, and this is confounded by party politics.

Proposition 10.10 Mandatory basic public health insurance
A mandatory but really basic public health insurance plan that allows room for private plans to supplement it will certainly be constitutional and can be made financially sustainable. A public health insurance option that runs alongside private plans and offers similar coverage either will not survive or will drive out the private providers.

10.7 Conclusions

The American healthcare system is the most costly in the world yet health outcomes are often no better than in many countries with much lower healthcare spending. Surveys conducted in 2007–2008 for ten industrial countries found that the US system is rated the worst among the ten, with one-third of Americans believing the US system "has so much wrong with it that we need to completely rebuild it."[21]

It is acknowledged that health outcomes depend on many factors, and the healthcare system is only one of them. As O'Neill and O'Neill (2007) observed, infant mortality is related to low birth weight, which is in turn related to substance abuse and smoking, Since there is more substance abuse and smoking among mothers in the United States than in Canada it is not surprising that America has a higher infant mortality rate.[22] While a number of surveys suggested Americans rate their healthcare system rather poorly, a Gallup Poll in 2006 found ratings rather similar for America, Canada and the United Kingdom.[23] A commentator also noted that people tend to report good experience and satisfaction with the care they actually get though they report dissatisfaction with the healthcare system.[24]

He was commenting on a recent (2011) poll commissioned by the Robert Wood Johnson Foundation, which dialed up 1,034 adults aged 18 and older and which found that 55 percent gave US healthcare quality a C or D and 11 percent gave it an F.[25] His observation that "respondents have little clear expertise for evaluating anything but their own personal experiences and [they] are perfectly happy with those personal experiences" is, however, consistent with the view that those who can afford it are happy with it, while those who cannot afford it and thus do not have much experience with it are unhappy with it. Indeed, grades of C, D or F were given by 43 percent of those with household incomes of less than $50,000, while only 21 percent of those with household incomes of $50,000 or more gave such low ratings.

American healthcare is certainly not an area in which Americans should be complacent. Spending over 17 percent of the GDP on healthcare is too far out of line with all other countries, regardless of how differences in demographic, cultural, and social factors may intervene into healthcare outcomes and needs. There is a huge potential to clean up the waste inherent in the current healthcare system. It appears that the waste has to do with the public insurance systems Medicare and Medicaid as much as the private healthcare and health insurance systems.[26] Indeed, to quote a recent article by Cutler and Ly (2011) "There are few other areas of the US economy where waste is so apparent and the possibility of savings is so tangible" (Cutler and Ly, 2011, p. 22). While the potential for reductions in waste is huge, realizing such savings is not at all easy, largely because of political economy factors.

Review questions

1. Cutler and Ly (2011) wrote that waste was more apparent and tangible in healthcare than in most other areas of the US economy. What are the sources of such waste, and how can they be tackled? If they are so apparent, why do they endure so long in America?
2. "Americans who actually use the healthcare system are generally satisfied with its efficiency. Public opinion polls which reflect the opinions of many who have not used the healthcare system are therefore biased." Comment.
3. Will a "public option" as an alternative to private health insurance work? Why?
4. How will a state-run healthcare system that provides protection meeting the minimum requirements of the public affect the private health insurance and private healthcare industries? What are the implications on the public interest?

11 The way forward

11.1 Introduction

We have now finished our survey of healthcare systems, and can now draw some conclusions.

First of all, the funding mechanisms can be summarized in Table 11.1. They are either mandatory or voluntary; publicly funded or privately funded; prospective or payment at the point of service; when publicly funded, they may be in the form of taxes or insurance premiums explicitly earmarked for healthcare, or appropriated from the general revenue.

In general, all these options can co-exist, and they often do. Indeed it makes sense to have a mix of different funding sources. Exclusively depending on any single funding mechanism will not be optimal: overly dependent on taxes to the exclusion of user fees will lead to moral hazard and wastefulness; overly dependent on user fees would undermine accessibility; ruling out private insurance would limit choices. Since healthcare does have public good aspects, in that the failure to care for the health of some people may lead to a failure to contain a contagious disease, and that good public health and healthcare may reduce the chances of epidemic outbreaks and may be a source of national pride and social harmony, there certainly will be an important role for tax-funded healthcare, and particularly for tax-funded promotion of public health and health-related research. We have seen that in France, healthcare protection is extended even to illegal aliens. Even in America, where the market dominates healthcare, there are public hospitals which will attend to the needs of the sick for free, if the patients cannot afford to pay – and if they can find one within reach that can help them. But with funding drying up, public hospitals in America are closing down – notwithstanding an obvious increase in demand that is in part a result of aging and in part a result of population growth.

It is argued throughout this book that when the sick and the ailing cannot get the care needed the public interest suffers. Defining the public interest as the *ex ante* welfare of the representative individual, our key question is how comfortable we are with the healthcare system if we imagine a scenario such that we could be anyone in the community including the sick and poor. In general, we would prefer to live in a society which provides for comprehensive basic care that is affordable. We have seen that from Hong Kong and Taiwan and Australia

Table 11.1 A taxonomy of alternative funding options*

Mandatory			*Voluntary*		
Direct/explicit		*Indirect/implicit*	*Traditional insurance plans*	*Managed care plans*	*User fees and charges*
Mandatory insurance premiums	*Mandatory Medical Savings Account (MSA) contributions*	*Tax-financed healthcare spending funded by taxes*	*Market insurance premiums*	*Membership fees*	*Fees or co-payments*
Disadvantages:					
Moral hazard on both supply side and demand side, if caregivers are profit-oriented private practitioners.	Not really a source of healthcare finance, although MSA holders can pay designated user charges. Savings may be inadequate or excessive. Individuals lose autonomy.	Demand-side moral hazard if fees are non-existent or too low. Possible loss of professional autonomy.	Moral hazard problems can be serious. Chronically ill and known high risk individuals may not get coverage.	Patients may not get needed services that are costly.	May render services financially inaccessible to some people. Needed medical treatment may be delayed. May cause excessive financial burden for patients and their families.
Advantages:					
Universal coverage can be assured.	Government has the comfort of knowing that patients have the means to pay the stipulated fees.	Containment of supply-side moral hazard because caregivers are salaried. Can provide for public healthcare needs which may be underprovided in the market place.	Consumers have autonomy over what to cover and what not to.	Less susceptible to moral hazard problems.	High fees and charges provide an incentive for preventive care. High fees cut waiting time for those who can afford. Consumers have greater autonomy, so long as they can afford. Doctors have a stronger sense of earning what they deserve.

Note
* Adapted from Ho (2001) in *Hong Kong Medical Journal* 7(2) June, 155–161.

in the east to Canada over in North America to France, Sweden, Switzerland and the United Kingdom in Europe, all have followed this approach, with different degrees of success that largely depends on the adequacy and reliability of the funding source.

We have seen that where user charges or co-payments for publicly provided care are very low or non-existent, such as in the United Kingdom, in Hong Kong and in Canada, the sustainability of the system is often called into question and queues have often become unacceptably long.

We have seen that a lack of regulations and supervision has given rise to serious abuse and fraud, as in the United States.

We have seen how the use of schedule fees, reference fees and government-set fees has helped contain cost escalation, as in Australia and in Switzerland.

We have studied the unique case of Singapore, where the bureaucracy has managed to cope with what others might regard as an administrative nightmare, as the healthcare system becomes more and more complex and embodies a combination of all the different approaches as discussed above.

11.2 Cost escalation and how much is enough

Table 11.2 shows that annual total expenditures on health in per capita, purchasing power parity terms, have been increasing at an average of 2.9 per cent per year for the OECD countries. Table 11.3 further shows that public healthcare expenditures in real terms have been rising annually at an average of 4.2 percent for the nine years up to 2009 among all the OECD countries. In this post-financial tsunami period, with many governments facing serious deficit and debt problems, it is generally and increasingly recognized that a more balanced budget over the long run is necessary for sustainability and that this will require containing public healthcare expenditures.

Given that most, if not all, countries are aging, and that public aspirations for health have been rising over the years, some increase in the percentage of the GDP devoted to healthcare is not a problem and should even be welcomed. It becomes a problem when the cost escalation is out of control. Some increase in resources devoted to healthcare is fine if this increase is the result of a conscious and cautious deliberation, and if the increases in spending are well spent. This requires mechanisms that promote cost-consciousness and incentives that minimize wasteful moral hazard.

It is noted that Australia, France, as well as Switzerland have all been able to contain the growth rate in the real per capita public expenditures on healthcare to the 2–3 percent range. In contrast, in the United Kingdom, where free healthcare has been taken for granted, real per capita public healthcare expenditures had been rising at an alarming 5.6 percent while in the United States, where Medicare and Medicaid benefits have been known to be abused and defrauded, real per capita public healthcare expenditures had been rising at 4.5 percent per annum. Among those that are more successful in containing cost escalation, Australia and Switzerland use schedule fees or reference fees to raise cost

Table 11.2 Annual total expenditure on health/capita, US$ purchasing power parity and rate of growth p.a., selected OECD countries, 2000–2009

	2000	*2001*	*2002*	*2003*	*2004*	*2005*	*2006*	*2007*	*2008*	*2009*	*% p.a.#*
Australia*	2,266	2,388	2,559	2,673	2,878	2,980	3,164	3,353	3,445	n.a.	2.30
Austria	2,862	2,906	3,057	3,199	3,390	3,472	3,629	3,792	4,128	4,289	1.97
Belgium	2,245	2,364	2,542	3,034	3,164	3,231	3,279	3,437	3,714	3,946	2.76
Canada	2,519	2,733	2,869	3,055	3,205	3,442	3,665	3,844	4,024	4,363	2.69
Chile	615	656	671	781	798	843	863	959	1,092	1,186	3.22
Czech Republic	981	1,081	1,195	1,338	1,387	1,475	1,556	1,661	1,839	2,108	3.76
Denmark	2,508	2,680	2,871	2,895	3,126	3,245	3,577	3,770	4,052	4,348	2.69
Finland	1,853	1,970	2,150	2,251	2,452	2,589	2,764	2,910	3,158	3,226	2.71
France	2,553	2,726	2,931	2,991	3,122	3,306	3,493	3,679	3,809	3,978	2.16
Germany	2,669	2,797	2,934	3,097	3,170	3,364	3,565	3,724	3,963	4,218	2.23
Hungary	853	970	1,114	1,283	1,305	1,411	1,486	1,433	1,495	1,511	2.80
Iceland	2,740	2,844	3,156	3,194	3,334	3,304	3,193	3,320	3,571	3,538	1.24
Ireland	1,768	2,069	2,344	2,550	2,777	2,959	3,200	3,494	3,784	3,781	3.74
Israel	1,766	1,882	1,870	1,750	1,835	1,829	1,897	2,012	2,142	2,165	0.99
Italy	2,064	2,228	2,235	2,265	2,373	2,516	2,725	2,771	3,059	3,137	2.04
Japan*	1,974	2,074	2,141	2,235	2,347	2,491	2,609	2,750	2,878	n.a.	2.07
Korea	771	918	966	1,046	1,136	1,291	1,469	1,651	1,736	1,879	4.39
Luxembourg	3,268	3,182	3,746	3,632	4,118	4,152	4,603	4,494	4,451	4,808	1.88
Mexico	508	552	584	629	688	731	776	842	892	918	2.90
Netherlands	2,340	2,555	2,833	3,097	3,309	3,450	3,613	3,944	4,241	4,914	3.65
New Zealand	1,607	1,709	1,841	1,850	2,044	2,197	2,467	2,525	2,784	2,983	3.03
Norway	3,043	3,265	3,628	3,835	4,078	4,301	4,507	4,885	5,230	5,352	2.76
Poland	583	642	733	748	807	857	934	1,078	1,265	1,394	4.30
Portugal*	1,654	1,714	1,780	1,894	1,996	2,212	2,303	2,419	2,508	n.a.	2.29
Slovak Republic	604	664	730	791	1,057	1,139	1,350	1,619	1,859	2,084	6.16
Spain	1,537	1,635	1,745	2,023	2,131	2,269	2,536	2,735	2,971	3,067	3.39
Sweden	2,286	2,501	2,702	2,832	2,954	2,963	3,193	3,432	3,644	3,722	2.38
Switzerland	3,221	3,428	3,673	3,777	3,936	4,015	4,150	4,469	4,930	5,144	2.28
Turkey*	433	423	442	447	520	591	712	798	902	n.a.	4.06
United Kingdom	1,828	1,996	2,184	2,317	2,540	2,735	3,006	3,051	3,281	3,487	3.17
United States	4,793	5,146	5,578	5,986	6,336	6,700	7,073	7,437	7,720	7,960	2.48
Average for all OECD countries											2.91

Source: OECD Health Data 2011, online, available at: http://stats.oecd.org/Index.aspx?DataSetCode=SHA.

Notes
* Growth rates are averages from 2000–2008 for countries with asterisks.
# Geometric average from beginning to end of period.

consciousness and help contain costs. In general, co-payments are charged in all the countries that were able to keep healthcare cost growth low. Because these co-payments are often rather low, as in Hong Kong and in Sweden, there is much room for raising the co-payments without undermining affordability. Because annual co-payments can be capped, as long as such caps are set not excessively high there is little worry that they will overburden the public. Indeed, raising co-payments and raising the annual "high cost ceilings" is what it takes

Table 11.3 Annual growth rate of public expenditure on health per capita, in real terms

	2000–2001	*2001–2002*	*2002–2003*	*2003–2004*	*2004–2005*	*2005–2006*	*2006–2007*	*2007–2008*	*2008–2009*	*Average*
Australia	2.7	5.9	0.8	5.7	0.7	2.1	4.2	2.3	n.a.	3.05
Austria	0.6	1	1.8	3.2	2.3	1.6	3.9	3.7	2.8	2.32
Belgium	3.7	0.8	20.5	5.8	0	−5.3	2.3	6.6	4.4	4.31
Canada	5.5	4.2	3.8	2.1	2.5	2.6	2.5	2.9	7.6	3.74
Chile	7.1	2.6	−18.9	2.1	2.6	4.4	10.6	13.6	17.4	4.61
Czech Republic	4.5	9	8	0.1	4.7	1.7	0.6	3.4	12.3	4.92
Denmark	5.4	3	2.1	3.5	3.4	4.9	1.5	1.3	6.5	3.51
Estonia	1.2	6.1	11	8.5	8.9	5.6	15.3	14.1	−4.3	7.38
Finland	6	7.5	9.3	5.1	5.9	2.2	0.5	4.4	0.4	4.59
France	2.4	3.8	2.9	2.7	2	0.8	1	−0.4	3.1	2.03
Germany	2	1.6	0.6	−3.2	1.8	1.8	1.6	3.4	4.5	1.57
Greece	17.5	1.7	6.9	0	14.2	8.7	1.2	n.a.	n.a.	7.17
Hungary	3.1	12.2	19.3	0.1	7.6	1.3	−9.9	−1.4	−5.4	2.99
Iceland	0.7	9.1	3.8	0.9	1.5	−0.9	3.8	−0.8	−2.1	1.78
Ireland	15.5	10.3	7.3	7.1	3.8	1.4	5.2	8.8	−3.2	6.24
Israel	3.3	−1.6	−3.8	0.7	1.1	0.5	1.8	4.9	0.2	0.79
Italy	6.7	1.5	−0.7	6.3	3.5	2.8	−3	4.9	−0.4	2.40
Japan	3.5	0.7	2	2.5	4.6	−1	3.6	3.2	n.a.	2.39
Korea	31.5	1.3	5.3	5.9	12.6	17	10.2	4.7	11.5	11.11
Luxembourg	−2.8	15.3	−9.2	9.8	−0.3	0	−6	−7	8	0.87
Mexico	2.1	0.6	3.8	8.9	0.3	1.2	4.6	5.1	5.3	3.54
Netherlands	5	5.7	n.a.	n.a.	n.a.	n.a.	n.a.	n.a.	n.a.	5.35
New Zealand	2.1	9.4	0.1	6	6.8	6.5	1.4	6.8	7.7	5.20
Norway	7.4	12.2	3	−0.6	−3.9	−3.2	4.8	−3.1	8.1	2.74
Poland	10.3	8.6	0.6	2.7	4.9	7	12.3	16.7	6.7	7.76
Portugal	1.1	3	3.2	2.9	3.3	−3.4	0.8	−0.6	n.a.	1.29
Slovak Republic	3.9	6.7	7.4	8.7	5	3.7	14	10.7	4.9	7.22
Slovenia	5.5	4.3	0.5	2.6	3.3	4.2	0.3	12.9	1.6	3.91
Spain	2.3	1.5	12.6	2.3	3.1	4.4	3.5	6.5	2.9	4.34
Sweden	4.5	6.8	3.6	0.6	2.2	2.4	2.5	2.3	1.8	2.97
Switzerland	7.7	4.1	3.3	2.3	3.1	−1.8	1.1	2.7	3.1	2.84
Turkey	4.8	12.9	5.3	7.6	3.4	13.4	6.6	12.4	n.a.	8.30
United Kingdom	6.3	6.2	5.5	7.2	6.9	4.3	1.4	4.9	7.5	5.58
United States	7.4	6.1	4.7	3.9	2.5	4.1	2.7	3.6	5.8	4.53
Average for all OECD countries										4.22

Source: OECD Health Data 2011, online, available at: http://stats.oecd.org/Index.aspx?DataSetCode=SHA.

to keep the healthcare system sustainable and to make the benefits of the latest medical advances accessible to the people.

Total healthcare expenditures per capita, in PPP dollars, ranged from below $3,000 to nearly $8,000 in 2009. The United States spent more than twice as much on healthcare per capita as the United Kingdom, which in turn spent some 85 percent more than Korea. Korea and many Eastern European countries started with a very low base and are rapidly increasing their healthcare expenditures. The rapid rates of increase reflect “catching up” and do not necessarily represent a problem, but if too little attention is paid to the subject of incentives, they may reflect wasteful deployment of resources that undermines the public interest.

11.3 Private–public interface

As discussed in the country chapters and summarized in Table 11.4, most countries distinguish between basic care and supplementary care. Coverage for basic care is often universal, and often paid through the tax system though may also require premiums or taxes earmarked for health insurance. Switzerland is a unique case in that basic statutory health insurance is always provided by private insurers on a non-profit basis. Basic healthcare services are also often provided publicly. The concept of what constitutes basic healthcare coverage varies from place to place. It is very generous in the United Kingdom and in Sweden, where coverage is truly comprehensive, and for that reason private supplemental insurance is rather uncommon. It is far less generous in Australia, where basic coverage is limited to schedule fees though safety nets are available to avoid excessive burden; and in Canada, where prescription drugs are generally not covered. In Singapore there is no formal provision of universal healthcare protection as such, but Singapore citizens and residents are charged concessionary fees and poor members of society have access to open wards that are heavily subsidized. Most Singaporeans also can pay out of their Medisave accounts for inpatient services and some specialist outpatient services.[1] Where coverage is less comprehensive or generous, supplementary insurance is bought by a much bigger segment of the population, especially in Australia, where such plans are subsidized.

While “basic coverage” is interpreted differently from country to country, the concept is surprisingly universal: even the United States defines mandatory benefits for its Medicaid program and all the elderly are given coverage in Part A (inpatient) and in Part B (outpatient services, plus some other specified items such as durable medical equipment, home health services). The almost universal coverage of basic healthcare is related to the anxiety that people may endure if such services are not covered or are not available when they need them. This takes us back to the discussion about mental goods and bads.

11.4 Mental goods and mental bads

Knowing that other members of society are protected, as well as knowing that one and one’s family members are protected, are “mental goods” that enhance a sense of security, caring society and justice. Some of these mental goods are "public goods" in nature, in the sense that everyone benefits from them and no one is excluded from these benefits. Such is the knowledge that the society in which one lives is a caring society and that it looks after the needs of the unfortunate. Other mental goods are more personal, which is a sense of being personally free from the worry of having to pay excessively for healthcare and of not being able to get needed medical care.

A significant mental bad is uncertainty. That is why transparency in medical charges is considered very important, and is an important objective in most jurisdictions. That is why the protection of a "high cost ceiling" is considered so important to the public interest.

It is hypothesized that all human beings are averse to big risks – the risks of a big loss. This is why catastrophic inpatient service insurance is considered basic healthcare – even more so than outpatient services. However, even for outpatient visits, fees should be at affordable levels, and most countries that choose to charge for these services would set them at very reasonable rates, which are also clearly stipulated to avoid the mental bad of uncertainty.

11.5 The political economy of healthcare reform

The discussion in this book should demonstrate that what makes a good healthcare system should be quite clear by now. It should be funded in part by taxes, and in part by user charges, in part by insurance funds. It should avail citizens of choice, but it should provide basic protection to all. Tax financing is appropriate to some extent, because there are public good characteristics in public health and in healthcare, and because medical infrastructure, research, and education benefit society at large and are significant outlays for any society. User charges are necessary, because they provide stronger incentives for prevention and for cautious use of precious resources, and they provide an important supplementary source of financing. Private insurance plans, whether of the managed care variety or the traditional third party type of insurance, belong to the free market, and supplement public healthcare by providing more choice.

There are many ways of cost containment: co-payments and coinsurance will restrain demand-side moral hazard; salaried staff would avoid supply-side moral hazard; official price setting and limiting reimbursements to official pricing guidelines; gate-keeping; making basic health insurance non-profit; building stronger governance mechanisms including capitation and financial accountability to promote efficient use of resources, and to prevent and punish abuses; global budgets; greater use of generic drugs and negotiating drug charges with pharmaceutical companies are among the ways to contain cost escalation, and have all proven to work, although sometimes with some undesirable side-effects.

While healthcare reform is an ongoing exercise all over the world, it is motivated by different forces. Sometimes it is clearly a matter of necessity, as in the case of the United States, where healthcare costs have catapulted to over 17 percent of the GDP and still leave large segments of the population unprotected.

Table 11.4 Healthcare plans in public and private sectors

	Basic healthcare		*Supplementary healthcare*	
	Services delivery	*Insurance*	*Services delivery*	*Insurance*
Australia	Primary care predominantly private. Hospitals predominantly public. Billing at schedule fees common but extra billing is allowed.	Mandatory. Co-payments apply for outpatient visits and for drugs. Funded by general revenue and a 1.5 percent levy on taxable income	Most elective surgery procedures are provided in private hospitals and day surgeries.	About 11 million Australians have bought supplementary coverage through private insurance. The insured gets a rebate at 30–40 percent of the premiums by the government depending on age.
Canada	Primary care predominantly private. Hospital care almost exclusively public. Doctors' fees fixed by provincial insurers. Extra billing not allowed.	Provincial, public insurers. Some segments of the population not covered.	Rare exceptions like the Cambie Surgery Centre provide private inpatient services. Doctors who opt out of provincial insurance plans charge fees freely but they are uncommon.	Roughly two-thirds of Canadians have supplementary private insurance coverage, mostly through their employers.
China (mainland)	Hospitals are predominantly public but all are inadequately funded. Increased funding in recent years, and in the future pledged.	Different schemes apply to different people: rural, urban workers and civil servants, with different benefits; Migrating to a single system aiming at covering all outpatient and inpatient on cost sharing principles	For-profit private hospitals and clinics are appearing.	Elective coverage by for-profit plans.
France	Primary care predominantly private; hospital care almost exclusively public; Reference prices serve as guidelines but extra billing allowed	Truly universal coverage extended even to illegal aliens. Specified non-reimbursable co-payments are subject to an annual ceiling of €50	Private practitioners and private hospitals subject to professional self regulation and minimal government regulation. Public hospitals may take private patients.	Elective coverage by for-profit plans
Hong Kong	Private practitioners dominate the outpatient market. Public hospitals dominate inpatient market. Private doctors' fees not regulated	All permanent residents can enjoy inpatient services in public hospitals at nominal charges	Private practitioners and private hospitals subject to professional self regulation and minimal government regulation	The share of private health insurance healthcare financing increased from 11.9 percent in 1989/1990 to 13.0 percent in 2006/2007 and has continued to increase in the more recent years.

New Zealand	Private practitioners dominate the outpatient market but are paid on a cost-sharing basis by patients and the government. Public hospitals dominate inpatient market;	Automatic. Co-payments apply for outpatient visits and for drugs.	Specialists often hold positions in public hospitals but maintain their private practices.	Private insurance often covers co-payments, elective surgery in private hospitals and specialist outpatient consultations.
Singapore	Private practitioners dominate the outpatient market; inpatient care predominantly public; government sets baseline prices	Medishield provides catastrophic coverage for inpatient services; primary care fees in public clinics kept low	Private practitioners and private hospitals are subject to government regulation and professional self regulation	Elective coverage by for-profit plans
Sweden	Predominantly public, operated by county councils locally	Automatic universal coverage.	Private hospitals specialize in elective surgery and work under contract with county councils.	About 5 percent of the population is covered by supplemental private health insurance.
Switzerland	Doctors are predominantly private. Hospitals are predominantly public or publicly subsidized	Universal coverage by non-profit private plans; co-payments and coinsurance apply	About one-quarter of inpatient services provided by private hospitals.	Elective coverage by for-profit plans, which are strictly regulated.
Taiwan	Services are mostly privately provided but paid by a single national insurer at set fees.	Universal, comprehensive coverage. Premium waivers or concessions for the poor. Co-payments and coinsurance apply.	Generally regarded as not necessary.	Very few people elect for coverage beyond the national health insurance
United Kingdom	Services are publicly funded but providers compete for resources in a quasi-market under purchaser-provider split model	Universal comprehensive coverage; co-payments sometimes but often not required.	Some private physicians as well as private hospitals set their own fees and are paid privately. Public hospitals may take some private patients.	Elective coverage by for-profit plans.
United States	States required to cover "mandatory benefits" to receive federal funding for Medicaid. Medicare covers inpatient and basic services (Parts A and B) for the elderly. Some 1,200 free and charitable clinics in the country.	The poor can use public and non-profit hospitals without paying but access is limited. Protection for the elderly (Medicare Part A and B) and for the eligible poor (Medicaid). Elective private insurance by others.	Private hospitals and service providers abound, many very well equipped. US boasts the highest magnetic resonance imaging (MRI) machines per million population, about four times that of Canada and three times that of Germany	Part C in Medicare for the aged over 65, covers vision, hearing, dental, and health and wellness. Part D covers drugs. Private "Medigap" insurance plans are optional; private insurance plans with dental and drug benefits mostly offered through employers.

Sometimes it is at least partly a matter of ideology, as in the case of the healthcare reform proposals forged by the Cameron coalition government. Our survey suggests that several systems are settling down into some kind of equilibrium. Singapore appears quite settled to its unique model combining mandatory Medisave with government-set user charges in combination with Medishield and Medifund, in combination with a big role of the private sector in primary care and a big role of the public sector in hospital care. Taiwan and Canada appear quite settled to their national or provincial/territory-based health insurance schemes. France and Switzerland apparently have found their systems of basic care insurance supplemented by for-profit insurance schemes sustainable.

Yet the interface between the private sector and the public sector almost always triggers ideological fights. We have seen how difficult it was for the United States to clean up all the apparent inefficiency that Cutler and Ly (2011) have noted. It was clearly by some stroke of luck that President Obama got his healthcare bill passed in 2010, and he certainly will need more luck if his reform package is not to be shot down as unconstitutional by the Supreme Court. In Canada, the Canadian Union of Public Employees (CUPE) has been fighting the threat of erosion of Medicare by private for-profit healthcare entrepreneurs for years. In Hong Kong, there is similar and widespread concern about the government's plans to invigorate the private health insurance market by spending HK$50 billion to subsidize the premiums of the high risk pool, and to build more private hospitals rather than public hospitals. As CUPE had predicted, the more profitable the private hospitals were, the more able were they to attract the skilled professionals from the public hospitals to their ranks. This would undermine the quality of services in the public hospitals and indirectly force patients to turn to private hospitals instead.[2]

Switzerland was able to mandate that basic health protection plans must be non-profit. But it seems unlikely that other countries could do the same: certainly not in America, because of the political economy of the health insurance market.

Canada was able to mandate that private doctors be reimbursed only at rates stipulated or negotiated with the provincial insurers, or they must not be reimbursed at all. This again is based on a unique interpretation of fair dealing. Both Australia and France allow extra-billing. Australia and France are able to do this without causing very serious problems because most doctors do not impose extra charges and in Australia supplementary insurance is subsidized. Will doctors in countries with a predominantly private primary care agree to charge at the schedule fees set by the government? Again it seems to be highly unlikely, again because of political economy considerations.

11.6 Conclusions

This closes our discussion of health policy and the public interest. We would reiterate the need for some kind of EBP in any healthcare system that takes the public interest seriously. We would reiterate the need for user fees, as an incentive for preventive care and for conscientious use of resources, subject to some annual "high cost ceiling" to keep the maximum cost of basic healthcare within the budget of every member of society. We proposed the concept of an LCS, which is based on the concept of cost sharing, to offer choices for optional care. The idea would limit the cost exposure of the government and yet would materially avail members of society to much greater choices over care.

Looking forward to a rapidly aging society, the imperative for cost containment is clear. But aging healthily may significantly reduce the trajectory for healthcare costs into the future. To motivate healthy aging, preventive care and a healthy lifestyle need to be adopted early in life. To provide greater incentives for healthy aging, and also to secure sufficient resources to ensure quality care, it is proposed that the annual high cost ceiling be raised gradually as people age beyond 50. The maximum high cost ceiling is proposed to be about three times the high cost ceiling for a younger person. This will tell a young person that if he takes good care of himself, he will save a considerable amount of healthcare costs, thus encouraging early prevention. Such incentives are obviously important, given that a healthier lifestyle can have a significantly positive impact on health and help reduce healthcare costs (Sassi and Hurst, 2008). The increase in the annual high cost ceiling with age, it should be noted, does not really imply an increase in the share of cost borne by the elderly. Given that older people generally spend well over five times what younger people spend, the degree of cost sharing for older people, even under these rising high cost ceilings, is actually smaller and the absolute amount of public money expended to care for the old per person, which covers all the costs for covered services beyond the ceilings, considerably bigger.

Finally, it should be recalled that health policy is not only about health. Health is a holistic concept and it takes a holistic approach to make a health policy that will best promote the public interest. It will be useful to repeat a point made in the concluding section of Chapter 9, that health policy is not just about financing healthcare and delivering healthcare services. Everything from food safety and driving habits to workplace safety and crime prevention has a place in health policy.

Notes

Preface

1 *Healthcare Financing and Delivery: A Model for Reform*, City University of Hong Kong Press, 1997.

1 Functional health and the health stock

1 This is obviously related to the "healthy year equivalent" (HYE) concept (Gafni and Birch, 1997, Birch *et al.*, 1998).
2 In this book we use household and consumer interchangeably, and treat household as a person.
3 In countries with a high infant mortality rate, life expectancy may rise after the initial couple of years when the infant is most vulnerable.
4 See Hubert *et al.* 2002.

2 A framework for risk and health policy analysis

1 For an evidence-based support of this argument, consider the willingness of people to pay for insurance against a hazard. The economic loss due to the outbreak of SARS in 2002–2003, too, is certainly far greater than the loss of lives and the damage to health of those directly affected because of fear. Witness the decline in air traffic in during that episode.
2 This decision utility is called "perceived utility" in my book *Public Policy and the Public Interest* (2012). "Decision utility" is probably a more accurate term.
3 Boldface in equation components signifies vectors, i.e., there may be many goods and many prices. The vector multiplication refers the sum of the expenditures on the different goods
4 David U. Himmelstein, Deborah Thorne, Elizabeth Warren, Steffie Woolhandler, (2009) "Medical Bankruptcy in the United States, 2007: Results of a National Study" *American Journal of Medicine*, 122(8): 741–746, August.
5 Many healthcare systems are very inefficient and wasteful because of bad incentives. For example "Japan has the longest hospital stays in the world. Patients often stay in the hospital much longer than they need to. People are prescribed a lot of medicines, and often get a lot of tests they don't need simply because they know that heath insurance will pay for it." See Facts and Details website, online, available at: http://factsanddetails.com/japan.php?itemid=838&catid=23&subcatid=151#13. Similarly, Chinese hospitals are known to make money from selling drugs, and they sell drugs at premium prices aggressively to patients. See Chapter 5 on China below. Misused drugs are not only wasteful but potentially harmful to health.

6 Nanfang Dushi Bao (Southern City Post) (Shenzhen edition) (南方都市報 (深圳版) January 20 2012.
7 Moral hazard may be of two kinds: endogenous probability and endogenous claims, as explained in Barr (1992).
8 "Fee reducing insurance" in the presence of information asymmetry may actually become "fee increasing" for the insurer who pays if it prompts service providers to overcharge. Stories about overcharges abound in China today. This may or may not have anything to do with insurance. For example, when a former chairman of the Hong Kong Reporters' Association suffered a stroke and was admitted to a hospital in Zhengzhou, he was charged 80,000 yuan (US$10,000) per day. That was subsequently reduced to 20,000 yuan upon intervention by the Hong Kong SAR Beijing Office (*Mingpao*, July 27, 2006). Overcharges may arise when it is perceived there is a high ability to pay and when a patient has little choice, for example in an emergency.
9 When a patient voluntarily receives and pays for premium services, which may be provided by a private medical facility, only the standard charges are recorded as eligible expenses.
10 These caps have not been changed for many years. See Sweden.SE website, online, available at: www.sweden.se/eng/Home/Society/Health-care/Facts/Health-care-in-Sweden/, accessed January 20, 2012.
11 The reform first started in Zhenjian and Jiujiang in 1994. In December of 1998 the Chinese government decided to extend the system across the nation, hoping that by the end of 2001 it would cover 80 million urban workers, but actual implementation could vary from locality to locality. See Hanvoravongchai, 2002: 31–33.
12 According to the officials of the Qinghai Employee Medical Insurance Regulatory Bureau (Qinghai Zhigong Yiliao Baoxian Guanliju),

> The Basic Employee Medical Insurance Plan for Urban Employees is a scheme demanding contributions from three parties: the state, the collective, and the individual. When a patient is admitted to the hospital, an out-of-pocket charge is payable as part of the individual's contribution. The state clearly stipulates that about 10 percent of the local average annual wage should be the standard for triggering socialized payments. For the Grade A hospitals in our province, 750 yuan is chargeable for the first admission, 650 yuan for the second, and 550 yuan for the third.
>
> (Xihai Dushibao, *Xihai City News* 西海都市报, July 13, 2006, p.A4)

13 Yew-Kwang Ng suggested this graduated pricing scheme, which resembles the system in practice in China. Unfortunately, however, an otherwise sensible healthcare system in China had been plagued by various problems such as overcharging and fraud as a result of the principal–agent problem under asymmetry of information in the context of inadequate public funding.
14 Meara *et al.*, 2004: 176–183. In China, even for the insured members of the urban population, medication costs are not covered at all unless the drug is on the Essential Drugs List. Similarly in Hong Kong, the Hospital Authority has established a "Hospital Authority Drug Formulary," that requires patients to pay for drugs that are not on the publicly provided drugs list.
15 The matching ratio may be reduced for the poor but otherwise should be 1:1.
16 Loading cost is the charge made by an insurance agency to cover its administrative costs and normal profit. Zero loading cost is assumed for simplicity. Assuming positive but identical loading costs for the two kinds of insurance schemes would not affect results.
17 These prospects actually have the same expected values. But expected utility under the Von Neumann–Morgenstern framework would be higher for the lower risk case, assuming that the utility function is concave. If the utility function is not only defined over the outcomes but also includes perceived risk as an argument, then the dominance of the less risky prospect is even greater (see Ho, 2001a, 2001b).

3 Insurance, moral hazard and adverse selection

1 See Rand Corporation (2006).
2 A HMO is usually a commercial entity that operates by merging the health insurance function with the healthcare function, and by such design successfully overcoming the principal–agent problem between the insurer and caregivers.
3 The discussion here follows the framework developed in Nicholas Barr, 1992.
4 See Bailey, 2004.

4 Health policy evaluation

1 Prior to December 2008 people were regularly turned away from hospitals in Japan, leading to the deaths of some patients. See Facts and Details website, online, available at: http://factsanddetails.com/japan.php?itemid=838&catid=23&subcatid=151#13. In December 2008, new rules were set up to prevent hospitals from refusing patients.
2 "Priorities for research to take forward the health equity policy agenda," *Bulletin of the World Health Organization*, December 2005, 83 (12).
3 There are lots of controversies about these estimates. A good discussion of the controversy is provided on the STATS website, online, available at: http://stats.org/stories/2011/value_statistical_life_jun27_11.html. Actually all such estimates that are based on behavior assume that people have accurate perceptions and are well informed, which generally is far from the truth.
4 An example of cost effectiveness analysis would be to compare work-site versus regular (physician office) care for effectiveness. See "Cost-effectiveness of a worksite hypertension treatment program" by A.G. Logan *et al.* (1981), which concluded that a worksite program is more cost effective than visits to clinics by workers.
5 The QALY approach translates life-years into standard, "full health" years by discounting life-years that are characterized by poor health.

5 Health policy in mainland China, Hong Kong and Taiwan: settling down to a model?

1 Private hospitals in Taiwan are not entirely private as most get partial government funding. According to *Taiwan Review* (February, 2008), hospitals that obtain Taiwan Joint Commission on Hospital Accreditation can claim government funding. Hospitals must renew their accreditation every three years. To the extent that most private hospitals in Taiwan are under contract with the BNIH they are akin to public hospitals. See section 5.2 below.
2 For example, although the employee's contribution is 2 percent in both Beijing and Shanghai, employers have to contribute 12 percent in Beijing but a higher 14 percent in Shanghai. The maximum payable, however, is higher in Beijing than in Shanghai. See AustCham website, online, available at: www.austcham.org/about-us/news/2011/jul/11/china%E2%80%99s-labour-revolution-continues-new-social-insurance-law.
3 Spending figures from *Chutian City Post* 楚天都市報, January 21, 2012. 2011 GDP figure from www.stats.gov.cn/english/newsandcomingevents/t20120117_402779577.htm.
4 "Shan Juan: Country Ramps Up Healthcare Spending," *China Daily* March 10, 2011).
5 Lo and Yaung (1998) gave evidence supporting this hypothesis.
6 According to the 2008/2009 Hospital Authority Budget, queuing time for specialist clinics was increasing. Waiting time for non-emergency surgical cases was extended to 221 weeks maximum in 2007, 89 weeks longer than that of three years ago. *Mingpao*, April 2 2008.
7 Since 1997 the Hospital Authority under budget constraint began to recruit doctors on contract terms with salaries and benefits much inferior to those applicable for existing

staff. Notwithstanding recent raises, there is still a big gap between doctors employed on contract terms and those on regular terms (*Oriental Daily*, August 29, 2007; *Hong Kong Economic Journal*, January 26, 2002).

8 This is according to Hsieh Yen-yao, executive-general of the Academy of Law and Medicine.

9 Doctors who are employed by an HMO may earn a salary plus bonus. Their behavior will be like "public providers acting like private caregivers," to be discussed in the next sub-section.

10 Doctors in Beijing typically had a monthly income of just over 2,000 yuan (US$250) per month in 2005. Collecting kickbacks from pharmaceutical companies is regarded as "understandable" (*Beijing Qingnianbao*, May 19, 2005). Some collect "red packets" from patients, who often understand this as an "implicit rule" (qian guize 潜规则) (*Shanxi Ribao*, May 19, 2005).

11 One particular notable case, though probably an exceptional case, involved a former chairman of the Hong Kong Reporters' Association who was admitted to a Zhengzhou hospital for stroke. He was charged 80,000 yuan (US$10,000 at the then prevailing exchange rate) per day. That was subsequently reduced to 20,000 yuan upon intervention by the Hong Kong SAR Beijing Office (*Mingpao*, July 27, 2006).

12 The BNHI has effectively become the dominant and informed purchaser of healthcare services in Taiwan on behalf of patients and accordingly assumes much bargaining power over pricing. This is an example wherein the much touted provider–purchaser split works.

13 See Hospital Authority website, online, available at: www.ha.org.hk/haho/ho/cs/v3/serviceguide_feenchg-en.htm.

14 A document downloaded from the Hospital Authority website suggested that the percentage of non-paying patients was around 30 percent in 2003. See Hospital Authority website, online, available at: www.ha.org.hk/haho/ho/cad_bnc/123594e.pdf accessed June 28, 2008.

15 But there is a qualifier: "for the same disease that causes the patient to stay no more than 30 days in an acute ward or 180 days in the chronic ward." These provisions apparently are intended to limit the cost to the government, and to encourage patients to agree to transfer to the less costly chronic ward in the event they need to stay over 30 days. Sweden runs a similar system, and Ho (1997, 2001) strongly argues in favor of such a system.

16 Beijing had an early healthcare scheme for urban workers in 2001. This was extended to migrant workers in 2004. Recently an overhaul of the health insurance system was announced and took effect from July 1, 2008, to provide coverage for all who live in the city including the jobless and the handicapped. Under the new scheme, the annual deductible was lowered; the reimbursement rate as well as the range of medications covered was raised; finally, for those requiring transplants, the maximum amounts covered were raised. These initiatives were expected to save 460 million yuan for Beijing residents. See *Zhonghua Gongshang Shibao* 中华工商时报 June 24 2008. See also *China Daily*, June 20, 2008.

17 DRGs classify the kinds of services that patients require according to their diagnosed ailment categories. They sometimes form the basis of government funding and insurance claims.

18 See "My Health, My Choice" publication, online, available at: www.myhealthmychoice.gov.hk/pdf/report/Executive_summary_eng.pdf for a summary of the government's position during the second stage of the consultation.

19 The annual notification of hepatitis E infection in Hong Kong jumped from 11 in 1996 to a record high of 118 in 2010. This is likely to be related to a diet change in the Hong Kong population as the disease is mainly transmitted through consumption of contaminated water or food. See Surveillance of Viral Hepatitis in Hong Kong, Centre for Health Protection, December 2011. Online, available at: www.chp.gov.hk/files/pdf/hepsurv10.pdf.

20 A merit good is a good deemed to be socially desirable so that its consumption is worthy of support or encouragement.
21 See Li Fan 李芃 (2009) "Exploring the healthcare insurance system in Zhenjiang: Migrating from Individual Account toward Family-based Account," in 21 世紀經濟 June 12, 2009.
22 See China Daily Clips.com website, online, available at: www.cdeclips.com/en/nation/Li_puts_focus_on_medical_reform/fullstory_73095.html.
23 *Beijing Daily* 北京日報 February 5, 2012.
24 Gaynor (2006)'s survey of the literature shows that competition would be a positive factor if prices are regulated but its effects would be ambiguous when prices are not regulated. The availability of a public sector that provides services at regulated prices provides an environment as if the prices charged by private caregivers were indirectly regulated.
25 See Lu and Chiang, 2011, for an excellent outline of the evolution of Taiwan's healthcare system.
26 *Beijing Daily* (北京日報) February 23, 2012.

6 Publicly funded healthcare systems: United Kingdom and Canada

1 "Commissioning and the Impact of the Purchaser–Provider Split on the NHS in England," online, available at: http://lookafterournhs.org.uk/wp-content/uploads/commissionign-and-purchaser–provider-split-with-links-03062.pdf.
2 "The impact of the NHS market: An overview of the literature, by CIVITAS: Institute for the Study of Civil Society" (2010). Online, available at: www.civitas.org.uk/nhs/download/Civitas_LiteratureReview_NHS_market_Feb10.pdf.
3 Subsequent legislations were passed in 1966 and 1984.
4 Detsky, A.S., Naylor, C.D. (2003) "Canada's Health Care System – Reform Delayed." *New England Medical Journal* 349: 804–810.
5 See Keep Health Care Public website, online, available at: http://keephealthcarepublic.ca/.
6 See Keep Health Care Public website, online, available at: http://keephealthcarepublic.ca/facts#longerwaittimes.
7 See Health Canada website, online, available at: www.hc-sc.gc.ca/hcs-sss/pubs/system-regime/2011-hcs-sss/index-eng.php.
8 Actually, the Canada Health Act excludes certain groups including members of the Canadian Forces and the Royal Canadian Mounted Police, federal penitentiary inmates and injured workers covered by workers' compensation, persons who have not completed a minimum period of residence in a province or territory, as well as refugee status claimants.
9 This is as true of the United States as it is of Hong Kong, where it was reported that in Tuen Mun Hospital the wait for an MRI in 2011 could be up to eight years. The Hospital Authority in Hong Kong expect the problem to be eased with the launch in 2012 of a public–private partnership scheme that will allow patients to get MRI services from private hospitals.
10 see NHS website, online, available at: www.nhs.uk/NHSEngland/Healthcosts/Pages/Prescriptioncosts.aspx.
11 The cap

> is grossly uneven between NHS trusts and foundation trusts as well as between foundation trusts themselves. Some FTS have a cap of 30 percent, some a cap of 5 percent and mental health foundation trusts have a cap of zero.

See NHS confederation website, online, available at: www.nhsconfed.org/Networks/FoundationTrust/Workstreams/Finance/Pages/PrivPatientIncomeCap.aspx The BBC release is accessible online, available at: www.bbc.co.uk/news/health-16337904.

12 See BMA.org, online, available at: www.bma.org.uk/images/part_tcm41–20061.pdf.

13 Madeleine Brindley (2009)"NHS 'new dawn' will focus on patients", October 1, *Western Mail*, online, available at: www.walesonline.co.uk/news/wales-news/2009/10/01/nhs-set-to-focus-on-patients-with-new-health-boards-91466–24824058/.

14 *Telegraph*, 18 October, 2008, online, available at: www.telegraph.co.uk/health/3223309/Doctors-paid-thousands-not-to-send-patients-to-hospital-for-treatment.html.

7 Singapore: Medisave, Medishield, Medifund and ElderShield

1 US Census Bureau projection. Online, available at: www.census.gov/compendia/statab/2012/tables/12s0104.pdf.

2 Apart from the favorable pricing of healthcare services for the poor and the Medifund, a recent initiative is the Interim Disability Assistance Program for the Elderly (IDAPE) scheme, which provides financial help to those who have become disabled and who are not eligible for coverage under ElderShield.

8 Universal publicly funded basic healthcare in Australia and New Zealand

1 The Australian government has signed reciprocal health care agreements with New Zealand, the United Kingdom, the Republic of Ireland, Sweden, the Netherlands, Belgium, Finland, Italy, Malta and Norway.

2 See Privatehealth.com website, online, available at: http://privatehealth.com.au/about-us/.

3 Online, available at: www.health.gov.au/internet/main/publishing.nsf/Content/elective-surgery-progress.

4 The Medicare benefits schedule (MBS) is a listing of the Medicare services subsidized by the Australian government. The schedule is part of the Medicare benefits scheme managed by the Department of Health and Ageing and administered by Medicare Australia. See for example, Medicare Australia website, online, available at: www.medicareaustralia.gov.au/about/stats/files/items_3_23_36_44_gp.pdf.

5 An Australian, New Zealander, a holder of permanent visa as well as a holder of specified temporary visas who lives in Australia is entitled to FTB(A) status if he has a dependent child under 21 years of age (including a foster child) or a dependant full-time student 21 to 24 years of age under care for at least 35 per cent of the time, if his income is under a certain amount.

6 A$80,000 in the 2011–2012 financial year for singles; and A$160,000 for a family in the 2011–12 financial year. The family income threshold increases by A$1,500 for each dependent child after the first.

7 Over 11.7 million Australians are covered by private health insurance (hospital and/or general treatment cover) and some ten million have hospital cover.

8 See *International Profile of Health Care Systems*, the Commonwealth Fund 2010.

9 See Privatehealth.com website, online, available at: http://privatehealth.com.au/about-private-health/.

10 According to the 2011 Commonwealth Fund report, "In financial year 2009–10, 74.3 percent of all Medicare services were bulk billed." Here bulk billing refers to reimbursement by the government according to schedule fees with no direct charges to patients.

11 See Department of Health, Victoria website, online, available at: http://health.vic.gov.au/casemix.

12 See for example: National Public Health Partnership (NPHP) (2006), Blueprint for nation-wide surveillance of chronic diseases and associated determinants, Melbourne, Australia. Australia is particularly noted for its pioneering work promoting mental

health and well-being. It conducts a National Survey of Mental Health and Wellbeing from time to time. The National Mental Health Report 2010 is the eleventh in the series, which monitors progress made under the National Mental Health Strategy.

13 See Menzies-Nous Group Survey 2010..
14 Menzies-Nous 2010 survey.
15 Posted May 5, 2011, online available at: http://parliamentflagpost.blogspot.com/2011/05/paying-for-health-care-how-can-we.html.

9 Three European countries: France, Switzerland and Sweden

1 Hospital-based physicians in Switzerland may supplement their income with fees charged on additional services that are paid by the patient or by the supplemental insurance policies.
2 Private doctors associated with HMOs may receive salaries.
3 According to Durand-Zaleski (2010), in France formal implementation of the DRG-based reimbursement system will not take place until 2012. In Switzerland, payments to hospitals by insurance funds may be DRG-based or per-diem based.

10 The American market-based system

1 See Alliance for Advancing Non-profit Healthcare website, online, available at: www.nonprofithealthcare.org/reports/1_community.pdf.
2 Based on OECD Health Data, online, available at: www.cms.gov/NationalHealthExpendData/downloads/highlights.pdf.
3 "Canadian Health Care, even with Queues, Bests US," Bloomberg September 18, 2009, on line, available at: www.bloomberg.com/apps/news?pid=newsarchive&sid=a_zs1Y1FspIM accessed February 23, 2012.
4 According to a recent study by Schoen *et al.* (2009), 58 percent of US physicians – by far the most among 11 countries surveyed – reported patient difficulty in paying for medications and care. Half of US doctors spend substantial time dealing with the restrictions insurance companies place on patients' care. See "A survey of primary care physicians in 11 countries, 2009: perspectives on care, costs, and experiences" by Cathy Schoen, Robin Osborn, Michelle M. Doty, David Squires, Jordon Peugh and Sandra Applebaum, Health Affairs Web Exclusive, November 5, 2009, w1171–w1183.
5 See the Commonwealth Fund website, online, available at: www.commonwealthfund.org/Surveys/2008/2008-Commonwealth-Fund-International-Health-Policy-Survey-of-Sicker-Adults.aspx. This corroborates with the result noted in Chapter 6 that Americans visit doctors far fewer times than Canadians and the British do.
6 Blanchflower and Oswald observed that:

> there is evidence that successive American generations became progressively less happy from 1900 to today.... In Europe, by contrast,... cohort well-being falls initially from the beginning of the century but, after bottoming out in the 1950s (which is the omitted base category) has actually been rising throughout the most recent generations.
>
> (2007, p. 12)

7 Ho (1995) proposed the concept of policy efficiency: that a policy should be evaluated in terms of the efficacy of achieving its intended goals given the resources committed.
8 See US Census Bureau website, online, available at: www.census.gov/newsroom/releases/archives/income_wealth/cb11–157.html accessed January 31, 2012.
9 See story in *USA Today*, online, available at: www.usatoday.com/news/nation/2010–09–17-uninsured17_ST_N.htm.

10 See CBS News website, online, available at: www.cbsnews.com/stories/2009/10/23/60minutes/main5414390.shtml.
11 See TopNews website, online, available at: http://topnews.us/content/236511-medicare-and-medicaid-fraud-reaches-estimated-47-billion.
12 It is nice to know that some $4 billion was recovered in fiscal 2010 by the Department of Justice, according to the CBS News story in the hyperlink given in note 15.
13 2006 Annual Report of the Office of the Auditor General of Ontario, online, available at: www.auditor.on.ca/en/reports_en/en06/308en06.pdf.
14 Henry Thomas Stelfox and Donald A. Redelmeier (2003) "An Analysis of One Potential Form of Health Care Fraud in Canada," *Canadian Medical Association Journal*, July 22, 169 (2).
15 The bill went through the senate on Christmas Eve 2009. For a good summary of what is in the bill, see CBS News website, online, available at: www.cbsnews.com/8301–503544_162–20000846–503544.html.
16 See CBS News website, online, available at: www.cbsnews.com/stories/2009/10/20/cbsnews_investigates/main5403220.shtml.
17 If the cost of health insurance takes up more than a stipulated percentage of one's income, which may vary with the income level, it is deemed by the Patient Protection and Affordable Care Act signed in 2010 to be beyond affordability.
18 See *Wall Street Journal* website, online, available at: http://online.wsj.com/article/SB10001424053111904006104576504383685080762.html.
19 See *Huffington Post* website, online, available at: www.huffingtonpost.com/2009/09/09/obama-health-care-speech_n_281265.html.
20 This view agrees with Robert E. Moffit's view. Robert Moffit is Director of the Center for Health Policy Studies at the Heritage Foundation. See: heritage Foundation website, online, available at: www.heritage.org/research/reports/2009/07/a-federal-health-insurance-exchange-combined-with-a-public-plan-the-house-and-senate-bills.
21 For France, Italy, Spain and Germany, *Financial Times*/Harris Poll for the *Financial Times*; for the United States and Great Britain and France, a Harris Interactive survey for the *International Herald Tribune*; and for the Netherlands, Canada, New Zealand and Australia, Harris Interactive survey for the Commonwealth Fund, all conducted in the 2007–2008 period. Online, available at: www.marketwatch.com/story/americans-rate-us-health-care-system-lowest-among-10-nations?pagenumber=1.
22 O'Neill, June E. and Dave M. O'Neill (2007) "Health Status, Health Care and Inequality: Canada versus the US," NBER Working Paper No. 13429.
23 Gallup poll, online, available at: www.gallup.com/poll/20821/americans-canadians-britons-similarly-rate-their-healthcare-systems.aspx.
24 He noted that when the same 1,034 respondents were asked how they would rate the "quality of health care YOU receive," 65 percent gave it an A or B and another 19 percent a C. Online, available at: www.frumforum.com/how-do-americans-rate-their-healthcare.
25 US News and World Reports website, online, available at: http://health.usnews.com/health-news/managing-your-healthcare/healthcare/articles/2011/04/14/majority-of-americans-give-quality-of-health-care-a-c-d-or-f.
26 For an excellent discussion of how this can be done, see Katherine Baicker and Dana Goldman (2011).

11 The way forward

1 Since people with different abilities and fortunes would have different balances in their Medisave accounts Hsiao (2001) noted that they therefore have unequal access to healthcare (p. 736).
2 CUPE website, online, available at: http://cupe.ca/updir/Private-For-Profit-Health-Care-Clinics.pdf.

References

Anell, Anders (2011) "The Swedish Health Care System, 2011" *International Profile of Healthcare Systems, 2011*, Washington, DC: The Commonwealth Fund.

Angell, Marcia (2008) "Privatizing Health Care is not the Answer: Lessons from the United States." *Canadian Medical Association Journal*, October 6.

Australian Department of Health and Ageing (2009) *Medicare Statistics*, June.

Australian Institute of Health and Welfare (2009) *Towards National Indicators of Safety and Quality in Health Care*, Canberra.

Australian Institute of Health and Welfare (2010) *Australia's Health 2010*, Canberra.

Baicker, Katherine and Dana Goldman (2011) "Patient Cost-sharing and Healthcare Spending Growth," *Journal of Economic Perspectives*, 25(2): 47–68.

Bailey, R. (2004) "Mandatory Health Insurance Now! It will Save Private Medicine – and Spur Medical Innovation." Reason.com website, November 2004. Online, available at: www.reason.com/news/show/29303.html.

Barr, Nicholas (1992) "Economic Theory and the Welfare State: A Survey and Interpretation," *Journal of Economic Literature*, June: 80(2): 741–803.

Baumol, William J. and David F. Bradford (1970) "Optimal Departures from Marginal Cost Pricing," *American Economic Review*, 60(3): 265–283, June.

Becker, Gary S. (1965) "A Theory of the Allocation of Time," *Economic Journal*, 75(299): 493–517.

Becker, Gary and Yona Rubinstein (2004) "Fear and the Response to Terrorism: An Economic Analysis," *mimeo*. Online, available at: www.ilr.cornell.edu/international/events/upload/BeckerrubinsteinPaper.pdf.

Berchtold, Peter and Isabelle Peytremann-Bridevaux (2011) "Integrated Care Organizations in Switzerland," *International Journal of Integrated Care*, 11 March.

Bercowitz, M., P. Fenn and J. Lambrinos (1983) "The Optimal Stock of Health with Endogenous Wages. Application to Partial Disability Compensation." *Journal of Health Economics* August 2(2): 139–147.

Birch S, Gafni A, Markham B, Marriott M, Lewis D, Main P (1998) "Health Years Equivalents as a Measure of Preferences For Dental Interventions." *Community Dental Health* 15: 233–242.

Blanchflower, David G. and Andrew Oswald (2007) "Is Well-being U-shaped over the Life Cycle?" *NBER Working Paper* 12935. Online, available at: www.nber.org/papers/w12935.

Blumenthal, David and William Hsiao (2005) "Privatization and Its Discontents – The Evolving Chinese Health Care System," *New England Journal of Medicine*, September 15, 1165–1170.

Boardman, A.E.; D.H. Greenbert, A.R. Vining and D.L. Weimer (2011) *Cost–Benefit Analysis: Concepts and Practice*, fourth edition, Pearson.

Broome, John (1993) "QALYs," *Journal of Public Economics*, 50(2): 149-167, February.

Carrin, Guy and Piya Hanvoravongchai (2003) Provider Payments and Patient Charges as Policy Tools for Cost-containment: How Successful are they in High-income Countries? *Human Resources for Health* 2003, 1.

Chalkley, Martin and Colin Tilley (2006) "Treatment Intensity and Provider Remuneration: Dentists in the British National Health Service." *Health Economics*, 15(9): 933–946.

Cumming, Jacqueline and Nicholas Mays (2011) "New Zealand's Primary Health Care Strategy: Early Effects of the New Financing and Payment System for General Practice and Future Challenges," *Health Economics, Policy and Law*, 6(1): 1–21.

Cutler, David M. and Dan P. Ly (2011) "The (Paper) Work of Medicine: Understanding International Medical Costs," *Journal of Economic Perspectives*, 25(2): 1–25.

Detsky, A.S. and C.D. Naylor (2003) "Canada's Health Care System – Reform Delayed." *New England Journal of Medicine*, 349: 804–810.

Department of Health (1997) *The New NHS: Modern, Dependable*, December 9. Online, available at: www.archive.official-documents.co.uk/document/doh/newnhs/contents.htm.

Dong, W. (2006) "Cost Containment Strategy – Medical Savings Account: the Shanghai Scheme and the Singaporean Model" *Paper Presented at the Annual Meeting of the American Sociological Association, Montreal Convention Center, Montreal, Quebec, Canada.*

Dong, W. (2001) "Health Care Reform in Urban China." Working Paper 2001/2. Munk Centre for International Studies at the University of Toronto.

Dranove, David and Michael L. Millenson (2006) "Medical Bankruptcy: Myth versus Fact" *Health Affairs*, 25(2).

Durand-Zaleski, Isabelle (2010) *The French Health Care System*, 2009.

Eggleston, K., L. Ling, Q. Meng, M. Lindelow and A. Wagstaff (2006) "Health Service Delivery in China: A Literature Review," *Policy, Research Working Paper;* no. WPS 3978. World Bank.

Ellis, Randall (1986) "Rational Behavior in the Presence of Coverage Ceilings and Deductibles," *Rand Journal of Economics*, 17, Summer.

Ellis, Randall P. (1998) "Creaming, Skimping and Dumping: Provider Competition on the Intensive and Extensive Margins," *Journal of Health Economics*, 7(5): 537–555.

Ellis, Richard and Thomas G. McGuire (1990) "Optimal Payment Systems for Health Services," *Journal of Health Economics,* 9: 375–396.

Ellis, Richard and Thomas G. McGuire (1996) "Hospital Response to Prospective Payment: Moral Hazard, Selection and Practice-style Effects," *Journal of Health Economics,* 15: 257–277.

Folland, Sherman, Allen C. Goodman and Miron Stano (2010) *Economics of Health and Health Care*, sixth edition, Prentice Hall.

Gafni, A. and S. Birch (1993) "Guidelines for the Adoption of New Technologies: A Prescription for Uncontrolled Growth in Expenditures and how to Avoid the Problem," *Canadian Medical Assn. Journal*, 148(6): 913–917.

Gafni, A. and S. Birch (1997) "Equity Considerations in Utility-based Measures of Health Outcomes in Economic Appraisals: An Adjustment Algorithm." *Journal of Health Economics*, 10: 329–342.

Gafni, A. and S. Birch (2003) "Inclusion of Drugs in Provincial Drug Benefit Programs:

Should 'Reasonable Decisions' Lead to Uncontrolled Growth in Expenditures?" [editorial]. *Canadian Medical Association .Journal*, 168(7): 849–851.

Gaynor, Martin (2006) "What Do We Know About Competition and Quality in Health Care Markets?" *NBER Working Papers* No. 12301.

Godager, Geir, Tor Iversen and Ching-To Ma (2009) "Service Motives and Profit Incentives among Physicians," *International Journal of Health Care Finance and Economics*, 9(1): 39–57, March.

Grossman, Michael (1972) "On the Concept of Health Capital and the Demand for Health," *Journal of Political Economy* 80 (2): 223–255.

Hanvoravongchai, P. (2002) 'Medical Savings Accounts: Lessons Learned from International Experience,' *EIP/HFS/PHF Discussion Paper* No. 52. Geneva: World Health Organization.

Himmelstein, D.U., Elizabeth Warren, Deborah Thorne and Steffie Woolhandler (2005) "Illness and Injury as Contributors to Bankruptcy," Health Affairs: w63–w73.

Ho, Lok Sang (1995a) "Market Reform and China's Health Care System," *Social Sciences and Medicine*, 41(8), October: 1065–1072.

Ho, Lok Sang (1995b) "Privatization of Public Housing: An Analysis of Policy Alternatives," *Contemporary Economic Policy*, 8(3), July: 53–63.

Ho, Lok Sang (1997) *Healthcare Financing and Delivery: A Model for Reform*, Hong Kong: City University of Hong Kong Press.

Ho, Lok Sang (2001a) *Principles of Public Policy Practice*, Boston: Kluwer Academic Publishers.

Ho, Lok Sang (2001b) "Health Care Financing and Delivery in Hong Kong: What Should Be Done," *Hong Kong Medical Journal*, 7(2), June: 155–161.

Ho, Lok Sang (2011a) "Worries Abound over Health Protection Scheme Proposal," July 26, online, available at: www.cdeclips.com/en/hongkong/Worries_abound_over_health_protection_scheme_proposal/fullstory_68438.html.

Ho, Lok Sang (2011b) "The Predicaments of the HK Public Hospital Care System," August 9. Online, available at: www.cdeclips.com/en/hongkong/The_predicaments_of_the_HK_public_hospital_care_system/fullstory_68718.html.

Ho, Lok Sang (2012) *Public Policy and the Public Interest*, new York: Routledge.

Hjertqvist, J. (2002) Meeting the Challenges to European Healthcare: Lessons Learned from the 'Stockholm Revolution' *Pharmacoeconomics*, 20: 47–53.

Hong Kong SAR Government (1999) *Improving Hong Kong's Health Care System: Why and For Whom?* (Health and Welfare Bureau) ("Harvard Report").

Hong Kong SAR Government (2001) *Lifelong Investment in Health, A Blueprint for Future Health Care System* (Health and Welfare Bureau).

Hong Kong SAR Government (2008) *Your Health, Your Life. – Healthcare Reform Consultation Document* (Health and Food Bureau).

Hornbrook, M.C. and M.J. Goodman (1996) "Chronic Disease, Functional Health Status, and Demographics: A Multi-Dimensional Approach to Risk Adjustment." *Health Services Research* August, 31(3): 283–307.

Hsiao, William (2001) "Commentary: Behind the Ideology and Theory: What is the Empirical Evidence for Medical Savings Accounts?" *Journal of Health Politics, Policy and Law*, 26(4): 733–738.

Hubert, Helen B., Daniel A. Bloch, John W. Oehlert and James F. Fries (2002) "Lifestyle Habits and Compression of Morbidity," *Journals of Gerontology Series A: Biological Sciences and Medical Sciences* 57:M347-M351. Online, available at: http://biomed.gerontologyjournals.org/cgi/content/full/57/6/M347.

Karatzas, George (1992) "On the Effect of Income and Relative Price on the Demand for Health Care-the EEC Evidence: a Comment," *Applied Economics*, 24(11): 1251–1253.

Kessler, Daniel P. (2011) "Evaluating the Medical Malpractice System and Options for Reform," *Journal of Economic Perspectives*, 25(2): 93–110.

Kington, R.S. and J.P. Smith (1997) "Socioeconomic Status and Racial and Ethnic Differences in Functional Status Associated with Chronic Diseases." *American Journal of Public Health* 87(5): 805–810.

Kotlikoff, L. and C. Hagist (2005) "Whose Going Broke? Comparing Growth in Healthcare Costs in Ten OECD Countries," NBER Working Paper No. 11833.

Lancaster, Kelvin (1966) "A New Approach to Consumer Theory," *Journal of Political Economy*: 74: 132–157.

Laupacis, A, G. Anderson, and B. O'Brien (2002) "Drug Policy: Making Effective Drugs Available without Bankrupting the Healthcare System," *Healthcare Papers*. 3(1): 12–30.

Li, J., K. Zhang and L. Tian (2006) "Multiple Facets of China's Health Inequality," *Lancet*, 367(9520): 1397–1397.

Lo, Hsuan and Chih-Liang Yaung (1998) "The Association of the Satisfaction with Compensation, Propensity to Leave, and Their Related Factors of Full-time Visiting Staff in a Medical Center-Application of Linear Structural Equation Model," *Taiwan Journal of Public Health*, 臺灣公共衛生雜誌 17(2): 125–138.

Logan, A.G., B.J. Milne, C. Achber, W.P. Campbell and R.B. Haynes (1981) "Cost-Effectiveness of a Worksite Hypertension Treatment Program," *Hypertension*, 3: 211–218.

Lu, Jui-Fen Rachel and William C. Hsiao (2003) "Does Universal Health Insurance Make Health Care Unaffordable? Lessons from Taiwan," *Health Affairs*, 22(3): 77–88.

Lu Jui-Fen Rachel and Tung-Liang Chiang (2011) "Evolution of Taiwan's Health Care System," *Health Economics, Policy and Law*, 6(1): 85–107.

Ma, C.A. (1994) "Health Care Payment Systems: Cost and Quality Incentives," *Journal of Economics & Management Strategy*, 3(1): 93–112.

Ma, C.A. (1998) "Health-Care Payment Systems: Cost and Quality Incentives – Reply," *Journal of Economics & Management Strategy*, 7(1), Spring: 139–142.

McClellan, Mark (2011) "Reforming Payments to Healthcare Providers: the Key to Slowing Healthcare Cost Growth While Improving Quality?" *Journal of Economic Perspectives*, 25(2): 69–92.

Meara, Ellen, Chapin White and David M. Cutler (2004) "Trends In Medical Spending By Age, 1963–2000," *Health Affairs*, 23(4): 176–183.

Mehrez, A and A. Gafni (1989) "Quality-adjusted Life Years, Utility Theory, and Healthy-years Equivalents." *Medical Decision Making*, April–June, 9(2):142–149.

Menzies-Nous Group Survey (2010) online, available at: www.menzieshealthpolicy.edu.au/mn_survey/Australian%20health%20survey%202010%20-%20short%20version.pdf

National Health and Hospitals Reform Commission (2009) "A Healthier Future for All Australians," Final Report, Canberra, June.

Newhouse, Joseph P. (2006) "Reconsidering the Moral Hazard-Risk Avoidance Trade-off." *Journal of Health Economics*, 25(5): 1005–1014, September.

OECD Health Data 2011.

O'Neill, June E. and Dave M. O'Neill (2007) "Health Status, Health Care and Inequality: Canada versus the US," NBER Working Paper No. 13429.

Pauly, M.V. and J.C. Goodman (1995) "Tax Credits for Health Insurance and Medical Savings Accounts." *Health Affairs*, 14(1): 125–139.

Picone, G., M.R. Wilson and M. Uribe (1998) "The Effect of Uncertainty on the Demand for Medical Care, Health Capital and Wealth," *Journal of Health Economics*, 17: 171–185.

PrivateHealth.com (no date) online, available at: http://privatehealth.com.au/about-private-health/understanding-private-health-insurance-premiums/.

Private Health Insurance Ombudsman, online, available at: http://privatehealth.gov.au/.

Propper, C., S. Burgess and D. Gossage (2003) *Competition and Quality: Evidence from the NHS Internal Market 1991-1999*, Bristol: University of Bristol.

Rand Corporation (2006) "The Health Insurance Experiment: A Classic RAND Study Speaks to the Current Health Care Reform Debate," Research Highlights.

Rudholm, Nikas; Arvid Nordmark and Per-Olov Marklund (2011) "Does Competition Increase Economic Efficiency in Swedish County Councils?" *Advances in Management & Applied Economics*, 1(2): 77–91.

Sassi, Franco and Jeremy Hurst (2008) *The Prevention of Lifestyle-Related Chronic Diseases: an Economic Framework*, OECD Health Working Paper no. 32.

Schoen, C., Robin Osborn, Michelle M. Doty, David Squires, Jordon Peugh and Sandra Applebaum (2009) "A Survey of Primary Care Physicians in 11 Countries, 2009: Perspectives on Care, Costs, and Experiences," *Health Affairs*, Web Exclusive November 5: w1171–w1183.

Schut, Frederik T. and Wynand, P.M. Van de Ven (2011) "Effects of Purchaser Competition in the Dutch Health System: Is the Glass Half Full or Half Empty?" *Health Economics, Policy, and Law*, 6(1): 109–123.

Squires, David (2010) "The Swiss Health Care System, 2009," *International Profile of Healthcare Systems, 2010*, Washington, DC: The Commonwealth Fund.

Sloan, Frank A. and Hirschel Kasper (2008) *Incentives and Choice in Health Care*, Boston: MIT Press.

Steinbrook, Robert (2006) "Private Health Care in Canada," *New England Journal of Medicine*. 354:1 661–1664 April 20. Online, available at: www.nejm.org/doi/full/10.1056/NEJMp068064.

Thomson, Sarah, Robin Osborn, David Squires and Sarah Jane Reed (eds) (2011), *International Profile of Healthcare Systems*, Washington, DC: The Commonwealth Fund.

Vaithianathan, Rhema (2006) "Health Insurance and Imperfect Competition in the Health Care Market," *Journal of Health Economics*, 25(6): 1193–1202.

Wagstaff, Adam; and Menno Pradhan (2005) "Health Insurance Impacts on Health and Non-medical Consumption in a Developing Country," *Policy Research Working Paper*; WPS 3563, April.

Wagstaff, Adam (2005) "Health Systems in East Asia: What Can Developing Countries Learn from Japan and the Asian Tigers?" *Policy, Research Working Paper*; WPS 3790, December.

Wagstaff, Adam (2008) "Measuring Financial Protection in Health," *Policy Research Working Paper*; WPS 4554, World Bank, March.

Wagstaff, Adam and Magnus Lindelow (2005) "Can Insurance Increase Financial Risk? The Curious Case of Health Insurance in China," *Policy Research Working Paper*; WPS 3741.

Wang, Kwan-I and Shou-Hsia Cheng (2006) "The Analysis of Level of Outpatient Visits and Healthcare Utilization: A Before and After Observation of the SARS Outbreak," *Taiwan Journal of Public Health* (臺灣公共衛生雜誌), 25(1): 75–82.

Woo, Wing Thye (2005) "The Structural Nature of Internal and External Imbalances in China," mimeo.

World Health Organization (2011) *World Health Statistics*, Geneva.

Yip, W. and K. Eggleston (2004) "Addressing Government and Market Failures with Payment Incentives: Hospital Reimbursement Reform in Hainan, China," *Social Science and Medicine*, 58(2): 267–277.

Yip, Winnie C. and William C. Hsiao (1997) "Medical Savings Accounts: Lessons from China, China's Medical Savings Accounts Coupled with Catastrophic Insurance have Yielded Mixed Results, So Far." *Health Affairs*, November–December, 16(6): 244–251.

Yip, Winnie C. and William C. Hsiao (2008) "The Chinese Health System at a Crossroads," *Health Affairs*, March–April, 27(2): 460–468.

Subject index

Name index